ARCHITECTURE

ARCHI

Movements and Trends from the 19th Century to the Present

TECTURE

edited by Luca Molinari

SKIRA

Design
Marcello Francone

Layout
Paola Oldani

Editorial coordination
Emma Cavazzini

Editing
Marco Abate

Iconographical research
Massimo Carmignani

Translations
NTL, Firenze

Photographic credits
Archivio Skira
Archivio Scala, Firenze
Andrea Jemolo, Roma

First published in Italy in 2015 by
Skira Editore S.p.A.
Palazzo Casati Stampa
via Torino 61
20123 Milano
Italy
www.skira.net

© 2015 Skira editore
© Giorgio de Chirico, Gerrit
Rietveld, Walter Gropius, Victor
Horta, Konstantin Melnikov,
Ludwig Mies van der Rohe,
Oscar Niemeyer, Amédée
Ozenfant, Rudolf Steiner,
UNStudio, Henri van de Velde
by SIAE 2015
© FLC, by SIAE 2015
© Frank Lloyd Wright
Foundation, by SIAE 2015

Printed and bound in Italy.
First edition

ISBN: 978-88-572-0473-4

Distributed in USA, Canada,
Central & South America by
Rizzoli International Publications,
Inc., 300 Park Avenue South,
New York, NY 10010, USA.
Distributed elsewhere in the
world by Thames and Hudson
Ltd., 181A High Holborn, London
WC1V 7QX, United Kingdom.

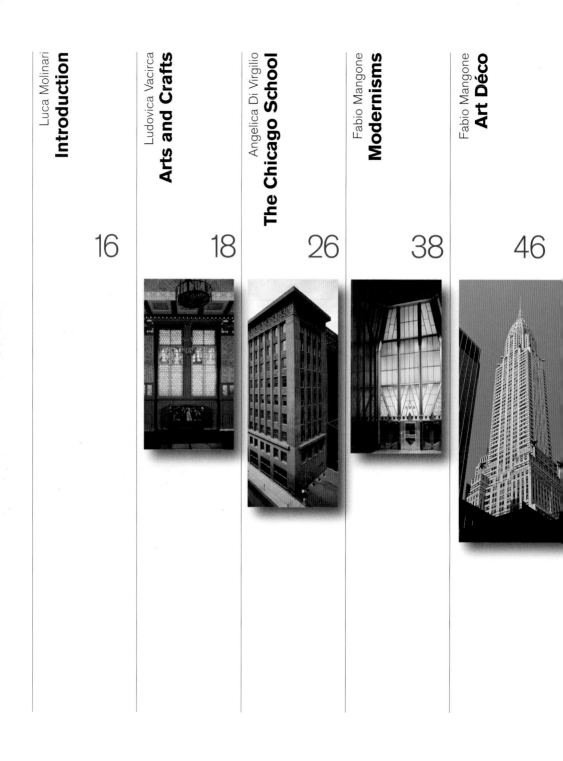

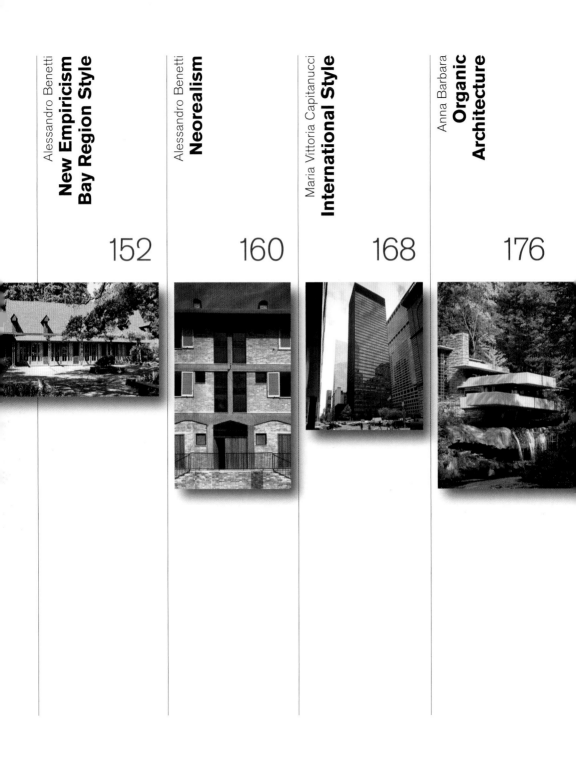

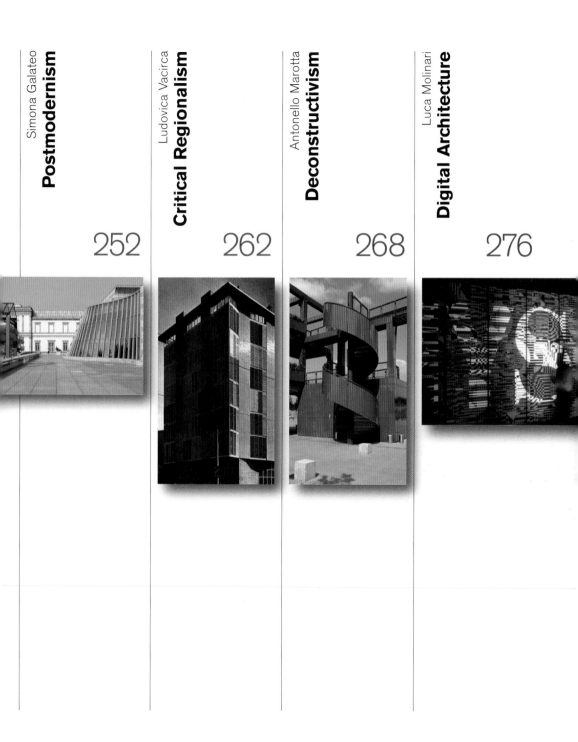

Luca Molinari

Introduction

Why is it of increasing importance today to rethink our histories of architecture and reinterpret the works, the lives of the architects, their writings and theoretical frames of reference? I believe that every era has the right/duty to renegotiate the boundaries and terms with which history and its events must measure themselves in each particular era and with the ongoing metamorphoses that produce new questions, expectations and trajectories.

There is no objective history; there are no manuals and written works that represent an absolute and unquestionable account of the events that took place, because every work is the result of a partial point of view that arises from the questions that produce research, specific selections and judgments. Every work that has attempted to interpret the past century is the product of a specific ideology and cultural vision of the world and the architecture that has heavily influenced the choices and standard criteria.

From this point of view, the twentieth century, inasmuch as it was a century that strove to be new and different, strove to be the vehicle for a novel idea of modernity, made use of history and its necessarily partial and very significant narratives, narratives that today we can begin to interpret with the necessary critical distance.

With the definitive advent of a widespread condition of post-modernity and with the fall of several walls at the end of the last century, there has been an opening up of large portions of the research areas, formerly unheeded by a historical-critical interpretation of the facts and the deeply occidental-centric, modernist and stylistic works. These works had obliterated architectural production and theory of entire parts of our world such as the whole bloc of Eastern Europe, Russia, China, Africa and the relevant areas of Central and South America. In addition to this geographical lapse of memory, we can find the same degree of amnesia with all those experiences and architects who could not be interpreted by the different cultural and linguist alliance systems that recognized themselves in the environments of modernism and post-modernism, establishing networks and areas of interest that were to prove useful for critical reinterpretations in the coming years.

With the fall of the walls and the many bureaucratic restrictions, archives and experiences known to just a very small world of specialized scholars were opened up to the larger academic world, greatly expanding the scope of our research and the perspectives from which to look at them. This condition, daughter of the XXI century, is an extraordinary opportunity for scholars and lovers of architecture to discover new experiences and works that were victims of the past century, bringing them back to life and into focus.

The task of this volume is to offer a problematic cross-reading that is inclusive of the major phenomena still capable of generating reflections worth remembering and carefully understanding.

The collection of 35 essays written by a new generation of architectural historians and students strives to be another of those contributions which at this stage is attempting to rethink the paradigms and the boundaries of our recent history, starting from the dawn of modernity in the twentieth century and venturing into present day. Without an understanding of the long-lasting phenomena, of the many courageous experiments, the failures that often followed, and the works that have marked our way of conceiving of and designing architecture in the contemporary world, we would not be able to interpret the historical density and depth that still exists today in the heritage of twentieth-century works and ideas.

This volume is intended as a light but not superficial remedy to the loss of memory that is accompanying us in this early part of the twenty-first century, and a tribute to an era that has permanently changed the way we think about, design and experience the space that surrounds us today.

Ludovica Vacirca

Arts and Crafts

The Arts and Crafts movement developed in England in the second half of the nineteenth century as a response to the profound changes that the industrial revolution had brought about in the arts. The new culture of progress and technology that gave priority to the role of the machine over craftsmanship provoked a response that entailed the defence of traditional production methods and a general rediscovery of medieval art. These became starting points for a research that was perhaps more theoretical than stylistic. This trend was rooted in the ideas of John Ruskin (1819-1900), whose writings on art and Gothic architecture had a broad circulation at the time.

William Morris (1834-1896), the main reference point for the movement, criticized the industrial system, starting with aesthetic and ethical objections. Mass-produced objects, apart from drawing from a historicist repertoire of dubious taste, was the result of a production process that transformed the craftsman into a worker, exploiting the labour force and limiting creative power.

After his studies at Oxford, he had the opportunity to become part of the Pre-Raphaelite circle of painters and study Ruskin's theories. Morris then frequented the studio of the architect George Edmund Street, a practitioner of the Victorian Gothic revival style. Here he met Philip Webb and together they travelled to France to discover that Gothic architecture representing, in its exact correspondence between form and function, the practical translation of the moral honesty to which they both aspired in their future works. Their opportunity was soon at hand. In 1859, in fact, Morris commissioned Webb to design his home-workshop in Bexleyheath, while he oversaw the design and construction of the furnishings. Because of the way the volumes are distributed, with the freedom of the planimetric layout and the use of local traditional construction techniques and materials, the Red House is considered by contemporary historiography to be the defining project in which Morris developed the principles of the Arts and Crafts movement. He broke away from the classical traditional academic codes and anticipated themes that modern architecture would eventually develop in a number of variations.

The ambitious renewal program of applied arts theorized by Morris, which aimed at overcoming the division of labour introduced by the industrial method (previously analysed by Adam Smith and harshly criticised by Ruskin in *The Stones of Venice*), began with the founding in 1861 of Morris, Marshall,

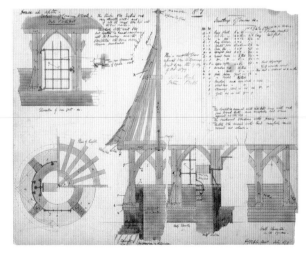

Richard Norman Shaw,
Adcote, Shropshire, 1875

Philip Webb, Red House,
Bexleyheath, 1859-1860

19

Faulkner & Co. This company brought together the Pre-Raphaelite painters Dante Gabriel Rossetti, Edward Burne-Jones, Ford Madox Brown, the architect Philip Webb, and others. One of the first successes of the company (which produced hand-crafted furniture, wallpaper, stained glass and tapestries) was the Green Dining Room, designed in 1867 by Webb for the present-day Victoria & Albert Museum in London. At the end of the nineteenth century, the movement had a large following in the English cultural *milieu*. Many of the architects who joined them (including Richard Norman Shaw, Arthur Heygate Mackmurdo, Charles Robert Ashbee, William Richard Lethaby and Charles Annesley Voysey) worked with dedication on Morris's cultural project. They founded schools and workshops of artisans, organized along the lines of the medieval craft guilds. Ruskin attributed to the guilds the educational value of places where, through cooperation between the various trades, it was possible to transmit the culture of the crafts and produce an art that was aesthetically and morally "beautiful." The Guild and School of Handicraft, established in 1887 by Charles Robert Ashbee (1863-1942), was one of the most active in this sense. Although strongly influenced by Ruskin's theories, Ashbee was a second generation designer who, at the turn of the century, was able to reinterpret the initial premises of the movement, recognizing that the machine had as much of a central role in modern society as the process of artistic revival. His work primarily revolves around the theme of the home. He built a number of residential buildings (including, in 1904, his own home in Cheyne Walk), developing all aspects of the project, according to the concept of a unique work already attempted by Morris with the Red House. Domestic architecture was indeed the area in which the Arts and Crafts movement achieved its most significant results, and especially in the work of Charles Annesley Voysey (1857-1941). In Voysey's vast output, which includes approximately forty houses built in the late nineteenth and early twentieth century, he continued to develop the compositional themes of free organization of space and "honest" use of materials developed by Webb. However, Voysey's style lay in the extraordinary ability to rigorously

"The past is not dead, but is living in us, and will be alive in the future which we are now helping to make"

William Morris

Charles Robert Ashbee,
House in Chelsea,
London, 1904

William Morris, *News
from nowhere*, Boston
1890

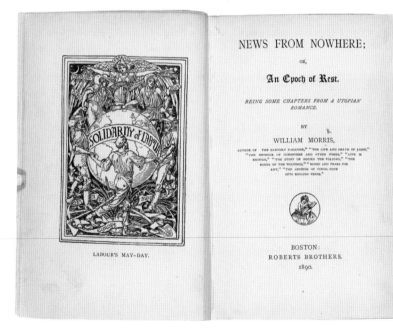

calibrate and measure the individual compositional elements, using a language that made reference to the traditional English country home without directly imitating the form. His most important creations include a house built in 1890 in the garden district of Bedford Park (designed by Richard Norman Shaw in the suburbs of London) and the Broad Leys House (1898), considered to be the highest manifestation of the poetics that were echoed in the architectural experiences of other countries.

At the end of the nineteenth century, the Arts and Crafts movement's experiments on the theme of the home became intertwined with those carried out in urban areas by the garden city theorists. The residential model described by Ebenezer Howard (1850-1928) in *Garden Cities of Tomorrow* (1902), based on urban sprawl in the countryside, the collective ownership of the land and an economy that could integrate industry and agriculture, in fact represented yet another reaction to industrial capitalism. It was a capitalism that Morris and his followers had opposed, with different orientations. As suggested by their writings (in particular, Morris's novel, *News from Nowhere,* from 1891), both Morris and Howard saw, in urban planning as well as architecture, the opportunity to establish a style of social reform with all the strength and limits of utopia. Although Morris's dream of an art that was not just for a chosen few soon had to struggle with the high cost of hand-crafted production, revealing his vulnerability on the practical level, he was nonetheless responsible for opening up new ways of thinking about the relationship between industry, art and craft, destined for a fruitful development in the twentieth century.

Bibliography
Barringer T., Rosenferl J., Smith A., *Pre-Raphaelites: Victorian Avant-Garde,* exhibition catalogue, Tate Britain, September 12, 2012 – January 13, 2013, Tate Publishing, London 2012.
Elia M., *William Morris e l'ideologia dell'architettura moderna,* Laterza, Bari 1976.
Frampton K., *Storia dell'architettura moderna,* Zanichelli, Bologna 1993.
Pevsner N., *I pionieri dell'architettura moderna: da Morris a Walter Gropius,* Garzanti, Milan 1999.
Richardson M., *Architects of the Arts and Crafts Movement,* London 1983.

Charles Annesley Voysey,
Broad Leys House,
Lancashire, 1898-1900

Philip Webb, Red House,
Bexleyheath, 1859-1860

23

Philip Webb, Red House,
Bexleyheath, 1859-1860

24

Philip Webb, Red House,
Bexleyheath, 1859-1860

Angelica Di Virgilio

The Chicago School

The "Chicago School" refers to the projects of a group of architects working in Chicago, the "Windy City", between 1871, the year of the city's great fire, and 1893, the opening of the Columbian Exhibition at the Chicago World's Fair on the shores of Lake Michigan. William Le Baron Jenney (1832-1907), Daniel H. Burnham (1846-1912), John W. Root (1850-1891), William Holabird (1854-1923), Martin Roche (1855-1927), Louis Sullivan (1856-1924) and Dankmar Adler (1844-1900) were the main protagonists; their work focused on rebuilding the Loop, the tertiary centre bounded by the Chicago River. Their work was united, on the one hand, by the experimentation in new building techniques, and on the other, by the more or less conscious research into formal solutions that would be best suited to commercial buildings. However, the results of these lines of research are less homogenous than the term "school" would suggest. The term was used for the first time by Sigfried Giedion[1] and, from there onwards, accepted by major historians of contemporary architecture.[2] The different backgrounds of the architects and their differing sensibilities meant that each of them carried out their research and experimentation independently, without creating an actual movement, to the point that some scholars dispute the uniqueness of the vision that critics of modern architecture attribute to them.[3] However, the most interesting aspect of the so-called "school" is not so much in the uniformity of the works, but rather in their having directed all the entrepreneurial, financial, technological and intellectual forces that at that time were working dispersedly in the American city, toward one goal and in one place, contributing to Chicago's urban and architectural developments, a Chicago still divided between functional new problems and preformed academic solutions.

The spark that literally triggered the fuse of this process was the great fire of 1871. In a single night it destroyed much of Chicago, whose buildings at the time were made of wood within a *balloon frame* system. The tabula rasa that followed was the perfect opportunity to experiment with the *laissez faire* of American liberalism. Thanks to its position as an internal hub for the nation and an efficient infrastructure system, Chicago quickly became an economic hub and the centre of an impressive flow of immigration.[4] The Loop, which was specialized in trade and business and the subsequent expulsion of residential areas, pushed toward the periphery, became the ideal area for enormous speculation. Land prices in the area increased from 130,000 to 900,000 dollars an acre after the fire, leading building contractors to adopt plans directed at high-income returns. The first skyscrapers, thanks to the advent of the elevator[5] and especially to the new building systems in iron and steel, made it possible to include higher floors in the rental market, rented at an equal if not higher price than the other levels. The Loop, which until 1871 had consisted mainly of low buildings, was radically transformed. In 1892, it became a compact group of buildings that consisted of between 10 and 21 floors.[6]

A pioneer in the field of new structures was William Le Baron Jenney. The Leiter Building (1879) and the Home Insurance Building (1883-1886) marked the transition from the earlier mixed construction in steel and masonry to the second, known to history as the first modern skyscraper. The skeleton, improved further in the Second Leiter Building (1889-1891) and in the Fair Building (1889), allowed for an increase in height without having to expand the foundations, freeing the perimeter walls from the load-bearing function and making it possible to open up the façade with almost continuous windows. Interested in

Advertisement of Otis
Bros & Co., New York,
19th century.

aspects of construction, Le Baron Jenney did not show the same attention to formal aspects: his language used ornamentation that was reduced and functional but still tied to an eclectic style, showing the lack of a true aesthetic research.

Unlike the most senior engineer, the architects of the next generation, such as Roche, Holabird, Burnham and Sullivan, who trained at his studio, instead tried to move away from the tired results of European academies and build a more original formal repertory. In particular, the partnership of Holabird & Roche focused on the stylization of the decor, entrusting details in the façades to standardized features, such as the *bow-windows* in the Tacoma Building (1887-1890) and the lightness of the large windows. Burnham & Root, who built the Monadnock Building in 1891, also worked with similar simplifications, but with completely different results: smooth façades, without any ornament, and curved joins on the surfaces bring out the grandeur of the load-bearing brick walls and highlight the monolithic volume, influenced by the work of Henry Hobson Richardson and his stylized Romanesque approach. A completely different approach was used in the design of the Reliance Building (1895), again designed by Burnham & Root, but built by Charles Atwood (1849-1895) after Root's death. The tower with bands of white tile and large windows that hide the structural cage was hailed by Giedion as "the Swan song of the Chicago School"[7] and is considered the most beautiful skyscraper in Chicago[8] in the classic historiography.

The work of Richardson and particularly the Marshall Field & Co. department stores (1885-1887) influenced the younger Sullivan as well. In collaboration with his partner Dankmar Adler, he designed Chicago's Auditorium (1886-1890). The large office block tower has something of the architecture of the master of Louisiana on the exterior, while inside behind the massive tripartite façades is a sophisticated structural system designed by Adler. Richardson's lesson in composition, rather than being formal, was absorbed by Sullivan in the following years, when he elaborated an original fully accomplished language with the Wainwright Building (St. Louis, 1890-1891), the Guaranty Building (Buffalo, 1894-1895) and especially the Carson Pirie Scott department stores: the structural clarity of the upper floors, which influenced the proto-functionalist solutions of Adolf Loos, is emphasized by contrast by the lush decorative cast iron base, a floristic game of art nouveau.

In 1893, the Columbian Exposition was inaugurated at the Chicago fair: the main pavilions which made up the White City were a hymn to classicism, to the architectural styles and the kind of ornament that L.H. Sullivan in his essay *Ornament in Architecture* defines as "mentally a luxury, not a necessity". The original solutions of Sullivan, Root and Roche seemed to suddenly disappear under the eclectic apparatus, back in vogue again due to the "fault" of the "corrupting seduction of public taste emanating from the pseudo splendour of the fair"[9] as pointed out by Giedion. While the Swiss critic exclusively imputes the Exhibition for the cessation of the "Chicago School," perhaps, as Benevolo noted, the end of that florid season might be found in the inability of the architects themselves to move completely outside the eclectic culture and the lack of one single theoretical base for all. This means that when a standardization of those experiences is required, their original content goes missing, highlighting the eclecticism that existed from the start.[10] So, while the tastes of customers were moving towards classicism, the architects of the so-called "School" had only two options: adapt, and then "betray" according to Giedion, as

Burnham chose to do, or isolate oneself as Sullivan did, shutting himself in with his writings and surviving thanks to small commissions, almost forgotten by the official culture.

Notes
[1] S. Giedion, *Space, Time and Architecture*, Harvard University Press, Cambridge Mass, 1941.
[2] See for all L. Benevolo, *Storia dell'architettura moderna*, Laterza, Bari (1960), and XX. 2006; or again W.J.R. Curtis, *Modern Architecture Since 1900*, Phaidon 1982. For more specific studies on the Chicago School, see. C.W. Condit, *The Chicago School of Architecture: a History of Commercial and Public Building in the Chicago Area, 1875-1925*, University of Chicago Press, Chicago 1964, still considered a fundamental work, or the more recent C. Gubitosi, *La scuola di Chicago e gli architetti della prateria 1871/1910*, Clean, Naples 2012.
[3] Allen Brooks was the first to express doubts about the term, preferring to include the Chicago experience in the more general history of the Commercial Style, see. H. Allen Brooks, *Chicago Architecture: Its Debt to the Arts and Crafts*, in "Journal of the Society of Architectural Historians", December 1971, pp. 312-317; Manfredo Tafuri states that "if the 'Chicago School' is that of Richardson, Root and Sullivan, then W. Le Baron Jenney is certainly not part of the 'Chicago School'"; see M. Tafuri, *Evoluzione dei grattacieli di Chicago*, in C. Gubitosi, *op. cit*, p.172, transcript of the speech of the conference of 1974. Francesco Dal Co also emphasizes that "the lowest common denominator of the Chicago School irreparably flattens the complexity, the contradictions, the multiplicity of responses in this unique circumstance"; see F. Dal Co, *Architettura e città negli Stati Uniti 1879-1910* in M. Tafuri, F. Dal Co, *Architettura contemporanea*, Electa, Milan (1974) 2009, p. 56. In this critical vein, among the most recent contributions, see. D. Bluestone, *Constructing Chicago*, Yale University Press, New Haven 1991.
[4] The city that in 1840 had only 4470 inhabitants in 1890 exceeded one million residents. See F.A. Randall, *History of the Development of Building Construction in Chicago*, The University of Illinois Press (1949) 2nd ed. 1999, p. 5.
[5] The steam elevator, installed for the first time by E.G. Otis in 1957 in New York, arrived in Chicago in 1857, while C.W. Baldwin built the first hydraulic elevator in 1870. The electric elevator began to spread from 1887. See. F.A. Randall, *op. cit*, p. 17.
[6] The first building to exceed ten stories was the Montauk Block (Burnham & Root, 1882-1883), and until 1905, the tallest building in Chicago was the Masonic Temple (Burnham & Root, 1892). See. *ibid*, pp. 16 and 18.
[7] S. Giedion, *op. cit*, p. 374. Instead, Tafuri makes a completely different judgement, considering the building to be the emblem of capitalism and "the heresy of organic American culture," which instead is expressed in the Monadnock, M. Tafuri, *op. cit*, p. 172. The historian draws broadly from a contemporary critic of Burnham and Root, Montgomery Schuyler, who in 1898 wrote that "If this [the Reliance Building] is the most and best that can be done with the skyscraper, the skyscraper is architecturally intractable", *ibid*, p. 158.
[8] See. L. Benevolo, *op. cit*, p. 242.
[9] S. Giedion, *op. cit*, p. 383. Giedion negatively interpreted the Exhibition inasmuch as it broke the continuity between the Chicago proto-skyscrapers and the works of the Modern Movement in Europe; the same critic places the Leiter Building in relationship with Le Corbusier's Maison Clarté (Geneva, 1930-1932), and the Reliance Building in relationship with the project for a glass tower designed by Mies van der Rohe (1921). See *ibid*, pp. 371-377.
[10] See. L. Benevolo, *op. cit*, p. 245.

Bibliography
Charernbhak W., Arbor A., *Chicago school architects and their critics*, UMI Research Press, Michigan 1981.
Colaianni D., Colaianni V.G., *I grattacieli e la scuola di Chicago*, Franco Angeli, Milan 2002.
Condit C.W., *The Chicago School of Architecture: a history of commercial and public building in the Chicago area, 1875-1925*, University of Chicago Press, Chicago 1964.
Denti G., *Morfologia e qualità della metropoli. Il caso di Chicago 1784-1910*, Franco Angeli, Milan 2005.
Frazier N., *Louis Sullivan and the Chicago school*, Crescent Books, New York 1991.
Gubitosi C., *La scuola di Chicago e gli architetti della prateria 1871/1910*, Clean, Naples 2012.
Randall F.A., *History of the Development of Building Costruction in Chicago*, The University of Illinois Press, Chicago 1949 (2nd ed. 1999).

Manhattan skyline,
New York, 1915

30

OFFICIAL BIRDSEYE VIEW—WORLD'S COLUMBIAN EXPOSITION, CHICAGO, 1893.

MARSHALL FIELD & COMPANY'S WHOLESALE STORE.
Fifth Avenue, Adams, and Quincy streets. One of the finest and most imposing stone structures in the city.

World's Columbian
Exposition, Chicago, 1893

Daniel Burnham, Marshall
Field and Company
Building, Chicago, 1892

Louis Sullivan, Carson,
Pirie, Scott and Company
Building, Chicago, 1899

32

Louis Sullivan, Carson,
Pirie, Scott and Company
Building, Chicago, 1899

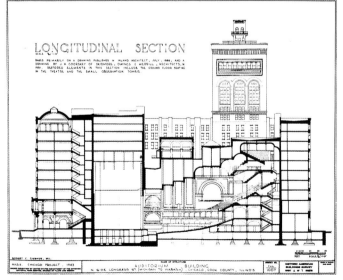

Louis Sullivan and Dankmar
Adler, Auditorium Building,
Chicago, 1877-1879

Louis Sullivan, Schlesinger
and Mayer Department
Store, Chicago, 1899-1904

Opposite
Louis Sullivan and Dankmar
Adler, Wainwright Building,
St. Louis, 1891

Fabio Mangone

Modernisms

odernisms affected much of Europe between the last two decades of the nineteenth century and the First World War. They rendered concrete the desire for renewal and the wish to move beyond revivalist languages that had been latent for the whole century, but until then never convincingly expressed. As regards such modernisms, it seems more appropriate to speak of a phenomenon rather than a movement, in that it involved currents that were articulated in various and independent ways in different countries, though they were contemporary to each other, shared significant cultural premises and were connected by a thick web of contacts and exchange. The wide circulation of illustrated architectural journals, periodical and otherwise, which often set "trends", facilitated the international dimension of the phenomenon. The modernisms consisted both of the more conspicuous movements such as Belgian and French Art Nouveau, Catalan Modernism, the Viennese and Prague Secession, the Scottish Modern Style, the German and Finnish *Jugendstil*, the Italian Liberty or *floreale* style and more unstable tendencies that emerged in various European nations, such as Switzerland, Hungary, Holland, Russia and Turkey. With the exception of Italy, where the name Liberty was

taken from the well-known English commercial enterprise, the names themselves of what was recognized as a fully modern "style" were already almost an embodiment of the desire for novelty, of a wish to move away from the academic tradition (Secession). The term "Art Nouveau", coined in the French-speaking nations to denote the local end-of-century progressive architecture, is often extended to indicate the whole phenomenon of modernisms. In the ambition to achieve a cosmopolitan dimension, the phenomenon of modernisms was posited in clear opposition to the various notions of a national style developed in the various European countries. Two important consequences derive from this. The first is that, no means by chance, the phenomenon found more fertile terrain in those contexts where the "administrative" sphere of the state was perceived as being limiting or antithetical with respect to the more authentic ethnic or cultural dimension of a given "people", as occurred in Catalonia, Sicily, Hungary, Scotland, Finland, contexts in which – and this is no accident – there was a particular propensity to draw on regional accents as well. The second is that this architecture met above all the aspirations of a cosmopolitan industrial bourgeoisie, and thus found its own natural field of application in homes (especially upper bourgeois ones) and in elitist establishments for leisure and tourism (big hotels, spas and bathing stations, Kursaal complexes and casinos, tea rooms), while it struggled to inform buildings intended to represent State officialdom, such as ministries, courts, parliament buildings (with the illustrious exception of Ernesto Basile's extension of Montecitorio in Rome). However, it should not be forgotten that where the best cultural conditions existed — such as, for example, the Brussels of Victor Horta and the Barcelona of Antoni Gaudí — modernisms were the expression of progressive and engaged bourgeois circles: it was in this ambit, for instance, that the no longer existent Maison du Peuple of Brussels was conceived in an Art Nouveau key.

From the point of view of languages, or of the "style", to use the terminology of the age, the various currents did not have a common identity. Indeed, they were rendered concrete in divergent formal ways. For example, while the Belgian and French Art Nouveau was characterized by a "graphic" style based on the sinuous line, the Viennese Secession favoured the expressiveness of two-dimensional elements and of orthogonal geometries, and Catalan Modernism was distinguished by markedly sculptural languages far removed from elementary geometry. Despite the extreme variability of the languages in which the various articulations of modernism were expressed, there were many common premises and the grounds for a shared poetics. Above all, these currents shared a desire to react to the contemporary eclecticism by searching for stimuli and sources of inspiration lying outside the tradition of historic styles: in some contexts, designers were bolder in drastically reducing the use of traditional elements; in other ones, such as Italian Liberty, attempts were made to find compromise languages, blending new modernist impulses with persistent eclectic approaches. In the longing to escape historic-stylistic revivals, to a large extent, and parallel to some contemporary experiences in painting and sculpture, possibilities were found for discovering new expressive ideas and stimuli in nature — in more evident forms in the case of Belgian Art Nouveau or Catalan Modernism or Italian *floreale*, and more latently in other cases. In some interesting instances, and in relation to some interesting figures — such as Henry van de Velde in Belgium or Peter Behrens in Germany or Ernesto Basile in Italy — the search for new languages also acquired substance in the stimuli deriving from the contemporary Middle European theories of artistic perception, like those of "pure visibility" and of *Einfühlung* or empathy, and of artistic creativity such as *Kunstwollen* or "artistic will". Another fundamental element unifying all the currents of modernism lay in the centrality assigned to the applied arts and the domestic project: a common presupposition was situated in the English movement of ideas whose leading exponent was William Morris, and in the Arts & Crafts experience. What was common in particular was the desire to bring art into everyday life, and to endow even commonly used objects and spaces with artistic qualities; the revolutionary idea of a socialism of beauty that should reach all levels of society was generally accepted, even though it did not really prove possible to bring new architectural and artistic products to every social class. No means by chance, almost all modernist works aspired to be a *Gesamtkunstwerk*, that is to say, a total artwork coherent right down to the smallest detail. On the one hand, designers tended to pursue absolute homogeneity even in the most minute architectural detail, carefully conceived even in very close-up scales; every functional element was interpreted in decorative terms, and value was also attributed to the use of high-quality craft products. On the other hand, the designing

his work achieved a synthesis of the permanent architecture of Joseph Olbrich, the staging by Josef Hoffmann, the sculpture of Max Klinger and the music of Ludwig van Beethoven.

The leading exponents of the modernist currents in architecture were: in Belgium, Victor Horta, Paul Hankar and Henry van de Velde (also an important theorist); in France, Hector Guimard and Henri Sauvage; in Catalonia, Antoni Gaudí, Lluís Domenèch i Montaner and Francesc Berenguer i Mestres; in Austria, Otto Wagner, Joseph Olbrich and Josef Hoffmann; in Scotland, Charles Rennie Mackintosh; in Germany (where Van de Velde and Olbrich were also active), August Endell; in Italy, Ernesto Basile, Giuseppe Sommaruga and Raimondo D'Aronco (also active in Turkey); in the area of the modern-day Czech Republic, Jan Kotěra; and in Finland, Eliel Saarinen.

Historiography has largely expressed the conviction that the phenomenon of modernisms constitutes the first complete episode of renewal under the influence of the so-called Modern Movement, though there are also the discordant views of those who, on narrowly ideological lines, have seen in this phenomenon an extreme outcome of the old nineteenth-century architecture, based on aestheticism for its own sake and pervaded by a conservative "class" principle. It remains clear, however, that it represents a crucial watershed between nineteenth-century eclecticism and the Neues Bauen of the twentieth century, besides being one of the rare moments in which an absolute coherence was achieved between architecture and design.

of the furniture and furnishings, and possibly of accessories as well, was not regarded as being separate from the architectural project, and there were some remarkable instances of "self-commissions": Henry van de Velde, in planning every detail of his home in Uccle, went so far as to design the clothes his wife was to wear, while Peter Behrens even designed the cutlery and the porcelain dinner services for his house in Darmstadt.

A further aspect of this poetics also took the shape of a search for fruitful collaborations with painters and sculptors, as occurred for instance in Secessionist Vienna. The aim was to achieve full-blown "synaesthesias", that is to say, aesthetically coherent works possibly liable to plurisensorial perception. One emblematic example is Gustav Klimt's *Beethoven Frieze*, produced for an exhibition held in the Secession Building in 1902, where

Bibliography
Duncan A., *Art Nouveau (World of Art)*, Thames & Hudson, New York 1994.
Russell F. (edited by), *Art Nouveau Architecture*, Academy Editions, London 1979.
Schmutzler R., *Art Nouveau*, Abrams, New York 1962.

Victor Horta, Hotel Tassel,
Bruxelles, 1893-1894

Opposite
Victor Horta, Hotel
Autrique, Bruxelles, 1893

41

Charles Rennie Mackintosh,
Art School, Glasgow,
1897-1899

42

William Van Alen,
Chrysler Building,
New York,
1928-1930

Opposite
Victor Horta, Hotel
Tassel, Bruxelles,
1893-1894

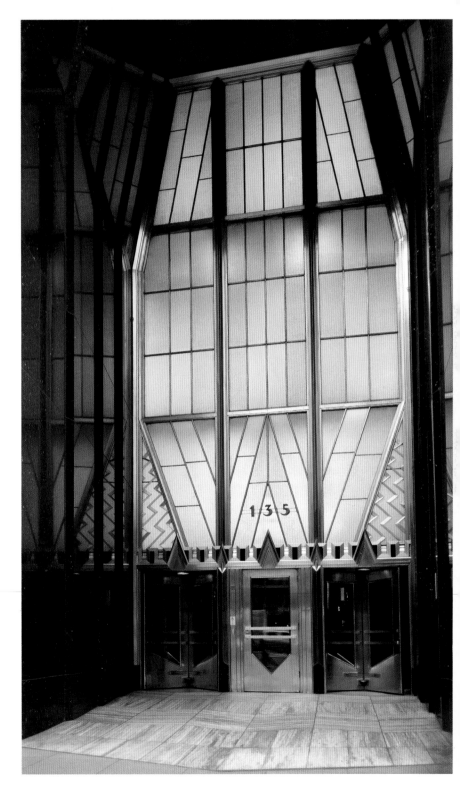

Fabio Mangone

Art Déco

Art Déco, or more simply Déco, is not a specific architectural phenomenon, but an intense season of taste that involves a number of the primarily "minor" visual arts, including painting, graphic design, furniture, jewellery, sculpture and clothing. The term defining it perfectly reflects the nature of this largely decorative phenomenon: its name derives from the famous exhibition of Decorative Arts held in Paris in 1925, which in many ways coincided with the height of the season of the bourgeois taste that prevailed throughout the 1920s and had a few tired survivors into the Thirties. But it must be said that in specific regard to architecture, that same exhibition was composite in nature and often lay outside that same notion of Art Déco. This was demonstrated by the more traditional pavilions, such as the one by Armando Brasini, and the more innovative ones, such as those designed by Perret, Le Corbusier, and Melnikov.

The concept of Art Déco, commonly applied to some of the architecture of the Twenties and Thirties, deserves some specification. There has never been a real theory of Art Déco. It was never a movement or school of architecture through which architects working in the Twenties and Thirties might be recognized. Nor is there a recognized Déco method to guide the overall approach to design, the composition of the plans, or the adoption of techniques and technologies. Critics defined the character of Déco after the fact. It was never programmed or recognized in the years in which it flourished. It was defined in some works that although were perhaps antithetical in some aspects, had a certain decorative modern but not too avant-garde orientation, thus limiting such a qualification primarily to the ornamental epidermis of the exterior volumes and the interior spaces. It was not by chance that some informed scholars felt that in architecture, it was more correct to speak in terms of Déco "taste" than Déco "style". The formal elements that distinguish Déco can be recognized primarily in the dominance of the line, no longer smooth and wavy as in Art Nouveau, but dry, sharp, and angular, with a Greek or zigzag motif, or flat swirl motifs. It was just such a line that often generated the clean, sharp, two-dimensional geometric figures that designed, adorned, and gave rhythm and order to architectural volumes and surfaces, with a special fondness for fan motifs, and the ziggurat. In some sense we could say that in architectural decoration as well, Art Déco lead, to some extent, to a routine in the crystalline and faceted forms of

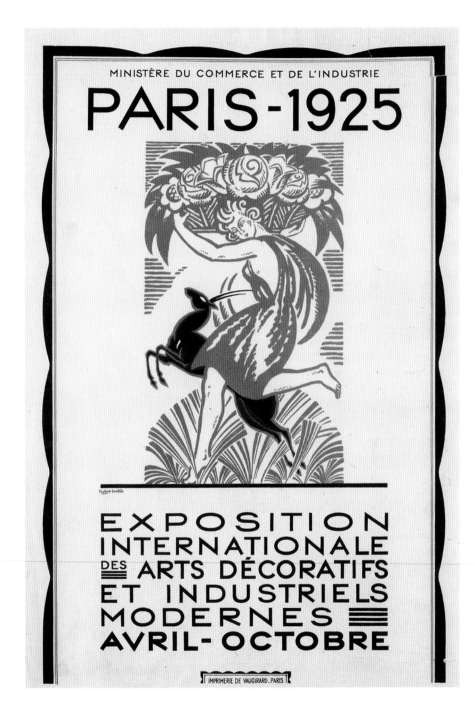

cubism and futurism. When the motifs are taken, rather than from the infinite repertoire of geometric shapes, from the figurative world - with a special preference for certain themes such as the cornucopia or the basket of roses - there is always a clear emphasis on the fact that it is a graphic stylization without any pretence to naturalism or mimesis. The fundamental role that decoration takes on is mostly declined with a strong preference for sophisticated finishes, for precious materials, for shiny surfaces, for fine handcrafted details. At the origin of these decorative patterns, one can primarily recognize certain trends that immediately followed Art Nouveau, widespread around the time of the First World War in Germany and Austria, and to some extent the lines of research of the Wiener Werkstätte and the same Josef Hoffmann. Born and developed in Europe, where while it might not have represented a more qualified modernity, it certainly represented a more widespread modernity, it was easy to proselytize to the Déco taste thanks to the ease with which its aesthetic principles could be transmitted, and its disengaged bourgeois and fashionable character, which eventually gave it a truly intercontinental reach. It met with considerable success in America, where not by chance, on the one hand, it provided a reliable line for the development of urban skyscrapers, especially in New York, and on the other hand, it informed entire neighbourhoods of vacation and recreation cities, such as Miami Beach, which has also been termed "tropical déco". In many places outside Europe, still subject to some extent to the European domain, and especially in North Africa - as the examples of Casablanca and Algiers bear witness - Art Déco represented the colonial style par excellence of the Twenties and Thirties. Finally, Déco taste even reached Asia, with limited but significant examples, as the extraordinary Bhawah Umaid Palace in Jodhpur in India bears witness.

In its various versions, Déco taste showed itself to be absolutely flexible in absorbing formal heterogeneous suggestions and ideas: secessionist and neo-secessionist (especially in Central Europe), Barocchetto and neo-eighteenth century (particularly in Italy), variously "exotic" and primarily Aztec and pre-Columbian (especially in the United States after the cultural expeditions to Mexico in 1924), and even rationalist or pseudo-rationalist ideas. Even certain works traced to avant-garde movements, but without a truly innovating inspiration, can be traced to Art Déco, such as the many works of the Twenties by the futurist Virgilio Marchi, and the many results of Bohemian "rondocubism".

Bibliography
Bayer P., *Art déco architecture: design, decoration and detail from the twenties and thirties*, Thames & Hudson, London 2003.
Bossaglia R., *L'Art Déco*, Laterza, Rome-Bari 1984.
Breze C., *American art déco: architecture and regionalism*, Norton & Co, London-New York 2003.
Larbodière J. M., *Paris art déco: l'architecture des années 20*, Charles Massin, Paris 2008.

Page 47
Exposition Internationale
des Arts Décoratifs
et Industriels Modernes,
Paris, 1925

Henri Sauvage, Studio
Building, Paris, 1926-1928

49

Henry Vaughan Lanchester,
Umaid Bhawah Palace,
Jodhpur, India, 1929-1943

William Van Alen,
Chrysler Building,
New York, 1928-1930

Antonello Marotta

Jugendstil, Sezessionstil, Catalan Modernism, the Glasgow School

The eclectic movements that characterized the nineteenth century involved a style that was intended to evoke the past in a blend of genres, while the Jugendstil was established to overcome the historical vision. It considered nature to be a teacher. In the same way that Impressionist painting left the studio and easel to go outside and work in nature, architecture was also seeking an idiom based on plant forms and organic lines.

The classicist and eclectic styles worked well in museum designs, and the buildings constructed in the main capitals of the time bear witness to this. These were complex architectures that incorporated grammatical memories of the past in their claddings and coverings. There was a return to the classic tympanum, the Ionic columns on the front that evoked the temple, the Roman pilasters and again, the spaces of vaulted ceilings or domes inspired by sixteenth-century architecture. In this interpretation, in which architecture again

gave a listing of its DNA, not only did the museum contain works as exhibitions and a conservation of the past, but more than anything, they framed all the other previous memories in their volumes as containers. The museum and the city were seen as inseparable. Between 1815 and 1830, in Munich, Leo von Klenze designed the Glyptothek, a classical temple designed to house marble statuary as well as the mental structures of that culture. Between 1823 and 1828, in Berlin, Karl Friedrich Schinkel designed the Altes Museum, a building with a portico and rooms in a telescopic configuration, an expression of the cultural, artistic, social and political level of the city. In 1891, in Vienna, Gottfried Semper completed the Kunsthistorisches Museum as a palace of culture, conceived on a Renaissance model in its organization of the spaces. The museum-building reached the heights of splendour during this phase in which culture and power

were fused together to communicate an image of memory, to provide a mirror for a renewed social sense, or an ideal aspiration. In these works, the past, through the use of the architectural quote, re-emerged as an archaeological memory.

The end of the nineteenth century was marked by great social and economic change, triggered by the industrial revolution. These profound changes created the need for a new style, a style that no longer made numerous references to the past, but rather to a renewed bond with nature, as already mentioned. It was in England that the historical connections and the foundations of the movement were to be found. William Morris began a dialogue with the Pre-Raphaelite movement, whose members included Dante Gabriel Rossetti and John Everett Millais, among others. This movement followed the common path to recover a tradition that predated the Renaissance. It opposed both industrialization and mass production. The Arts and Crafts movement, founded on the principles developed by Morris, aimed at returning to craft, to an anti-mechanization approach, and an idea of the integrated and cohesive society. What was happening from the mid-nineteenth century developed into a new material concept. In fact, the materials changed with the emerging industrial transformation, and while Morris built the Red House (1850), again using a "traditional" model, when the great works were built, such as infrastructures, bridges, bold new buildings, iron became the conveyer of a new aesthetics.

While eclecticism was characterized, as we have seen, by a revival of different styles taken from the past, the Jugendstil sought an expression for the new era. Underlying this style were elements from the Arts and Crafts movement, the Gothic Revival, the tie to Pre-Raphaelite painting, and the revolution

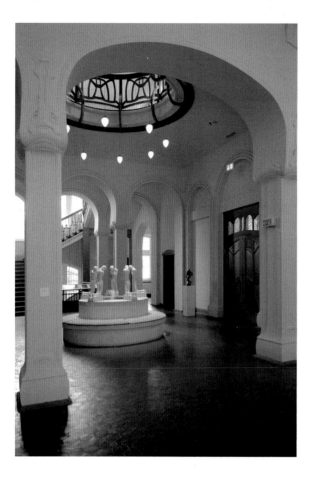

triggered by Impressionist and Symbolist art. Furthermore, the experiments on curving wood for Thonet chairs identified this need for a technique to bend surfaces, following nature's lines, just as Pre-Raphaelite painting sought a new vision related to the senses in the body's fluidity.

We shall now analyse the architectural achievements of the Jugendstil, the Sezessionstil, the Glasgow School and Catalan Modernism. The Jugendstil took its name from the German periodical "Die Jugend", published in Munich, Bavaria since 1896. This trend, which soon had several names – Art Nouveau in France, the Modern Style in England, Modernism in Spain, Liberty in Italy, and Sezessionstil in Austria – was a success throughout Europe.

In the late nineteenth century, the theory of the *Einfühlung* aesthetic was developed in German culture. It addressed the themes of *empathy* and *symbolic sympathy*. This *feeling together* established a new relationship between the subject and the object, between being and the phenomenological reality. Combining the idealistic thinking and new-born studies in psychology, investigations were beginning, investigations into the relationships between the forms of nature and those of man. This research was formalized by the aesthetic scholars Vischer and Lipps, but owes much to Worringer for its diffusion. In 1908, he wrote the text *Abstraktion und Einfühlung*, where he shed light on two approaches, one which tended to be organic, applied according to aesthetic principles of nature, and an opposite one that tended toward abstraction, typical of the early phase in which feelings related to order and geometric purity prevailed. Associated with *Einfühlung* are the experiments in concave and convex form which found ample space in the research of the new style: we only have to think of Gaudí's Catalan Modernism, and the more strictly geometric-abstract experiments

Page 55
Joseph Maria Olbrich,
House of Secession, Vienna,
1897-1998

Henri van de Velde,
Karl Ernst Osthaus, Hagen,
1906-1908

Antoni Gaudí, Casa Batlló,
Barcelona, 1877

Antoni Gaudí, Casa Milà,
Barcelona, 1905-1912

57

Joseph Maria Olbrich,
Mathildenhöhe, Darmstadt,
1908

Page 60
Otto Wagner, Austrian
Postal Savings Bank, Vienna,
1906

by Wagner and Mackintosh. We should mention one of the most important figures of the Jugendstil, the Belgian Henry van de Velde and his work.

As a supporter of the importance of craft and the workshop, from 1906 to 1914 he was the director of the Weimar Kunstgewerbeschule, a school of applied arts in craft that brought together artistic processes and applied processes. In 1919, the school, under the direction of Gropius, was transformed into the Bauhaus School, following the merger with the Hochschule für Bildende Künste, a school of fine arts. Van de Velde believed in the fundamental role of defending the crafts, to the point that throughout his life he worked in various artistic fields, such as the design of furniture, book binding, the design of graphic characters and clothing. A constant feature of the Jugendstil was the idea that the new style would extend not only to architecture but also to all objects that were part of life, according to the principle of total art.

At the behest of patron Karl Ernst Osthaus, between 1901 and 1902, van de Velde designed the furnishings and décor of the Folkwang Museum in Essen. The materials, such as stone, wood and metal, were used in a floral style, with stylized forms that clarified the need to surpass the principle of ornament tied to historicist models. In 1899, the German Grand Duke Ernst Ludwig von Hessen invited the Viennese architect Joseph Maria Olbrich to Darmstadt to work in an artists' workshop, a colony which became a centre for the Jugendstil. In 1908, the year of Olbrich's death, the Wedding Tower in the Mathildenhöhe complex was completed. The tower, made of bricks, was crowned by five arched elements, covered with blue tiles. Ernst Ludwig's wish was to build a centre for the reform of the visual arts. In Germany, no great works were created, but the aesthetic and cultural foundations were laid for the development of the movement in Europe. In Vienna, the Sezessionstil came into being. It was characterized by a compositional vision aimed at total art, bringing together the various artistic disciplines in a unique style. The architects Otto Wagner and his students, Joseph Maria Olbrich and Josef Hoffmann created a language that adhered to the spirit of the time, in line with the modern needs of construction and utility. In those years, Vienna was a vital centre of culture, art, literature and music. In 1897, the painter Gustav Klimt, the sculptor Max Klinger, and the architect Josef Hoffmann created the Viennese Secession movement. The intention was to break down the stagnant rules of the academy and build a centre, the House of Secession, where a total art would be developed. In 1898, Hoffmann designed the Secession building, a rectangular complex in the shape of a Greek cross, characterized by a symmetrical axis, in a classical configuration that was completed by a cupola of laurel leaves in gilded iron. The building aimed at summarizing the complexity of the secessionist movement and at the same time, was a venue for artists, with an atrium and office space, and an area for exhibitions which could also be held outdoors in a triangular shaped garden. Everything communicates a use of decoration in which the plans of the graphics, the interiors and the architecture are combined, where space and design are meant to be unified. The volume is generated by four cubes, modelled by the openings, which in their abstraction communicate a dialectic between classicism and the reduction to elemental forms. Vienna was the home of Sigmund Freud and his research aimed at unravelling the complexities of the mind. It is no accident that memory and the unconscious were being combined in the Viennese experiment, in the dialectical confrontation between the persistence of classicism and the origins of modern thought. Between 1904 and 1906, in Vienna, Otto

Wagner designed the interior of the Austrian Postal Savings Bank. Built a few years after the construction of the House of Secession, in this design we can see substantial language changes that open the field to modernity. The use of steel pillars and the arched vault, and the total absence of decoration, show a reduction to essentiality. The space is dignified but lacks any citation and clarifies research that was increasingly directed toward the industry's potential to build a modern and objective space. While in the House of Secession the link with the classical tradition was still intense, in this work by Wagner there are no nostalgic leanings toward the golden past, paving the way for a new relationship between architecture and modern construction.

It was Charles Mackintosh, with the creation of the Glasgow School of Art (1896-1909) in Scotland, who characterized a variant of Art Nouveau in the United Kingdom. The school, with its necessary and monumental forms, is a stereo-metric square volume, in which the entrance is modelled like a sculpture that gives the whole a more meaningful aspect in the excavation of the stone. The large windows that illuminate the drawing studios show a rational approach to the design, which in some ways anticipates modern research. The internal space is flexible and characterized by mobile wings. A rationality of intent prevails in the architecture, while many details such as the bay window, the decorations, and the wooden furnishings, confirm a love for decoration, a product of these years, and show an adherence to dynamic and stylized organic forms. In 1900, the Scottish architect was invited to Vienna to exhibit his works at the Secession exhibition, curated by Olbrich. This occasion was a milestone in Viennese culture and in particular for the design vision of Josef Hoffmann, who drew from it a lesson in rigour and essentiality, the prescient feature of modern thought.

In Barcelona, Antoni Gaudí was carrying out some of the most interesting research into the new style, with a movement known as Catalan Modernism. He was a shy and problematic man who found his inspiration in nature, and that empathy (*Einfühlung*) with living forms that he transposed into his architecture. He used to state, "The tree is my master," an affirmation that interpreted the clay and the skeleton, the structure and nature fused together. It was an organic world that brought something Gothic to the dynamic and complex spaces to give life to history. Count Eusebi Güell offered him the opportunity to create the famous park, built between 1900 and 1914, where Gaudí gave proof of his qualities as an architect, landscape architect and decorator, in the sinuous surfaces of the benches, in the monumental staircases, the sloping arcades and the multi-coloured buildings. The Catalan architect had also a strong interest in majolica surfaces but especially in the structures, to which he devoted intense studies that converge in his famous sculptural works. Between 1904 and 1906, he designed the Casa Batlló whose façade is decorated with balconies that evoke an imaginary and primitive world. This is sculptural architecture, where, in polychrome cladding, the cylindrical tower grows, and a large courtyard with blue tiles floods the indoor spaces with coloured light.

Certainly with the Casa Milà Gaudí designed one of his most powerful works, in which the plan is shaped by an organic concave-convex force. All of this has the telluric action of a base of carved rock. Inside, two large courtyards and three sets of stairs solve the problems of distribution and lighting, while the exterior, free from restrictions, seems symbolic and material, driven by a vital energy, similar to the action of wind and water on rock. The construction seems to respond to the possibilities of reinforced concrete, for its formal freedom, but was made of limestone blocks and iron beams.

This work anticipates the visionary and expressive poetics of Le Corbusier's Unité d'Habitation in Marseilles (1947-1952), but instead of the roof garden, the Catalan architect designed a system of small towers, of chimneys that recreate, in the space trodden by the roof, a highly imaginative environment full of symbolism.

The currents of modernism, full of different cultural views, in their complex confrontation with tradition and modernity anticipate the research that began in the Twenties and Thirties, marked by the relentless confrontation with industry and the machine. These currents eventually decreed the abandonment of an artisan approach in favour of the rationality of mass production.

Bibliography
De Fusco R., *Storia dell'architettura contemporanea*, Laterza, Rome-Bari 1992.
Fanelli G., Godoli E., *Josef Hoffmann*, Laterza, Rome-Bari 2005.
Fiell C. e P., *Charles Rennie Mackintosh (1968-1928)*, Taschen, Cologne 1995.
Lahuerta J.J., *Antoni Gaudì 1852-1926. Architettura, ideologia e politica*, Electa, Milan 2003.
Pevsner N., *I pionieri dell'architettura moderna. Da William Morris a Walter Gropius*, Garzanti, Milan 1999.
Trevisiol R., *Otto Wagner*, Laterza, Rome-Bari 2006.

Anna Barbara

Wiener Werkstätte and Deutscher Werkbund

At the turn of the late nineteenth and early twentieth centuries, architecture, art and the applied arts underwent the most radical innovation ever seen before: the industrial revolution. It was within this framework that countries such as England, firstly, and then Austria, Germany, Switzerland and Belgium, established actual organizations to assist and sanction the transition from artisan production to industrial production. These transitions were by no means natural and painless. They involved artists, architects, academies, training schools, companies, corporations, journals and above all, exhibitions. These exhibitions were a synthesis of all that was taking shape.

Two major organizations, the Wiener Werkstätte and the Deutscher Werkbund, provided the cultural, creative and productive models that gave rise to the Modern Movement. The great novelty introduced by these two organizations was the idea that architecture, furnishings, art and what later became known as design, all needed an element of entrepreneurship as well as creativity. Only when there was a meeting between vision, manufacturing and the market did the modern twentieth

century design project come into being. The main representatives of the Austrian architectural culture at the end of the nineteenth century, despite coming from a classical tradition, realized the need for a revival, something for which the Empire also felt a need. Otto Wagner, like his Belgian (Victor Horta) and Scottish colleagues (Rennie Mackintosh), understood that the future of architecture did not lie in revisiting and imitating the styles of the past, but in combing the potential offered by modern technology. Wagner began a process of renewal that also involved the Viennese Secession group and the key figure of Joseph Maria Olbrich, and completed it with the assistance of Joseph Hoffmann and the Wiener Werkstätte.

Joseph Maria Olbrich worked in Wagner's studio for five years, and in 1897 joined the Secession and designed its Vienna headquarters. He was invited to Darmstadt by Prince E.L. von Hessen to create a full scale project for a residence for artists. He was to design the architecture, its exhibition spaces, the decor, the gardens, the clothes, the dishes ... anything that could be designed.

The Secession, like the Wiener Werkstätte, had

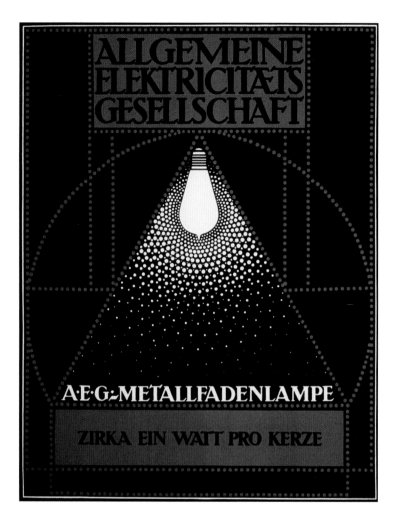

Page 63
Josef Hoffmann, Purkersdorf
Sanatorium, 1904-1905

Peter Behrens, Turbinenfabrik,
AEG, 1908-1909

Above
Peter Behrens, Advertising
poster, AEG, 1910

Opposite
Weissenhof, Stuttgart, 1927

a special character: they were not an avant-garde group breaking with the past, but rather connected to the intellectual bourgeoisie who became their client from the outset.

The relationship with the journals was strategic, because it was precisely through these that they introduced a synthesis between visual culture, graphic design, and art theory. The journals also acted on two other fronts: they used the language of the buyers of the new art, in other words, that middle class that was looking for a taste other than that of the aristocrats. For this emerging and wealthy class, they created complete stylistic scenarios as reference points from which to choose, decorate, and direct their tastes.

The main author of the Wiener Werkstätte was Joseph Hoffmann. A student at the Academy with Wagner, in 1898 he joined the Secession and subsequently began to teach at the Kunstgewerbeschule. In 1903, together with Koloman Moser, he founded the Wiener

Werkstätte, the Vienna workshops, as a consequence of the Secession and in response to the Academy of Art.

The Wiener Werkstätte were financed by Fritz Wärndorfer, who transformed a simple workshop into a real brand, capable of producing furniture, objects, fabrics, bookbinding, jewellery and so forth, with an unprecedented formula. The Wiener Werkstätte products were marked with the brand name and signatures of the designers and craftsmen, emphasizing the close relationship between all parties. The manufacturers dealt in unique pieces, were hostile to mechanization and placed importance on the materials, with the intention of emphasizing simplicity and functionality.

In their early years, the Wiener Werkstätte were incredibly successful and all the artists of the time, including Gustav Klimt, Oskar Kokoschka, Egon Schiele, Josef Hoffmann, Dagobert Peche, Otto Prutscher, Koloman

Joseph Hoffmann, Palais Stoclet,
Bruxelles, 1905-1911

Moser, Ernst Lichtblau and Josef Frank began
to produce objects in this environment that
was creative, productive and commercial.
Hoffmann was also the designer of the
Purkersdorf Sanatorium (1904-1905) and the
Palais Stoclet (1904). In these designs, the
intention was to purify forms into pure
geometry, forms that would shortly lead to the
Modern Movement.
At the Deutscher Werkbund too, the
relationship between art, craft and industry
was the central theme of the production
between the nineteenth and twentieth
centuries. In Germany, the debate on these
themes took on an emblematic tone because,
on the one hand, it was trying to promote
products on the domestic market that were

still in the hands of artisans, while on the
other, it attempted to penetrate foreign
markets with German products.
The positions were not aligned just as they
were not aligned in other countries because
some conceived this combining of art and
industrial production as a strength in an
expressive attempt to give aesthetic qualities
to industrial production. Others regarded it as
a threat, and others, more pragmatically, an
inexorable union in which both one and the
other would be reshaped.
A pioneer in the synthesis process was
Hermann Muthesius, who was sent to study
the English educational and manufacturing
systems, and on his return he reformulated
the national program *Kunstgewerbeschule*
(School of Applied Arts).
Once again, as had happened in Austria, it
was the England of John Ruskin and William
Morris that became the cultural reference.

Muthesius was opposed to imitating the styles of the past, as well as the extreme freedom of the Jugendstil, so between 1906 and 1907, on the occasion of the German arts and crafts exhibition in Dresden, he founded an association of manufacturers, traders and artists to revive applied art and architecture in Germany. In this case, the woodworking industrialist Karl Schmidt was also involved, as well as the chief architect of the municipality of Hamburg, Fritz Schumacher, and the liberal Friedrich Naumann. The signatories in 1906 were 12 architects and 12 companies, but in 1908, 492 had already joined and by 1920, there were 1870 members.

At the Deutscher Werkbund, the members were Germany's most prominent architects, but there were also the Belgian Henry van de Velde, the Dutch Hendrik Petrus Berlage and by affinity, also the Austrians Hoffmann and Wagner. One key figure to understanding the Deutscher Werkbund is Peter Behrens. He began in an artists' colony in Darmstadt, in the climate of novelty and uniqueness that was attempting to hold together various art forms. Behrens became strategic when he was appointed artistic adviser at the Aeg turbine factory. There he designed some of its buildings, but also the products and advertising. Behrens' studio became a hotbed of young architects who from there were soon to become the masters of the Modern Movement: Gropius, Mies van der Rohe and Le Corbusier.

The most significant events for understanding the momentous influence of the Deutscher Werkbund were the exhibition in Cologne in 1914 and the one in Stuttgart in 1927. During the exhibition in Cologne some highly paradigmatic works were created: Gropius and Meyer designed the pavilion to exhibit the production of the Deutscher Werkbund. Bruno Taut designed the Glaspavilion, completely made of glass, an extraordinarily imaginative and virtuosic work, and Van de Velde designed the theatre. But it was precisely at this moment of comparison that often contradictory differences arose: the proponents of "typification" or those of the *Kunstwollen*. In substance, on the one side there was industrial serialization and design, and on the other, the individualism of the artist and the artisan.

The other exhibition that sums up the debate and research was the one held in Stuttgart in 1927, which can be considered the concrete manifesto that gave birth to the Modern Movement. The most significant architects of the time were invited, such as Le Corbusier, Hans Scharoun, J.J.P. Oud, Ludwig Hilberseimer, and Walter Gropius. They had the task of designing the residential district of Weissenhof, following a master plan conceived and coordinated by Mies van der Rohe. The outcome was a work of extraordinary quality, which summarized the communality of issues and visions that crossed Europe.

The Deutscher Werkbund was closed in 1934 by the Nazi regime. It was reopened in 1950 and remained so until the Sixties.

Bibliography
Baroni D., D'Auria A., *Josef Hoffmann e la Wiener Werkstätte*, Electa, Milan 1981.
Benevolo L., *Storia dell'architettura moderna*, Laterza, Bari 1985.
Bisanz-Prakken M., Mainoldi C., Fabiani L., *Gustav Klimt e le origini della Secessione Viennese*, Mazzotta, Milan 1999.
Bressan M., De Grassi M. (edited by), *Ver Sacrum. Rivista d'arte della secessione viennese 1898-1903*, preface by R. Bossaglia, text by C. Benedik, Edizioni della Laguna, Mariano del Friuli 2003.
De Benedetti M., Pracchi A., *Antologia dell'architettura moderna*, Zanichelli, Bologna 1988.
Di Stefano E., *Secessione viennese. Da Klimt a Wagner*, Dossier d'art, Giunti, Florence 1998.
Fanelli G., Godoli E., *Josef Hoffmann*, Laterza, Rome-Bari 2005.
Gresleri G. (edited by), *Josef Hoffmann*, Zanichelli, Bologna 1981.
Sekler E.F., *Josef Hoffmann 1870-1956*, Electa, Milan 1991.
Witt-Dorring C. (edited by), *Josef Hoffmann. Interiors 1902-1913*, Neue Galerie, Museum for German and Austrian Art, Prestel, New York-Munich 2006.

Anna Barbara

The avant-garde movements: Futurism, Czech Cubism, Suprematism, Constructivism, Expressionism, De Stijl

The first decade of the twentieth century was marked by the emergence of numerous avant-garde movements in art, theatre, literature and architecture.
Although related to national contexts for the most part, they were all united by similar issues: the same desire to break with tradition; the use of journals as vehicles for propaganda; the invention of new languages capable of expressing the near future.
The first *Manifesto Futurista* (*Futurist Manifesto*), by Filippo Tommaso Marinetti, was published in 1909 in "Le Figaro" as an attack on traditionalism and unconditional praise of speed, dynamism, the machine and the active

experience of the senses in the creation and enjoyment of art, poetry, writing, music and sound, colour, the electric light, dynamic space and architecture. The legacy of the past, mummified in museums and academies, was attacked in favour of a new vitality. The privileged setting of Futurism was the modern metropolis, the stage for the community's strength. In 1910, the *Manifesto futurista di pittura* (*Futurist Manifesto of Painting*) was published, and in 1912, one on sculpture. The themes ranged from energy as a metaphor, to the electric light, the speed of movement and means of transport, which were among the privileged subjects, large-scale infrastructures, stations, factories, and power plants. Futurist architecture had no actual buildings, but it did have the extraordinary visions of Antonio Sant'Elia, who in 1914, with the Great War at the gates, printed *L'architettura futurista. Manifesto* (*Futuristic architecture. Manifesto*) in Milan. The outcome of these visions for "The New City" demanded not only new forms, but materials suited to structuring these virtuosic visions. These would be materials such as "cement, iron, glass, cardboard, textile fibre, and all those wood surrogates, stone and brick" that could highlight visible elevators, stairwells and high metal walkways, in order to achieve "the maximum of elasticity and lightness".

In parallel to Futurism in Italy, Picasso and Braque's theories on Cubism took root in architecture between the 1910s and 1920s in Prague, where large buildings, mansions, churches and their furnishings were being built. The theorist of Czech Cubism was Pavel Janak, who began with a sort of "pyramid-shaped cubism" that after the First World War was translated into the Czech culture as "rondocubism", blending misaligned and angular geometry with traditional Slavic semi-circles and signs. The most significant work by Pavel Janak was the headquarters of the Bank of the Foreign Legion (1920-1932) and numerous industrial buildings.

Among the works by Josef Gočár (1910-1912), the House of the Black Madonna was one of the liveliest representatives not only of Czech architecture, but of European avant-garde architecture of the time. Gočár was also the author of the State Railway Building, the church of St. Wenceslas and the Czechoslovak Pavilion at the Paris Exposition of 1925. Perhaps the best example of Czech Cubism is a small apartment building, the Hodek House, by Josef Chochol (1913), built just before the First World War. Bound by the acute shape of the lot on a slope, this small building exhibits many Cubist details: angles, plumes and

faceted frames, the composition of the façades superimposed on a clear structural grid, as well as corner recessed porticos, come directly from the Cubist dictionary. Czech Cubism was not a real movement and it lasted only five years, but it still occupies as important a position as other movements such as Wendingen, Futurism and German Expressionism and perhaps it is a necessary step to introducing the functionalism that followed the First World War.

The avant-garde trends were not only movements of semantic and formal experimentation, but also political and social movements. The Soviet avant-garde movements, which preceded the political revolution in Russia, felt the need from the outset to redesign and reconfigure the objectives in art in order for this to become an effective social and political tool, above all a tool that was capable of making the promised

Page 69
Antonio Sant'Elia, *Generating station*, 1914

Vladimir Tatlin, Monument to the Third International, 1919

Bruno Taut, Glashaus, Deutscher Werkbund, Cologne, 1914

changes visible. The relationship between political revolution and the avant-garde often consisted in giving concreteness to art, and as such its products and artefacts.

The *Manifesto of Suprematism* of 1915 is a work by Kazimir Malevich and the poet Mayakovski, and according to this, the abstract painting model ought to assume a spatial dimension provided by the geometric shapes of colour. The works by Malevich had architectural titles to emphasize the desire to work on pure plasticity, on the art that leads to art. For Malevich, art was not supposed to represent anything. It had to break free from reality to produce a new unprecedented reality. The straight line and the square were signs with which to build Suprematist art. Malevich set aside reality and brought it to absolute zero to make paintings of "white on white". For Malevich, art had to be disconnected from society in order for the artist to achieve spiritual independence.

In its first five years of life, the Russian Revolution swept through the bourgeois state institutions and abolished private property. Within this framework, the avant-garde movements lacked mediation and the new social models needed new and experimental forms to contain them. On the one hand, it legitimized classical architecture as the only architecture capable of embodying civic virtues, and on the other hand, the research and experimentation was carried to the extreme.

Of the Soviet avant-garde movements, constructivism also worked on materialist principles of labour under the pressure of the political and social revolution that was transforming Russia after 1919. Tatlin, Gabo, and Pevsner worked on the principle of surpassing art to immerse oneself in the concrete world and in the technical world of machines. Tatlin's Monument to the Third International (1919) was the symbol of this: a 400-meter high steel spiral that was supposed to contain a cube, a pyramid, a cylinder and a hemisphere in glass. It was intended to host meetings, be an information centre, but in particular, it would celebrate the fusion of the arts into a single "constructive" activity.

Elsewhere, under the banner of expressionism, all those creative and artistic phenomena that between 1910 and 1925 crossed through Germany and the Netherlands, were becoming more intense. The definition is very controversial because it sometimes refers to a concept, sometimes a style with sinuous forms, at times generating simplifications or inclusions that range through the works of Michel de Klerk, Bruno Taut, Hans Poelzig, Pieter Kramer, Otto Bartning, Hugo Häring and in part, Gropius's experiments as well.

A starting point of Expressionism in architecture could be the *Glashaus* by Bruno Taut, for the Exposition of the Deutscher Werkbund in Cologne in 1914. This crystal

and steel pavilion dematerialized form and left the task of building volumes to the light, a literary translation of the writings of Paul Scheerbart on "glass architecture". Taut not only wished to exalt the expressive and technical potential of glass, but also succeed in formulating a representation of an ideal future.

Another form of expressionism came from Erich Mendelsohn, a Prussian who, in 1911, came into contact with the Blaue Reiter (Blue Rider) movement and espoused the idea that form originated from a tension capable of fusing the parts and the whole. Architecture was a synthesis in a unique and central image of all the compositional, structural, and formal tensions. In the Einstein Tower in Potsdam (1920-1921), Mendelsohn tried to accomplish this synthesis by modelling the cylindrical body as a fluid sculpture.

Mies van der Rohe also attempted to engage in expressionist poetics, with a paradigmatic project of German expressionism of those years: the skyscraper at the Friedrichstrasse station (1921) in Berlin. It was a vision of a vertical prism that was supposed to have been completely made of glass, without pursuing a play of light and shadow, but rather the reflection of light on the individual fixed points of the design, which are the stairs and elevators.

In the same years, in the Netherlands, the first issue of "De Stijl" was published, affirming plastic art in architecture as an abstract matrix and therefore radically new as an architectural reference. In this case too, the past is understood as nostalgia and then denied almost unconditionally. The journal was edited by Theo van Doesburg and for years it

Bruno Taut, Glashaus, Deutscher Werkbund, Cologne, 1914

Erich Mendelsohn,
Einstein Tower, Postdam
1919-1922

Gerrit Rietveld,
Rietveld- Schröder House,
Utrecht, 1924

published pieces by the architect J.J.P. Oud, the painter Mondrian, the poet Kok and others. The most direct references are those to cubism and futurist visions, while forms of expressionism that could have had subjective or purely emotional value are denied. The single principle is the unity of the decorative arts called "Neoplasticism".

In fact, De Stijl was not a true and proper avant-garde movement and was always very much tied to the journal and its director and almost only editor. The members of De Stijl were not in contact with each other and some of them never even met. Apart from the first years in which there was intense collaboration at the international level as well, with Lazlo Moholy-Nagy, Richter and El Lissitzky, over the years the contributions to the journal diminished until they became almost authorial, and in 1928, with an issue dedicated to architecture and movement, "De Stijl" closed its doors. The compositional idea of Neoplasticism was methodologically very similar to the ideas that were circulating in the other avant-garde movements: juxtapose two-dimensional elements capable of generating tension and new plasticity. From painting, this method was transferred to the built urban space in the minds of urban planners. The Schröder House (1924), designed and built by Gerrit Rietveld in Utrecht, is the translation of the architectural theories on neoplasticism. At the head of a series of terraced houses, the house is on two floors, of which the ground floor has a fairly traditional plan with a kitchen and a bedroom, while the upper floor is a unique space that provides the possibility – by moving and rotating baffles – of being divided into bedrooms, living rooms and bathroom. The façades follow a functional composition and colour scheme that is also respected in furnishings and interiors.

Bibliography
Curtis W.J.R., *L'architettura moderna del Novecento*, Bruno Mondadori, Milan 1999.
De Benedetti M., Pracchi A., *Antologia dell'architettura moderna*, Zanichelli, Bologna 1988.
Scheerbart P., *Architettura di vetro*, Adelphi, Milan 1982.

Fabio Mangone

Neo-eclecticism

Known also as "return eclecticism", neo-eclecticism developed in Italy in the first decades of the twentieth century, in an ambiguous relationship of continuity with and reaction to the modernist Liberty trend. It cannot be considered a movement in the strict sense, in the absence of any genuine theorization clarifying its goals and ideological content; instead it should be seen as a strand of architecture with its own distinct and recognizable characteristics, found in the works of many architects active between the Tens and the early Thirties. Critics of the time often spoke of them in relation to the concept of the "fantastic".

On one hand neo-eclecticism was embodied in the Tens and Twenties in the lively and widespread practice of the utopian, highly imaginative and imaginary project, with a special enthusiasm for the monumental and celebrative theme. This is demonstrated by, amongst others, the designs of Giuseppe Mancini, Antonio Sant'Elia and Mario Chiattone when they were not pursuing Futurist or para-Futurist lines of inquiry, and of Giulio Ulisse Arata, Piero Berzolla and Silvio Gambini. On the other, it yielded a highly decorative architecture that was fairly lively in terms of its plastic values and emphatic in its monumental connotations,

which developed both in urban contexts – with public and private buildings – and in cemeteries. A greater concentration of this type of construction can be found in Genoa and along the Ligurian coast (with the buildings of Dario Carbone, Gino Coppedè, Giuseppe Mancini and Gaetano Orzali), and in Milan (with the works of Ulisse Stacchini, Giulio Ulisse Arata, Cesare Penati and Cesare Tenca, Achille Manfredini and, until the early Thirties, of Aldo Andreani). However, it is also present in many other cities, in the remarkable output of the architects who embraced this trend, such as Adolfo Avena in Naples or Paolo Bonci in Palermo, or in totally emblematic buildings such as the Mantua stock exchange by Andreani himself, or Palazzo Mincuzzi in Bari, the work of Aldo Forcignanò and Gaetano Palmiotto, or finally, in entire neighbourhoods such as the Coppedè in Rome.

The common elements are above all a kind of return to the use of historic stylistic features, as in the previous period of nineteenth-century eclecticism, but with a marked preference for showy neo-Mannerist and neo-Baroque traits, and above all with a totally new manner. The academic historic-stylistic features were deprived of their nature as elements of a shared and reassuring code,

Gino Coppedè, Coppedè
neighbourhood, Rome,
1913-1926

being blended instead into variegated composite mixes, often with exaggerations of scale or, alternatively, with a packing of the volumes and surfaces with signs. In this way, an absolutely new effect was produced in the name of a kind of absolute creative "individualism". What's more, critics read some of the most significant works of this phase in terms of personal idioms, speaking of the "Coppedè style" or the "Arata style" in relation to two leading exponents of this strand of architecture. The individualistic trait did not just concern the architect's ability to produce new compositions starting from fragments of history, but also to the building tendency to become an absolute and dominant cornerstone of an urban or landscape setting. Although neo-eclecticism may, on an initial approximate view, appear to be a delayed phase of nineteenth-century eclecticism, and therefore a mere rethinking of remote styles, in actual fact this tendency took shape by way of an important reflection on contemporary architectural experiences, including modernist ones: from the recent wave of monumentomania in Emperor William's Germany it drew a propensity for gigantism and for truncated pyramidal or at any rate prevalently vertical compositions; from Liberty, and more generally from

European modernisms, it inherited the possibility for a certain freedom in plani-volumetric composition, and the longing for a total artwork coherent right down to the last detail; from the exercises of the Wagnerschule, Otto Wagner's Viennese school, it took suggestive ideas of fantasy archaeological compositions. It shared many elements with Expressionist currents, albeit in a reactionary and historicist vein: the centrality attributed to the sketch, as a go-between linking individual creativity and architectural formativeness; the passion for architectural design as a research tool endowed with meaning in its own right; and the search for forms of individual expression able to interpret a more general state of mind or a collective taste.

Bibliography
Bossaglia R., "Dopo il Liberty: considerazioni sull'Eclettismo di ritorno e il filone dell'architettura fantastica in Italia", in *Studi in onore di Giulio Carlo Argan*, Multigrafica, Rome 1984.
Bossaglia R., Cozzi M., *I Coppedè*, Sagep, Genoa 1982.
Mangone F., *Giulio Ulisse Arata. L'opera completa*, Electa-Napoli, Naples 1993.
Mangone F., "La morte e l'eroe: archiscultura monumentale in Italia, 1890-1922", in *Nuova città*, Florence, no. 9, 1995.

Armando Brasini, Palazzo del Governo, Taranto, 1930-1934

Giuseppe Mancini, Villa Sem Benelli, Zoagli, 1914

Opposite
Gino Coppedè, Coppedè neighbourhood, Rome, 1913-1926

Ludovica Vacirca

Return to Order

At the end of the First World War, a part of the European architectural culture, excluded from contemporary historiography, beat a path toward modernity in the name of tradition and a renewed relationship of continuity with the past. This phenomenon led to a number of experiences in quite different contexts that were neither the result of a language nor of a single style, to the extent that any attempt at narrative runs the risk of falling into facile simplifications. If on the traditionalist horizon there is a common point that connects the individual isolated facts, it might be the quest for continuity with the past and the rejection of any historicist attitude. This continuity was based on the constant transmission of knowledge and values through which the new architecture was legitimized.

The need to "return to order" that had manifested itself in much of Europe before the war, both in literature as well as the visual arts, became more urgent when the war ended. In Italy, the art review *Valori Plastici* and the literary review *La Ronda* brought together a group of artists who opposed the recent avant-garde experience and called for a return to classical values and the ideals connected with them. Around 1919, in Milan, the twentieth-century movement was born as a reaction to the climate that had prevailed in the Italian architecture of the time, still tied to eclecticism. The new movement drew its ordaining principles for a new design method from history. These principles were close to the metaphysical painting of Giorgio de Chirico and Carlo Carrà and advocated by the art critic Margherita Sarfatti. "It is understood that there will be no slavish copy or elaborate contamination," wrote Giovanni Muzio (1893-1982) in an article that appeared in *Dedalo* in 1931, "but free choice in inspiration, and I would almost say that this classicism was none other than the touchstone by which to measure their efforts, so that every element sounds right and is straightforward."

Muzio, along with the protagonists of the Novecento group, such as Giuseppe De Finetti, Alpago Novello, Ottavio Cabiati, Gio Ponti and Gigiotti Zanini, in Via Moscova in Milan, designed the building destined to become the stone manifesto of a movement that, unlike the avant-garde and the rationalist movements, eschewed any rigid written program. The Ca' Brütta (1919-1922), as it was renamed with hostility by the Milanese, was an experiment in housing that broke away from the tradition of the bourgeois building, deriding it, with a combination of intentionally improper stylistic quotations, using tired and vulgar decoration on the façade, revealing its modernity in the typological and distributive solutions adopted. Echoes of Palladio can be found in the architectural designs of Muzio and those of Gigiotti Zanini (1893-1962). Their achievements, of which the working-class housing in Affori (1927) is an emblematic example, manage to reinterpret the classical idiom while focusing on local culture.

Despite the heterogeneous achievements of the individual members of the group, the constant focus on the urban aspect of the architectural object and its rootedness in place, which was manifested in the use of traditional construction techniques and materials, was one of the recurring themes both in the experiments of the Novecento group and those conducted by the traditionalist movements in other countries. In Germany, Paul Schmitthenner (1884-1949), a student of Theodor Fischer (first president of the Deutscher Werkbund) and professor at the School of Stuttgart (one of the most

important centres for the dissemination of traditional architectural culture), brought up the issue of the relationship between architecture and place in his studies on housing. For Schmitthenner, the dwelling, which had nothing to do with the functionalist idea of *machine à habiter*, was to be built with traditional techniques and materials and integrated into the landscape. In the numerous *Siedlungen* designed by him, including the Haus Deutschtums in Stuttgart (1924-1926), he was able to translate theory into practice, experimenting on a path parallel to that of rationalism. This path found its most fertile ground for experimentation in Germany.

In 1927, Schmitthenner was excluded from the Weissenhofausstellung in Stuttgart for his conservative ideas, along with Paul Bonatz (1877-1956). Also a student of Fischer, Bonatz, together with Friedrich Scholer, designed the Central Station in Stuttgart (1911-1928), a work that became the emblem of a research project whose object

was to simplify form. This monumental architecture played on the composition of pure volumes, and responded both to functional needs as well as those imposed by a cherished continuity with local tradition. Bonatz was commissioned by the Nazi Party to design the entire infrastructural network in Germany, but neither he nor Schmitthenner (among the first architects to openly support Hitler), were ever called upon by the Third Reich for the construction of those buildings that were to publicly represent power. The Party preferred the monumental classicism that found its voice in Albert Speer. It was a classicism reduced to an empty exercise in rhetoric and its premises were far removed from the results achieved, along different paths, by Auguste Perret (1874-1954) in France and Edwyn Lutyens (1869-1944) in England.

The classicism of Perret was the formal outcome of research focused on the possible relationships between structure, form and new building materials. As noted by Pigafetta, Abbondandolo and Trisciuoglio, these made up the cornerstone of the traditional French architectural culture. In the Musée des Travaux Publics (1936), classical order is used as an element of continuity with the past and then reformulated according to the rules of constructive logic which, thanks to the use of reinforced concrete, provided many new solutions to explore. The approach most certainly differed from the one taken by Lutyens, who achieved a "progressive classicism" – according to Gavin Stamp's

definition – after producing a wealth of domestic architectural designs, in line with the principles of the Arts and Crafts movement, returning to the forms and materials of local tradition. Public architecture such as the Palace of the Viceroy in New Delhi (1912-1929) and the monument to the fallen in the battle of the Somme at Thiepval (1924) were an opportunity to reinterpret classical tradition in a modern light. In memorial architecture of this type, which becomes the guardian of a common memory, the use of archetypal models was common practice. However, the triple arch of the monument to the fallen of Thiepval rejects any rhetoric, relying on the evocative power of its volumes and the abstraction of its form.

This forgotten story is linked to the quest for another route to modernity, rich in reflections and contradictions. However, it rarely managed to escape ideological evaluations (in part due to the relationships between theories and individual professionals and the twentieth century totalitarian regimes) and the interpretive categories on which the history of the modern movement is built.

Bibliography
Burg A., *Novecento milanese. I novecentisti e il rinnovamento dell'architettura a Milano fra il 1920 e il 1940*, Federico Motta, Milan 1991.
Ciucci G., *Classicismo-Classicismi. Architettura Europa/America 1920-1940*, Electa, Milan 1995.
Cohen J.L., *The future of architecture since 1889*, Phaidon, London-New York 2012.
Gambirasio G., Minardi B. (edited by), *Giovanni Muzio. Opere e scritti*, Franco Angeli, Milan 1982.
Pigafetta G., Abbondandolo I., Trasciuoglio M., *Architettura tradizionalista. Architetti, opere, teorie*, Jaca Book, Milan 2002.
Schmitthenner P., *Gebaute Form*, Leinfelden-Echterdingen 1984.

Above
Giovanni Muzio, Cà Brutta,
Milan, 1919-1922

Opposite
Gigiotti Zanini, Low-cost house,
Affori (Milan), 1927

Page 79
Giorgio De Chirico, *Piazza d'Italia*, 1915

Paul Bonatz, Central Station,
Stuttgard, 1911-1928

Edwin Lutyens, Monument
to the fallen in the battle
of the Somme, Thiepval, 1924

Chiara Ingrosso

L'Esprit Nouveau

L'Esprit Nouveau was an important aesthetics review founded by Charles-Edouard Jeanneret and Amédée Ozenfant in 1919. It was the first director, Paul Dermée, who chose its name, inspired by Guillaume Apollinaire's definition of the cultural atmosphere in modern Paris. In fact, its 28 issues, published between 1920 and 1925, were fully inspired by the avant-garde climate in Paris between the wars, where the plastic arts, but also music and poetry, enjoyed a particularly rich and lively moment.

The review was responsible for spreading the "purist" movement, whose manifesto, Après le Cubisme (1918), by Ozenfant and Jeanneret, expressed the need to overcome the decorative aspects inherent in cubism through research into an art that is focused on order and geometry, symbol of the new mechanical era. Of the pseudonyms chosen by the Swiss architect to sign his articles, from 1920, the name Le Corbusier continued to be associated with his entire architectural production.

The research into architecture by Le Corbusier that appeared in the pages of L'Esprit Nouveau was compiled in the book Vers une Architecture. The first edition of 1923 bears the signature of Saugnier, Ozenfant's pseudonym, as well as Le Corbusier. The sum of Le Corbusier's theory of the early Twenties, Vers une Architecture contains a collection of articles from the review, some of which were rewritten and further developed.

The L'Esprit Nouveau years represent the most intense phase of the Swiss architect's cultural formation. In 1917, thanks to Ozenfant, he moved to Paris permanently and began to frequent numerous artists such as Georges Braque, Juan Gris, Pablo Picasso, Jacques Lipchitz, Fernand Léger and others. From 1918, he also began to paint continuously, exhibiting in numerous galleries. His were "purist" paintings which portrayed "objects-types" in cold colours, arranged according to clear and stylized geometric patterns.

The premise underlying the theory of Jeanneret and Ozenfant is that the advent of the machine was a true revolution, practical as well as spiritual and aesthetic. Mechanization, being based on geometry and therefore involving mathematical order, has an artistic value. The modern steamship fully represents this aesthetic; to the point that the chapter Des yeux qui ne voient pas in Vers une Architecture defines it as: "The first step in the realization of a world organized according to the new spirit." Like the steamship, cars, airplanes and everything designed by

engineers must therefore be admired as free from academicism and the stylistic forms of the past.

With a short circuit typical of the avant-garde, mechanization was associated not only with the work of engineers but also classical art. In the pamphlet, *Après le Cubisme*, it was already stated that the new art of machines reflected that same "ideal of perfection" that the Greeks had in mind when they built the Parthenon. There is an important description of the temple in the chapter *Architecture, pure création de l'esprit* in *Vers une Architecture*, where Le Corbusier compares the plasticity of marble to the shininess of steel.

Both man's senses and spirit were therefore attracted to systems that were ordered by numerical proportions. Hence the importance, in architectural and figurative compositions, of rediscovering the planning schemes or blueprints that had already been used since ancient times, to which Le Corbusier devoted a chapter in *Vers une Architecture*. A similar scheme, such as the golden section or golden mean, gives a sense of unity which is the key to harmony and proportion in a classical composition.

Many of his works were based on these principles from 1922 onward, when he embarked on his professional career in Paris, working with his cousin Pierre Jenneret. In those years, he worked on his studies of housing units and their aggregation. La Maison Citrohan (1922), whose name evokes a well-known brand of automobile, a reworking of the Masion Dom-Ino (1915), is based on the Hennebique system, as well as

Poster for the exhibition *Amédée Ozenfant-Pierre Jeanneret Peintures Puristes*, Druet Gallery, Paris, 1921

Le Corbusier, *Vers une architecture*, Paris 1923

Le Corbusier, Ozenfant House,
Paris, 1926

Le Corbusier, L'Esprit
Nouveau pavilion,
International Exposition
of Modern Industrial and
Decorative Arts, Paris, 1925

Le Corbusier, Plan Voisin,
1922-1925

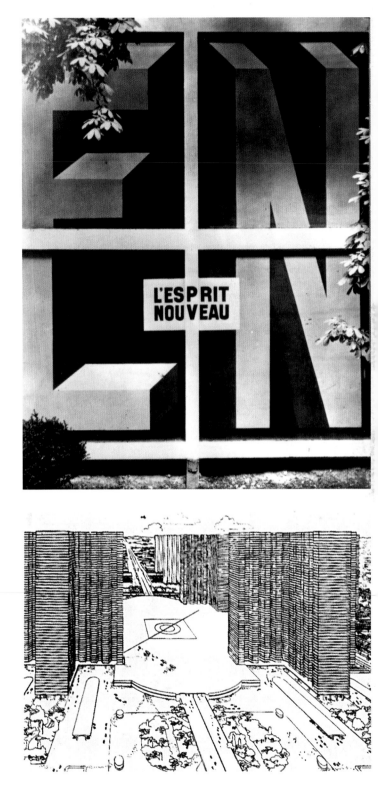

the *Immeuble-Villa* residential unit, which in turn was to become the general type of working-class housing that Le Corbusier developed in height and re-proposed in the project for the *Ville Contemporaine de 3 millions d'habitants* (1922). In 1925, in the *L'Esprit Nouveau* pavilion in Paris – which was actually the prototype for Maison Citrohan – he presented his project for the Ville Contemporaine accompanied by the Plan Voisin (1925), which was its practical application for the city of Paris. The houses in the garden city of Pessac (1926) and the two Wiessenhof buildings in Stuttgart (1927) are later versions of the Maison Citrohan.

At the same time, Le Corbusier and his partner designed a series of bourgeois villas in and around Paris, gradually experimenting with a new architectural idiom. Belonging to that period are Maison Ozenfant (1922), Maison La Roche-Jeanneret (1923), Maison Cook (1926), Villa Stein-de Monzie in Garches, and the Villa Savoye (1929).

To all intents and purposes these are "purist" villas, devoid of any stylistic reference, based on simple geometric and clear forms, characterized by novel structural elements introduced thanks to the contemporary revolutions in technology, first and foremost, reinforced concrete, and therefore a structural system based on a rigid frame.

As Robert Slutzky pointed out, there are strong similarities between the curved surfaces of the stairwells or the shaped partitions in Villa Stein-de Monzie with the "object-type" of the contemporary "purist" paintings, to the point that Jean-Louis Cohen defines this villa as "a painting decompressed in space."

But the cross-references between architectures, paintings and theoretical reflections did not stop there. In fact, the classical world was a constant reference and the façade elevations of both Maison La Roche-Jeanneret and Villa Stein-de Monzie

are based on planning schemes. Proven similarities between the plans for Villa Stein-de Monzie and Villa Savoye, and, respectively, the Malcontenta and Rotonda by Palladio, reinforce the references to antiquity. There are also constant references to the works of engineers, such as the large terraces of Villa Stein-de Monzie and Villa Savoye that clearly allude to the decks of steamships.

The villas constitute the most brilliant synthetic formulation of the direct consequences of mechanization applied to architecture, whose theoretical formulation goes back to *L'Esprit Nouveau*, then stigmatized since 1927 in the essay *Les cinq points de l'architecture nouvelle*. The introduction of the famous "five-points" (*pilotis*, free ground plan design, free façade design, "horizontal" window, roof-garden), regularly found in Le Corbusier's designs in those years, in fact responds to the need to introduce technological innovations in architectural design, a central assumption in Le Corbusier's theoretical formulation in the first twenty years.

The period of the first theoretical training and architectural experimentation lasted until the competition for the Palace of Nations (United Nations Office) in Geneva (1927), and came to a definitive end with the Swiss architect's leadership of the CIAM at the beginning of the Thirties, when his mature phase began, characterized by a long series of large-scale and highly representative commissions.

Bibliography
Boesiger W. (edited by), *Le Corbusier - Oeuvre Complete*, 8 vol., Zurich 1930-1970.
Cohen J.-L., *Le Corbusier: an Atlas of Modern Landscapes*, New York 2013.
Le Corbusier-Saugnier, *Vers une Architecture*, Paris 1923.
Olmo C., Gabetti R., *Le Corbusier e "L'Esprit Nouveau"*, Turin 1975.
Ozenfant A., Jeanneret C.-E., *Après le Cubisme*, Paris 1918.
Ozenfant A., Jeanneret C.-E., *La peinture moderne*, Paris 1925.

Amédée Ozenfant, *Untitled*,
c. 1927

Pages 90-91
Le Corbusier, Villa Savoye,
Poissy, 1929

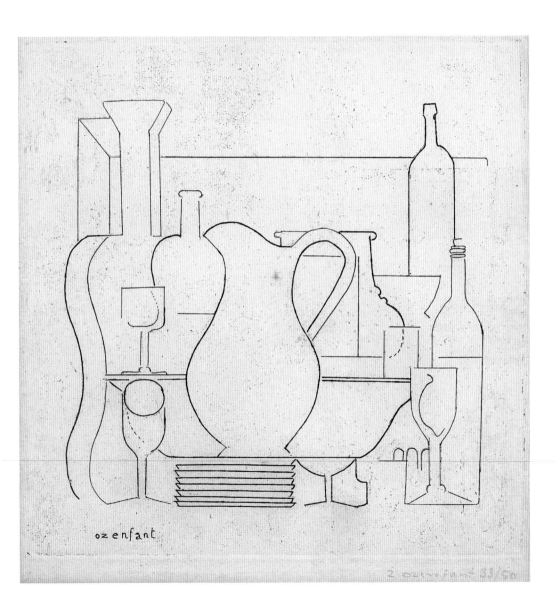

ozenfant

2·ozenfant 83/50

Antonello Marotta

Bauhaus and Vkhutemas

In 1919, Walter Gropius established the Staatliches Bauhaus, literally the "house of construction" which was a fusion of a school of applied arts in craft, the Kunstgewerbeschule in Weimar, and a fine arts school, the Hochschule für Bildende Künste The Bauhaus was founded with a revolutionary aim, to combine art and technology, painting, sculpture and architecture, in order to break down the distinction between the craftsman and the artist. Gropius developed the ideas of William Morris and Henry van de Velde, on craft and the importance of the workshop, but integrated them into the industrialisation process. Various different personalities were invited by him to form the school's core. These included Lyonel Feininger, Johannes Itten, and Gerhard Marcks. Paul Klee and Oskar Schlemmer began to teach there in 1921 and Wassily Kandinsky from 1922. The early phase followed an expressionist model, and Feininger's manifesto with its dynamic cathedral is reminiscent of this. Johannes Itten was certainly the teacher who embodied the school's direction with his basic course *Vorkurs*. The intention was to create a community that could practically and theoretically develop a sense of form and colour based on empathy. Itten was

introduced to Gropius by his wife Alma Mahler, for having worked, in Vienna, on a teaching method based on tact and the theory of colours. In 1923, Gropius theorized a new path for the Bauhaus coining the slogan "Art and technology: a new unity." This sanctioned greater adherence to the world of the factory, resulting in the crisis with Itten's training model. The Hungarian László Moholy-Nagy, who strengthened the line of Soviet Constructivism, was called on to replace him. This change of course was not painless, inasmuch as it shifted the direction from craft to industrial production, with the political contradictions that a similar openness would have generated. In those years, there was also a great leaning toward the theories of the Dutch De Stijl, characterized by basic shapes, primary colours, and the central role of the right angle, in a spatial construction decreed by the use of plates. The ostracism of the conservative regional government of Thuringia, in 1925, marked the end of Bauhaus activities in Weimar. The mayor of Dessau, Fritz Hesse, welcomed the school and teachers. In 1926, Walter Gropius completed the Bauhaus in Dessau, where it concentrated organizational, structural, and material models of industrialization in the

Ivan Leonidov, Lenin Institute of Librarianship, 1927

Liubov Popova, Sketch for "The magnanimous Cuckhold" by Fernard Crommelynck, 1922, Moscow, Tret'jakov Gallery

Page 94
Woman (Lis Beyer or Ise Gropius) sitting on the armchair by Marcel Breuer, photo by Erich Consemuller, 1926

functional and spatial program. The German master was looking to America, to the Fordist model of mass production of automobiles and transposing the same methodology to architecture. Giulio Carlo Argan explains the nature of Gropius' functionalism as a response to a phase marked by the irrationality of the war. This needed to be countered by a lucid, rigorous program, as a reaction to the historic chaos and despair. Argan interprets it as a factory and school model merged into a single structure to give shape to the vision of *work as education*. It is a building with a bridge design, anti-monumental, crossed through by a road. Composed of two parts, there is a rectangular section and an L-shaped section. The first section houses the classrooms and physics lab, the second, in a wing, the workshops and exhibition hall and the other, the theatre, canteen and kitchen. A two-storey section houses the administrative offices and that of the Director, and the meeting room for the Board. The section that connects the parts, suspended from the ground and supported by four pillars, is the fulcrum of the entire system. The Bauhaus in Dessau is a model of functionalism, where the parts fulfil their specific tasks. Emblematic of this is the body of workshops, with four stories that are all windows, for carpentry, metal working, wall decoration, weaving, printing, sculpture and theatre arts. Transparency, as Rudolf Arnheim clarified in 1927, is an expression of a political ideal of purity, order and clarity. The Bauhaus School is a pure white cathedral, where the body of the housing-workshops, six levels and twenty-eight rooms with jutting balconies, shows a vertical tension. The design is a dynamic and kinetic expression, where asymmetry, movement, and the rotation of the levels are triumphant. Klee's studies on the origin of the line and Kandinsky's on the theory of tensions gave Gropius principles

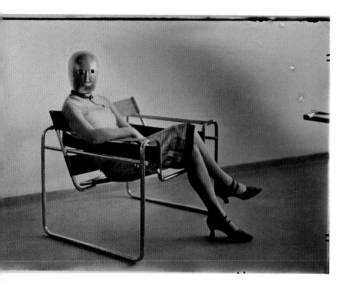

simplicity. Bayer invented new typefaces, which were strongly linked to Soviet constructivist experiences and were used in Bauhaus publications, while Breuer began to experiment with metallic materials, taken from industry, to produce furniture, such as his famous Wassily chair in chrome tubing. In 1928, Gropius resigned as director of the Bauhaus in an unstable political climate, marked by considerable in-fighting. The Swiss designer Hannes Meyer took his place, running a program that leaned more and more toward industrial production. The subjectivity of craft was counterbalanced by a more collective vision of the factory's mass production process. This highly politicized direction led to his dismissal by the city of Dessau. Finally, it was the turn of Mies van der Rohe, the last director. He moved the school to Berlin in 1932, making it private, until it was closed in 1933 by the Nazis. The Bauhaus was certainly one of the most important training workshops of the twentieth century, distinguished by the quality of its teachers and founded on democratic principles of ethical transparency, in a historical period marked by the tragedy of war. It was one of the great utopias of the industrial century.

Less well known but just as extraordinary were the Vkhutemas, the higher State technical and artistic schools, based in Moscow, between 1920 and 1926. Like the German experience, the goal was that of joining artistic and industrial production. The purpose was to train architects, artists and designers, in a climate of experimentation dictated by the Soviet constructivist theories, to overturn a vision of creativity founded on the ancient world. After the October Revolution of 1917, which marked the end of the Tsarist regime, the Vkhutemas absorbed the avant-garde experiments in art and architecture. Its manifestation was an expression of a social art. In 1918, the

for shaping the volumes and internal functions. The historian Sigfried Giedion explains that with the recession of the pillars, a new dimension of composition is created, in which the façades are designed as glass curtain-walls. In his book and manifesto *Space, Time and Architecture*, he speaks of suspended floors and transparency, of a building that has incorporated the space-time principle, and in which lives interior-exterior simultaneity. There is no longer a single perspective but multiple spaces and endless views, as Purist and Cubist research predicted. The Bauhaus materialized the desire to build a democratic society, based on progress.

The move to the new building in Dessau also saw the passing of the baton from the masters to the students. A decisive role in the new structure was now played by alumni who were now professors, Josef Albers, Marcel Breuer, and Herbert Bayer, and who established a utilitarian direction. Albers was convinced that the school's new paradigms should be linked to the world of the factory, where creativity had to meet affordability and painting *White on White Background* by Kazimir Malevich was the first in the Suprematist painting movement, on the idea of an abstract art that cancelled out the nineteenth-century stylistic codes. In 1919, Vladimir Tatlin, with the *Monument to the Third Socialist International*, transposed the victory of the Bolshevik Revolution into spatial research. The design was a dynamic steel spiral, a double helix, three hundred metres high, where three volumes would rotate: a meeting room in the form of a cube, a pyramid for the administrative offices and, finally, a press centre in the shape of a cylinder. Parallel to this, in 1920, El Lissitzky, architect, painter, typographer and photographer, began to create the series of *Proun*, in which the various fields of art, architecture and design were blended into abstract compositions of urban spaces and primary elements, in line with Malevich's Suprematist research. The establishment of the Vkhutemas was the result of the profound political and social changes that sanctioned the end of art as it had been traditionally understood, anchored in the nineteenth-century model, in favour of a technical and artistic training related to industry and the factory. Open to everyone, the school was divided into eight faculties: painting, sculpture, architecture, metalworking, woodworking, ceramics, textiles, and graphics. The intention was to combine technical-productive and artistic training. To this end, a dominant role was played by the *Basic Course*, which was initially for two years and divided into four teaching units that explored space, volume, surface and colour, and graphics. The aim was to investigate the basics of each discipline and introduce into the minds of the students the ability to combine the properties of proportion, rhythm, and dynamics. The rules of visual perception were taught with an educational and scientific objective. This analytical and combinatorial method found a reference in Tatlin's *Corner Counter-relief*. These compositions were based on the difference and contrast of materials and spatial shapes. Plexiglas, wood, iron and cement were assembled in compositions where the spatial and formal research generated a new art. The series of *Proun* by El Lissitzky, as anticipated, represented in the union between art, architecture and graphic design, another reference in the *Basic Course*. Following the first phase, between 1920 and 1922, marked by a teaching model that was emotional, subjective and linked to the subconscious, there was a methodology of objective transmission, which gave a central position to technique, construction, and mathematics, with a rational and objective direction. Aleksandr Rodchenko played a dominant role in this, and his workshops had a productivist orientation. The teachers Tatlin, El Lissitzky, Gabo, Popova, Rodchenko, and Stepanova proposed abstract compositions, adhering to an objective view of the world, tied to a political interpretation of the left. Nikolai Ladovsky, architect and educator, understood the importance of adding the psychology of perception and applying this approach to architecture and space, to create a new composition. Some architects who developed this vision include Krinsky, Melnikov, and the Vesnin brothers.

There was by no means just one orientation in the school: for some teachers the avant-garde experiences had severed the link with tradition, for others it was still necessary to investigate an applied and decorative art. In 1923, with Favorsky as director, a productivist orientation was removed from the *Basic Course* in favour of a more conservative general education. This generated discontent among students and in parallel with the new direction at the Bauhaus School, a school of design that was

closer to the needs of industry was developed further. Rodchenko, who in 1923 became the director of the Faculty of Metalworking, realized that the only way for an enlightened teaching was to take industrial mass production as a model, removing all decoration to produce an art of necessity. From the line to the constructed form, the method aimed at identifying the rules of construction. In those years, they dealt not only with abstract themes, but themes that were also valuable for society. In 1925, Konstantin Melnikov created a masterpiece with the Pavilion of the USSR at the Exhibition of Decorative Arts in Paris, with two wedge-shaped bodies in wood and glass, crossed by a monumental ramp, on which hovered inclined planes. This was one of the best examples of the principles of Suprematist and Constructivist art. Around 1925, at the Faculty of Architecture of the Vkhutemas, there were two main currents: that of the constructivist Aleksandr Vesnin and that of the rationalist Nikolai Ladovsky. Vesnin asked students to pay close attention to the function and program as these would not be sufficient for a valid project, which had to counter an expressive form. Of Vesnin's more talented students, it is worth mentioning Ivan Leonidov, who was able to make artistic aspects interact with rational and constructive aspects. He gave proof of this ability in his thesis (supervisor A. Vesnin) with the project for the Lenin Institute of Librarianship (1927). His rigorous and innovative composition, a spherical auditorium in iron and glass, was the apex of design. The suspended auditorium was supported by taut cables. This was counterbalanced by the glass tower housing the library, while a suspended monorail linked the new institute to the city.
In 1926, the school changed its name from Vkhutemas to Vkhutein (Higher Artistic Technical Institute), the name it kept until the official closing in 1930. The name change sanctioned a change of direction in favour of the professional preparation that was certain to outweigh an art training in terms of relevance. The Russian experience was certainly one of the most important of the twentieth century, paving the way for an interrelationship between the ideal and the real. Ultimately Bauhaus and Vkhutemas represented two of the most innovative approaches in the relationship between architecture, design and art, beating a path on which experimentation continues to this day.

Bibliography
Argan G.C., *Walter Gropius e la Bauhaus*, Einaudi, Turin 1951.
Droste M., *Bauhaus 1919-1933*, Taschen, Cologne 1991.
Gropius W., *Per un'architettura totale*, con uno scritto di Manlio Brusatin, Abscondita, Milan 2007.
Komarova L., *Il Vchutemas e il suo tempo. Testimonianze e progetti della scuola costruttivista a Mosca*, Kappa, Rome 1996.
Lisitskij-Küppers S., *El Lisitskij. Pittore, architetto, tipografo, fotografo*, Editori Riuniti, Rome 1992.
Ray M., *Tatlin e la cultura del Vchutemas: 1885-1953, 1920-1930*, Officina Edizioni, Rome 1992.

Walter Gropius, Bauhaus,
Dessau, 1925-1926

Pages 100-101
Wagenfeld Wilhelm,
Table lamp, 1924

El Lissitzky, *Proun 3A*,
c. 1920, Los Angeles,
Los Angeles County Museum
of Art

Walter Gropius, Bauhaus,
House of masters, Dessau,
1925-1926

98

100

101

Antonello Marotta

Functionalism, Neue Sachlichkeit, Gruppo 7, Rationalism, Mars Group, Tecton

The terms function, rationality, economy, and again seriality and reproducibility mark the historical period of the First World War.

The word "functionalism" is derived from Dankmar Adler's famous definition: "Form follows function" and refers to a modern attitude of thinking of architecture as a response to the functions. In the eighteenth century, the theorists of the Enlightenment were already putting these principles prominently into practice: we can think of Lodoli, Laugier, Milizia, Algarotti, and Durand, but it was in the twentieth century and especially in the period after the First World War that the term functionalism acquired a new value.

With the end of the war the political landscape changed, as did the geography of power, with the disappearance of monarchies and the end of the Austro-Hungarian Empire. The war crushed dreams and social desires, destroyed cities and homes, transforming the relationship between inhabitant and urban environment, leaving deep desolation and ruin in centuries-old Europe. The problems of the post-war period turned to reconstruction, the great theme of dwelling places and housing. The philosophy that developed in these years, prompted by the world of art and literature,

was aimed at a functional language, the concrete art that found a real answer to one of the most severe crises to strike humanity in the market and industry. While Henry Ford's automobile production model established a new method that saw in seriality, reproducibility, and economy, one of the winning factors in the economics of the new American manufacturing policy, soon many modern designers such as Walter Gropius and Le Corbusier were looking at the machine as a model in architecture: Le Corbusier in the well-known definition of *machine à habiter* and Gropius in the desire to embody an architecture based on the industrial model, aimed at building, with reduced costs, a home for everyone.

It was in the Germany of the mid-1920s that the functionalist tendency was the strongest and the term "Neue Sachlichkeit" (New Objectivity) was coined. The term indicated an ever more strongly felt and rooted need to

Giuseppe Terragni, Casa del Fascio, Como, 1933-1936

think of architecture in objective and functional terms. The Neue Sachlichkeit was opposed to the expressionist delirium and sought more human and socially conscious motivations. This nourished the creation of the Bauhaus school, established in Dessau (1925-1926) by Walter Gropius, and it also nourished the construction of low-cost housing or housing for the masses.

With the building of the Bauhaus in Dessau, historiography recognized the application of a functional architectural model, where the different parts of the school were arranged and interrelated according to their roles. The windowed sections of the workshops inspired the photographs of Lucia Moholy-Nagy for perfectly meeting the functional need, the

103

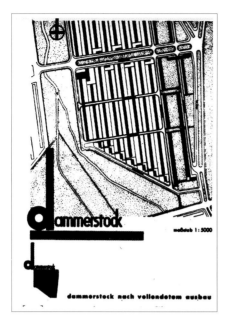

Walter Gropius, Dammerstock neighbourhood, Karlsruhe, 1927-1928

Opposite
Walter Gropius, Törten neighbourhood, Dessau, 1926-1928

Behren's work is still tied to history: one only has to think of the façade that evokes a pediment of a temple, but that is definitely modern in its constructive logic, made of steel and masonry. With the Fagus building, the German designers created a model of modern architecture in their use of new materials, such as iron and glass, and in the total and absolute battle against ornamentation and the eclectic styles that had characterized the movements of nineteenth-century architecture. In the streamlining or rationalization of the supporting structure, separated from the façade with doors, in the use of a glass curtain walls and metal floors and finally the entirely transparent right angle, Gropius and Meyer conceived a work capable of resolving functional, economic and social problems. The issue of transparency becomes central and assumes a political connotation in the idea that glass, as claimed by the philosopher Walter Benjamin, was an enemy of the secret, so as to create a new civilization. Over time, a modern utopia was born that was particularly driven by the physical and ethical transparency.
Other memories resurface in this project, such as photos of the American silos, used by Gropius in 1911 in the atlas compiled by Karl Ernst Osthaus. The German master glimpsed in those cathedrals of function, the perfect model for the nascent modern architecture, a beauty equal to the Egyptian pyramids, because he saw authentic and necessary

need to flood the interior with light. The Bauhaus is a white cathedral, a factory of culture, the expression of the clinical dream of modernity. Asymmetry, movement and the rotation of planes characterize its system, which denies the historical relationship with the street.
Between 1911 and 1914, Walter Gropius and his assistant Adolf Meyer designed the Fagus workshops in Alfeld an der Leine, where in fact they produced one of the first manifestoes of modern architecture. Parallel to this, in 1907, in the Paris art world, cubism and the avant-garde were coming into being, marking a new perspective for the modern man. Gropius was twenty-eight years old when he built the Fagus building. From 1907 to 1910, he trained in the studio of Behrens, where they had helped two other giants of modern architecture: Mies van der Rohe and Le Corbusier. Gropius had the good fortune to work on the Turbinenfabrik AEG project by Behrens, completed in Berlin in 1909.

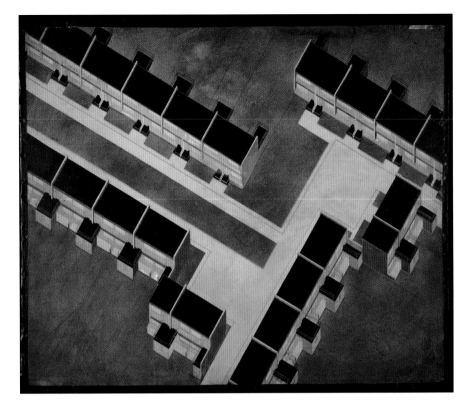

structures in them, a pared-down aesthetic and aspiration to a social principle.

In Germany, after the end of the First World War, the reconstruction of housing became a pressing need to the point that it inspired a new style known as Neues Bauen, aimed at streamlining manufacturing and building processes. Berlin and Frankfurt were becoming centres of experimentation in collective housing. In 1931 in Berlin, Hans Scharoun designed the Siemenstadt housing complex; Ernst May, the chief engineer, was responsible for building the Siedlungen Riedhof-West housing estate (1927-1934) and Römerstadt (1927-1928) in Frankfurt; Margarete Schütte-Lihotzky designed the prototype of the Frankfurt Kitchen in 1928, where she streamlined the space into a

simple and functional environment for the housewife. Walter Gropius was the architect who felt an intense need to resolve the issue of affordable housing. He designed various projects along these lines: the Törten district in Dessau (1926-1927), characterized by a radial layout, the Dammerstock district in Karlsruhe (1927-1928), where a certain independence of the residential block from the road could be observed, and the Siemenstadt district in Berlin (1929), an extremely simple housing design. In those years, Gropius was so focused on problems of feasibility and cost that he studied mechanisms for increasing ease of construction: the Törten district comes to mind, where the arrangement of the housing estates is a result of the location of the tracks for the transport of prefabricated beams: a solution that lowered the building costs. Gropius, Klein, and May pushed the rational model to the limits to generate *Existenzminimum*, a minimal living space that would meet the industrialization, serialization and particularly the affordability criteria. The living space or cell was studied as a *machine for living,* through flow diagrams to streamline movements inside the dwelling.

In 1927 in Stuttgart, the Weissenhof District was built for the exhibition of architecture organized by the Deutscher Werkbund. The aim was to promote the ideas of the Modern Movement. Compared to the districts in Frankfurt and Berlin which had been intended for the poorer classes, the Stuttgart district was designed for a middle class. Originally, Mies van der Rohe's was to draft the masterplan and the invitation to assign the different lots. Some of the most important names in modern architecture were called upon: Le Corbusier, Jacobus Johannes Pieter Oud, Walter Gropius, Ludwig Hilberseimer, Bruno Taut, Peter Behrens, Hans Scharoun, as well as Mies van der Rohe himself. Limiting the different participants to using reinforced concrete and a flat roof generated results that were basically similar, in accordance with the Neues Bauen, which now prevailed.

In 1929, Mies van der Rohe produced his masterpiece, the Barcelona Pavilion, which remains one of the most important works of rationalism. Destroyed after the exhibition, it was rebuilt in 1986 by Ignasi de Solà-Morales, Cristian Cirici and Fernando Ramos. The Pavilion condenses years of research and experimentation. A travertine base, containing a rectangular tank, anchors the architecture to the ground while eight cruciform chrome pillars support the reinforced concrete level. The space has green marble and onyx slabs and glass partitions that create a multiplication of the interior space and a fluidity and virtual perspective. At the end, a sculpture by Georg Kolbe is immersed in a smaller pool. The block of onyx, which Mies recovered from a quarry in Hamburg, became the module for the Pavilion's height, simply by doubling the size of the slabs obtained. In this project, Mies van der Rohe united tradition with the avant-garde.

It was Peter Behrens who brought Schinkel's work to the attention of Mies van der Rohe, who went to apprentice at his studio. Mies was drawn to his work throughout his life. In 1834, Karl Friedrich Schinkel designed the Palace on the Acropolis for King Otto of Greece. His proposal consisted of a large building that incorporated the entire Acropolis, to enhance the presence of the ruins of the Parthenon. In 1838, Schinkel prepared the Project for the summer palace in Orianda, in Crimea. The sacred mountain, the base, the rock which opposes its resistance to time and the forces that act on nature, offered the young Mies van der Rohe the starting point to what were to become his poetics. Schinkel's idea the ground or land offered him a solid steady research base, despite being mediated by other experiences: the Twenties of De Stijl and the Suprematists. In the Barcelona Pavilion the conceptual relationship to the Proun by El Lissitzky and the Dutch neoplastic theories were fundamental. The pavilion condenses research on slabs that can generate multiple points of view, while the stable ground brings architecture into a deeper history.

Between 1929 and 1931, Le Corbusier created the Villa Savoye in Poissy, a manifesto of rationalist thought. In this house, the Swiss master applied his five programmatic points developed in 1926: the pilotis, the free designing of the ground plan, free design of the façade, the horizontal window, and roof-gardens. Le Corbusier had experimented with purist research, conducted

Berthold Lubetkin,
Penguins' swimming pool
at London Zoo, 1931-1933

Page 108
Ludwig Mies van der Rohe,
Reinforced concrete
building, Berlin, 1923

with the painter Amédée Ozenfant, into a new composition where a central perspective was absent and multitude of points of view prevailed. That experimentation, through the use of reinforced concrete, which had liberated architecture from the weight of the wall, was transposed by him into the Ville Savoye. The ground plan is structured on the shape of the square, where the pilotis are 4.75 meters apart, a plan which was derived from the arc of curvature of the automobile, which becomes the metric reference of the ground floor where the garage is located, a garage which has a curved side. The design of the villa involves a superimposition of layers: the ground floor is supported by pilotis which liberate the architecture from the ground and make it almost fly, while the first level contains the living space on three sides, consisting of a living room, three bedrooms and bathroom facilities. A ramp provides spatial fascination to this slowing-down of perception. The first level has an inner

courtyard that faces the living room. Le Corbusier creates an *architectural promenade*, a system of slow connections that eventually lead to the roof garden. Here he generates an additional landscape, sculpting the curved bodies of the solarium and the stairs. The Swiss designer puts into practice his concept of architecture based on rationality: the pilotis, which are set back, allow him to create the free ground plan and façade, but all the focus is on the force and discovery of space, on reversing the concept of the garden, transposed into the courtyard and onto the rooftop, on finally creating a sculptural form, shaping the interior walls. These almost seem to be sculpted and are close to his artistic research, in painting and in sculpture, where he had made the wall containing life concave.
Rationalism spread first in Europe and then in the United States as an international movement, characterized by a logical and practical approach to the urban, architectural

and construction problems. The rise of Nazism forced the modern masters into exile in the States, to continue the research into rationalism through designing, building and teaching.

Rationalism arrived late In England, a nation heavily anchored to history with respect to what was happening in Germany, the Netherlands and Switzerland. The historian Sigfried Giedion asked Morton Shand to bring together a group of designers and theorists to represent England in modern architecture. In 1933, the Mars Group (Modern Architectural Research Group) was founded, which became the English section of Ciam. In 1935, the movement brought together many notable figures including Wells Coates, Maxwell Fry, Francis Reginald Stevens Yorke as well as Amyas Connell, Colin Lucas, and Basil Ward, establishing an exchange with the extraordinary personalities who had taken refuge in England: Berthold Lubetkin, László Moholy-Nagy, Walter Gropius and Serge Chermayeff. In 1938, they worked on a plan to develop London, which was aimed at radically requalifying the British capital in the post-war period and showing how the style of the Modern Movement had not crystallized but rather was to be understood as an open approach to change. An important contribution to British rationalism was made by the Russian Constructivist Berthold Lubetkin, who had immigrated to England. In 1932, Lubetkin had founded the collective of architects known as the Tecton Group (which included Lindsay Drake, Denys Lasdun, Godfrey Samuel, and Francis Skinner) which only disbanded in 1948.

In Italy, rationalism had some valid interpreters, but the complex political situation following World War I did not foster a favourable development. In 1926, Gruppo 7 was founded. The Lombard collective was formed by young architects who had graduated from the Politecnico di Milano:

Luigi Figini, Gino Pollini, Guido Frette, Sebastiano Larco, Carlo Enrico Rava, Giuseppe Terragni and Ubaldo Castagnoli, who was replaced by Adalberto Libera. Gruppo 7 was inspired less by the ideas of futurism than those of the international rationalism that had come to life in Germany, Belgium, France, Holland and the Ussr. In 1928, the collective merged into Miar (Italian Movement for Rational Architecture). In the same year, the first exhibition of Italian rationalist architecture was held in Rome, promoted by Adalberto Libera and Gaetano Minnucci. The Miar had about fifty architects, including, in addition to the Gruppo 7 participants, Gino Cancellotti, Louis Piccinato, Alberto Sartoris, Giuseppe Capponi, Mario Ridolfi, Giuseppe Pagano, and Mario Labò. In the Italian political climate, the movement found an open attitude from the fascist regime in the early stages. But after the Second Exhibition, held in Rome in 1931, the Miar met strong opposition from the fascist forces, and was dissolved. Some designers went to Rami (Regrouping of modern Italian architects), at the behest of the fascist union. After 1935, the line of the neoclassical monumentality of Piacentini was preferred. In those years, Italy was no outsider to the international debate: in 1928 Giò Ponti founded the magazine *Domus*. In 1933, Giuseppe Pagano was director of *Casabella*, joined in 1935 by Edoardo Persico. The magazines played an important role in the spread of Italian architecture of the Thirties. The results are seen in the works: in 1935 Giovanni Michelucci built the train station, Firenze Santa Maria Novella. In 1933, Luciano Baldessari completed the press Pavilion for the 5th Triennial of Milan. Giuseppe Pagano designed the Bocconi University (1937-1941) in Milan. In 1930, Figini and Pollini, together with the Gruppo 7, at the Fourth International Triennial Exhibition of decorative and industrial arts in Monza,

Ludwig Mies van der Rohe,
Glass tower, Berlin, 1922

designed La Casa elettrica: a pavilion to show the developments in electrical equipment for homes. Adalberto Libera and Guido Frette designed the furniture, while Piero Bottoni designed the kitchen and the bathroom. The Casa elettrica perfectly embodied the rational model of the home, leaning more and more toward comfort and the alliance with industrial production.

But Giuseppe Terragni was the one who pushed the furthest in those years. Between 1927 and 1929, he designed Novocomum, in Como, with offices on the ground floor and residences on the four upper levels. It is a building where rational research and Soviet constructivist influences emerge in the solution of the right angle.

Between 1936 and 1937, the architect completed the Asilo Sant'Elia in Como. The plan is built on a square base of about forty metres along one side, enlivened by a courtyard carved into the volume. To the south-east are four classrooms, at the centre a large atrium that opens onto the garden and on the opposite side, the refectory. The plan is rotated to meet the needs of the light. The result is a horizontal composition which reveals a constant relationship between the interior and exterior, and in which the articulation of the bodies between the transparency of the glass surfaces and the presence of the frame which is detached from the façade is the salient feature. From the garden, bordered by a portico, a dynamic stairway provides access to the roof-terrace, from which it is possible to see the tower of the Baradello. The organism lives in the gathering and the expansion of the transparent walls and frames that create a continuous spatial tension. The nursery is designed to provide interaction between life and nature.

With the Casa del Fascio, Terragni designed one of the most important works of modern Italian architecture. Built between 1933 and

1936, the building has a square plan, with seven bays on each side. A central open area characterizes the interior. The project includes asymmetrical features that coexist in the different façades, and in the off-centre courtyard. This project celebrates volume, which is anchored to the ground, but at the same time the frame denies the massiveness. Located in a strategic point in Como, near the historic city walls, in relationship to the apse of the Duomo, the façades are distinguished by openings that create strong tension in the hollow spaces. It is a return to the Dutch De Stijl literature, in the compositional play of empty space, stabilized by corner bands where the wall is full. Inside Terragni creates the double-height courtyard overlooked by an atrium and balconies. The space opens up, in a clearly legible structure, where the light emerges at the bottom of the arcades, and the use of glass blocks celebrates the depletion of internal shadows. With the Casa del Fascio, Terragni makes the Italian tradition of the courtyard coexist with the abstract and metaphysical research of Rho, Radice and De Chirico. The project was to be completed with the help of Nizzoli who had devised a system of decorative panels intended to celebrate the regime. The war put an end to the debate on the monumental value of the work, giving Terrigni's abstract force of thought back to history, thought which in the following decades shaped the America of Peter Eisenman, in the Seventies, and later the Portuguese and Spanish scene of today.

Bibliography
Cohen J.L, *Ludwig Mies van der Rohe*, Laterza, Rome-Bari 1996.
Giedion S., *Spazio, tempo ed architettura. Lo sviluppo di una nuova tradizione*, Hoepli, Milan 1984.
Gregotti V., Marzari, M. (eds), *Luigi Figini - Gino Pollini. Opera completa*, Electa, Milan 1996.
Le Corbusier, *Verso una Architettura*, Paris 1923.
Nerdinger W., *Walter Gropius. Opera completa*, Electa, Milan 1988.
Saggio A., *Giuseppe Terragni. Vita e opere*, Laterza, Rome-Bari 1995.

Walter Gropius, Fagus
workshops, Alfeld an der
Leine, 1911-1914

Giuseppe Terragni,
Novocomum, Como,
1928-1929

113

Ludwig Mies van der Rohe,
German Pavilion, Barcelona,
1929

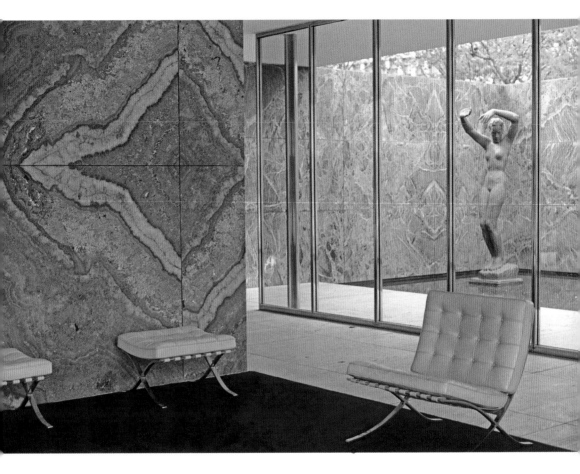

Ludwig Mies van der Rohe,
German Pavilion, Barcelona,
1929

115

Chiara Ingrosso

Ciam Congrès Internationaux d'Architecture Moderne

The CIAM was an international organization for modern architecture that, over the span of the three decades from 1928 to 1959, promoted a series of periodic conferences. Through numerous documents and publications, the CIAM became the most important organization for the diffusion of the so-called Modern Movement and its ideas. The Modern Movement's canonical image was primarily constructed by certain members of CIAM, including Sigfried Giedion, Le Corbusier, Walter Gropius, and Mies van der Rohe. Eventually, the thinking of the diverse personalities who attended the first congresses, and who also characterized the ways of understanding modern architecture, came to be incorporated and crystallized into the single coherent formula of the Modern Movement. According to Reyner Banham, this process of homogenization, which began primarily with the 1933 CIAM when Le Corbusier began to lead the group, marked the beginning of the academic stage of modern architecture. Surely the fact that the Modern Movement spread around the world from 1945 until 1965, making it a mainstream rather than avant-garde movement, was undoubtedly due to the CIAM's activities as well.

According to Kenneth Frampton, the CIAM can be divided into three phases: the first, up to 1930, was primarily focused on functionalist theories of a social nature and was dominated by German-speaking architects; the second phase, up to the war, and then the third phase, sanctioned the triumph of liberal idealism (ratified by *The Athens Charter*, a document from the 1933 CIAM) on the initial materialism. According to this line of argument, the congresses that took place after the war were all characterized by the emergence of a new orientation that directly opposed both functionalism and idealism in the architecture of the old masters.

These tensions led to the definitive rupture between generations, and this was sealed precisely by the dissolution of CIAM in 1959 in Otterlo, and by the concomitant rise of Team 10, made up of the new generations of modern architects.

The first CIAM, chaired by Karl Moser, with Giedion as Secretary-general, was held from June 26 to 28, 1928, in La Sarraz, Switzerland, in the castle of Madame Hélène de Mandrot, the true godmother and patron of the organization. This marked the founding of the organization, and a declaration of the desire to establish a program of studies and discussions on modern architecture was made. The Declaration of La Sarraz, signed by twenty-four European architects, clearly enshrined the need to begin again from scratch and go back to the academicism of the past and place architecture in a wider economic and social context, as well as advocating a standardized form of

Group photo of the first Ciam,
La Sarraz, 1928

construction that could be easily replicated. The second congress chaired by Ernst May was held a year later in Frankfurt and was dedicated to minimum subsistence housing (or *Existenzminimum*). May expressed the political soul of the CIAM: since 1925, he had been the director of municipal building in Frankfurt, and was the promoter of a massive social housing program that led to the formation of a number of functionalist *Siedlungen* on the outskirts of the German city; in the early Thirties, with Mart Stam and Hans Schmidt, both members of the CIAM, he moved to the USSR, taking charge of the reconstruction of the socialist settlement system.

The Frankfurt CIAM focused on the rational

Le Corbusier at the third
Ciam, Bruxelles, 1930

Page 120
Team 10 at Ciam 11,
Otterlo, 1959

Page 121
Cornelis van Eesteren
at Ciam 4, Athens, 1933

118

"The key points of urbanism consist of four functions: living, working, recreation (in one's spare time), circulating"

Le Corbusier

analysis of housing for the working classes in order to identify the minimum requirements, not so much on the level of survival as on the level of social existence. According to the rational approach used by May, the housing design was closely connected to the city design, and architecture's task was to integrate the individual housing cells or units into the urban context, guaranteeing equally favourable conditions for everyone.

In Frankfurt, there were three executive organizations of CIAM: the Congrès (general meeting of members); the Cirpac (Comité International pour la Résolution des Problémes de l'Architecture Contemporaine); the working groups for specific themes. All the members were divided into national delegations.

The theme of affordable housing that had been broached in Frankfurt was taken up again at the next CIAM, dedicated to rational construction methods applied to newly constructed settlements. This took place in 1930 in Brussels under the direction of

Cornelis van Eesteren, who designed the project for the expansion of Amsterdam. Although the Brussels CIAM was closely connected to the one that followed in 1933, dedicated to the functional city, the later Congress broke away sharply from the previous one due to the transition in leadership from the Germans to Le Corbusier. In addition, due to the difficult political situation in Europe, the fourth CIAM did not take place in a city as the others had, but on board the ship *Patris II*, during the July and August voyage from Marseille to Athens (a return trip). The stances of the Congress, not always unanimous, were summarized in a series of papers, the most famous of which is *The Athens Charter*, formulated by Le Corbusier in 1943, ten years after the congress. *The Athens Charter* is considered by Françoise Choay to be the most successful synthesis of propositions for progressive urban planning or, according to those same members of CIAM, the manifesto of modern urban planning *tout court*; Paola Di Biagi has

observed that it is undoubtedly the symbol, even the myth (in a negative sense as well), of urban planning in the twentieth century. Banham defined it as the CIAM's most ruinous document.

Making a comparative analysis of thirty-four European cities, the *Athens Charter* actually proposes eliminating the traditional elements found in the urban space (streets, squares, lots, blocks, monuments) and sets out an urban planning method based on the division of the city into four functional areas (residential, leisure, work and traffic circulation), as well as building appropriately situated residential blocks.

The 1937 CIAM in Paris, dedicated to housing and leisure, perfected the postulates of the *Athens Charter* and closed the series of meetings that preceded the Second World War. The work of the CIAM members continued even after 1939 in the USA, where many of them had moved, and particularly the

important proponents such as Gropius, Giedion, Mies and Sert.

In the aftermath of the war, when the bombing had in fact made historical city centres into the coveted *tabula rasa* and the city revealed itself to be a physical entity loaded with meaning, ridden with peculiar symbolic networks, the historical and emotional dimensions were definitively established in CIAM's debates regarding cities. Already in 1942, José Lluís Sert, a prominent member of the Spanish delegation (Gatepac) and later chairman of the CIAM congresses from 1947 to 1956, had included a chapter devoted to the city centre in his book, *Can our cities survive?*, thus recognizing the preeminent role played by this part of urban design. The Bergamo CIAM of 1949 was dedicated to the theme *The Heart of the City*. Here, the Italian delegation's role was growing in importance, as was Hoddesdon's in 1951. Their debate questioned the rigidity of the analytical and

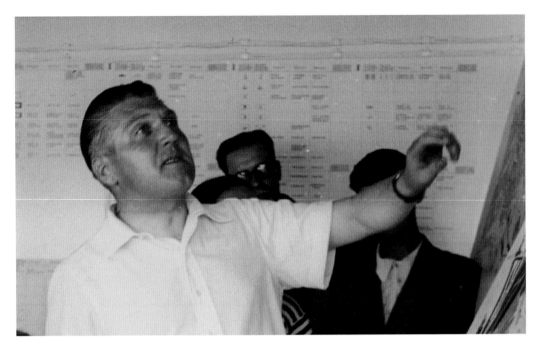

prescriptive approach of the *Athens Charter*. But the conflict between old and new generations finally exploded at the Congress in Aix-en-Provence (1953), where the theme was habitat. Young people came together in the CIAM X Committee in charge of organizing the conference. During subsequent preparatory meetings, the nucleus that came to be known as Team 10 began to form and among those who gradually took part were Jaap Bakema, Georges Candilis, Rolf Gutmann, Peter Smithson, Bill and Gill Howell, Aldo van Eyck, Sandy van Ginkel, Alison Smithson, John Voelcker, Shadrach Woods and Giancarlo De Carlo.

At the tenth congress, held in Dubrovnik in 1956, and which recorded the meaningful absence of Le Corbusier, Gropius and Van Eesteren, Team 10 was the protagonist in a series of studies aimed at overcoming the rigidity and abstraction of modern architecture, and immersing the project in everyday life.

Finally, in Otterlo in 1959, there came the handover between CIAM and Team 10. The Congress which was held in the Netherlands was organized according to the new informal rules that later became characteristic of the subsequent Team 10 meetings.

Bibliography
Aymonino C., *L'abitazione razionale. Atti dei congressi C.I.A.M. 1929-30*, Padua 1971.
Di Biagi P. (edited by), *La Carta d'Atene. Manifesto e frammento dell'urbanistica moderna*, Rome 1998.
Die Wohnung für das Existenzminimum, Stuttgart 1930.
La Charte d'Athènes, Paris 1943.
Logis et loisirs, Paris 1938.
Mumford E., *The Ciam Discourse on Urbanism, 1928-1960*, Cambridge Mass 2002.
Newman O. (edited by), *Ciam '59 in Otterlo*, Stuttgart 1961.
Rationelle Bebauungsweisen, Stuttgart 1931.
Rogers E.N., Sert J.L., Tyrwhitt J. (edited by), *The Heart of the City*, New York, London 1952.
Sert J.L., *Can Our Cities Survive?*, Oxford University Press, London 1942.

Poster of Ciam 7, Bergamo,
1949

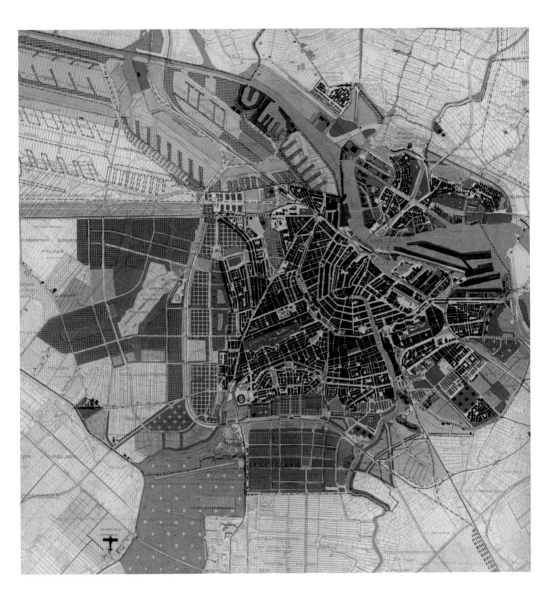

Cornelis van Eesteren,
Project for the expansion
of Amsterdam, 1931-1934

123

Alessandro Benetti

Totalitarian Architecture

The establishment of the communist dictatorship in Russia (1917), the Fascist dictatorship in Italy (1922) and Nazism in Germany (1933) were destined to greatly influence the architectural debate and landscape construction in those three countries.

Each regime, with different timing and methods, examined their own state architectures, the three-dimensional translation of the ideology of central power. Despite the specific nature of the Russian, Italian and German approaches, some common tendencies can be found in all of them and, more generally, in most of the "totalitarian" architectural currents in Western history.

As emphasized by Deyan Sudjic, the monumental aspect is one of its fundamental components for two reasons: firstly, because of the evocative power of large scale construction, which supports and stimulates the *pathos* of the masses; and secondly, the reference to the mnemonic aspect of the monumental object, which becomes the voice of historical memory (often rewritten in retrospect), and providing young regimes with a form of legitimation. The frequent return to "classic" architecture should also be interpreted in the light of self-legitimization:

often interpreted oversimplifying as aschematic juxtaposition of styles, it becomes the guarantor of the timeless, perpetual and absolute power it represents. The resulting architecture is generally one that "speaks" loudly, with an exuberant symbolic aspect that is inherently compromised by the ideology that produced it (Biraghi), an ideology that, a posteriori, proves very difficult to assess objectively and in terms of quality. In principle, it is safe to say that, between the Twenties and the early Forties, we find in totalitarian architecture a tendency toward poor quality and less experimentation. This occurs in parallel to the political, social and cultural environment under question, becoming increasingly more extreme.

The process was anything but straightforward, and instead characterized by some key turning points: the most striking of these is undoubtedly the raid by the Gestapo on the Berlin headquarters of the Bauhaus, on April 11, 1933. In the same year as their coming to power, with this *coup de theatre,* the Nazis reaffirmed their distaste for the "Bolshevik" avant-garde, and thus accelerated the mass exodus of the leading exponents of German rationalism and expressionism.

124

Albert Speer, Germany, Project for the Great Berlin, 1937-1943

Russian and German pavilions, Universal Exhibition of Paris, 1937

Pages 126-127 Albert Speer with Adolf Hitler

Albert Speer, Zeppelinfeld, Nuremberg, 1934-1936

In 1934, the results of the competition for the schools for the party's hierarchy bear eloquent witness to the Reich's architectural orientation: the heavy masses of masonry in exposed brick and stone in the winning designs by Hermann Giesler and Clemens Klotz conform to gloomy neo-medieval aesthetics, the official expression of the dreadful philosophy of "Blut und Boden" (Blood and Soil), that preached the German people's attachment to the land and their home.

One of the many architects who worked in various capacities with the Nazi leadership was Albert Speer (Mannheim, 1905 - London, 1981). He occupied an absolutely dominant position. As a trusted advisor to Adolf Hitler, he transformed many highly ambitious visions into projects: the Zeppelinfeld in Nuremberg (1934-1936), a colossal theatre seating area for party meetings, in proportions so extreme that they cancelled out the architectural objects surrounding it; the urban plan for Germany (1937-1943), the new capital of the empire that was to have risen from the ashes of Berlin, organized around a monumental axis

120 meters wide and 5 km long; the Große Halle, an enormous pantheon whose axis was to represent the conclusion; and the Reich Chancellery (1938-1939), the only fragment of Germany that was built.

Speer was also the designer of the German Pavilion at the Universal Exhibition of Paris in 1937, where the images of the period, taken from the Palais de Chaillot, immortalized it along with the Russian Pavilion by Boris Iofan. Positioned on the banks of the Seine, in a symmetrical position with respect to the Eiffel Tower, the two buildings are strikingly similar results of architectural parables that are very different.

The Russian architectural research of the early Twenties looks to the futurist, constructivist and supremacist avant-garde of the pre-revolutionary period for a direct source of inspiration: the Monument to the Third International by Vladimir Tatlin (1919), for example, is a "cumbersome construction seeking revolutionary dynamism, a dream of romantic engineering" (Zevi) that articulates the time of the new era through the movement of solids suspended within it.

Thanks to the work of free associations like Asnova and Osa (but also university workshops Vkhutemas, and the Institute of Artistic Culture, Inkhuk) the various efforts by rationalists and constructivists blended to become a progressive vision of Soviet architecture, which at first seemed to find practical implementation due to the start of the five-year plans (1928).

Dating from this crucial period of change are major works such as the Rusakov Club for the Union of Municipal Workers and the home studio of Konstantin Melnikov (both in Moscow, 1927-1929), as well as the residential unit of Narkomfin (again in the capital, 1928-1930) by Moisej Ginzburg. These buildings are the verification of the "social condenser" theory, aligned with contemporary experiments by Le Corbusier on the theme of collective living.

The victory in the competition for the Palace of Soviets (1933) by Boris Iofan's project (an abnormally large architectural mass with graded exterior walls, surmounted by a colossal statue of Lenin) bears witness to the regime's abandonment of any avant-garde ambitions.

In 1932 all the cultural associations were incorporated into the SSA, under direct state control. In 1937, the Congress of the Union of Soviet architects enshrined the advent of "socialist realism." Promoter of an architecture that "spoke" to the masses, and the unequivocal exaltation of triumphant communism, the new orientation was fully realized in the plans for the city of Moscow (Vladimir Semenov, 1935), which entailed radio-centric urban plans and a return to the style of Haussmann, particularly in the metro stations (starting in 1931), whose opulence contrasts sharply with the proletarian reality. After Second World War, the Soviet government launched a campaign to systematically export socialist realism to all the states of the USSR, also organizing veritable study trips to Moscow for local professionals.

Socialist realism was more broadly applied in the post-war reconstruction period (for example, in the devastated city of Warsaw), as the "style" of reference in the creation of new urban centres, often attached to large industrial complexes that were part of the five-year plans (such as Nowa Huta in Poland and Stalinstadt in the German Democratic Republic), and as the image of large institutional buildings throughout the Union. The Palace of Culture and Science in Warsaw (1952-1955), clearly inspired by the Seven Sisters in Moscow (the "tall buildings" built by Dmitry Chechulin in strategic points in the Russian capital, beginning in 1948), are the colossal testimonials to the tendency toward cultural homogenization in the Soviet world.

Each republic of the people, on the other hand, reacted differently to the new directives, partially hybridizing the content with local experiences of the previous

Zeppelinfeld mit Saalbautribüne

Spira

Konstantin Melnikov,
Club Rusakov, Moscow,
1927-1929

Moisej Ginzburg,
Narkomfin, 1928-1930

Opposite
Boris Iofan, Palace
of Soviets, 1933

decades. Czech architectural modernism, for example, was particularly strong. This was confirmed by the new cities of Ostrava, Nová Dubnica and Poruba, which owed much more to the trends in Scandinavian urban planning (Jean-Louis Cohen).

In Italy, the *Duce* (Mussolini) was interfering with all the major sites during the Fascist era. By approving or rejecting the projects submitted to him, he guided the progressive definition of his own "style" for the regime. Mussolini took on the most important intellectuals of the time, who, in different ways, regarded European modernism as a model for a new Italian architecture: Giuseppe Pagano and Edoardo Persico (co-directors of *Casabella*), Pier Maria Bardi and Massimo Bontempelli (directors of *Quadrante*), the architects of the Gruppo 7 and Miar (Italian Movement for Rational Architecture).

The support that was given by Mussolini at the Exhibition of Rationalist Architecture (1931) and the design by Adalberto Libera and Mario De Renzi for the Exhibition of the Fascist Revolution (1932), on the other hand, should be understood primarily as the opportunistic desire to grab the esteem of fervent young fascists.

In the light of Mussolini, in fact, the function of architecture was primarily related to educating the masses as to the magnitude of the regime. The reference to one or the other trend was not defined a priori, but responded to contingent needs.

This was the basis for the support given to the building of the Santa Maria Novella train station in Florence (1932-1934, Giovanni Michelucci). Its stereometric volumes, barely softened by the glass roof of the atrium, vaguely reminiscent of a *streamline* style, "would please the Italian people". But there was also the complete lack of interest in the Casa del Fascio in Como (1932-1936, designed by Giuseppe Terragni), because it

was too icy and hermetic to garner the enthusiasm of the masses.

As part of the extensive plan for the ruralisation of the urban population promoted by the regime, on receiving initial approval for the plan for Sabaudia (1933-1935), in a timidly modernist "style", a decidedly more vernacular language was promoted (and therefore more eloquent) for Pontinia (1934-1935). In Sardinia, Saverio Muratori was creating the mining centre of Cortoghiana, where the endless porticos of Piazza Venezia defined atmospheres that were clearly inspired by De Chirico's metaphysical works. In the intricate political landscape of Fascism, Mussolini's approval was won by such chameleon-like figures as the Milanese

architect Piero Portaluppi – one of his best works is the straightforward volume of the tower of the Italian Fascist headquarters in Piazza San Sepolcro in Milan (1935-1940) – and the Roman Luigi Moretti, designer of the Casa delle Armi at the Foro Mussolini, designed by Luigi Moretti (1933-1936), and whose refined spatial designs culminated in the sculpted element of the spiral staircase. In the second half of the Thirties, as the regime became gradually more rigid and aligned with Hitler's Germany, the Fascist "style" took on more precise connotations. The obsessive reference to Roman and Classical architecture was the *leitmotif* of an architectural language by that time entirely devoted to constructing the history and myth

129

of Fascism, to be transmitted to posterity. Marcello Piacentini, already appreciated for designing the Piazza della Vittoria in Brescia (1927-1932, one of the most impressive and complete demolitions of the Fascist era) and a skilled coordinator of the events surrounding the City University of Rome (1936), was put in charge of the ambitious experiment E42, conceived as the seat of the Universal Exposition of 1942 that never took place, dominated by the "very Roman" bulk of the "Square Colosseum" (the Palazzo della Civiltà del Lavoro designed by Ernesto La Padula, Giovanni Guerrini, and Mario Romano, 1937-1940). Piacentini confirmed himself to be a diligent and shrewd interpreter of the central directives, a loyal right-hand man to Mussolini and, ultimately, the Fascist architect par excellence.

Bibliography
Biraghi M., *Storia dell'architettura contemporanea II*, Einaudi, Turin 2008.
Ciucci G., *Gli architetti e il fascismo. Architettura e città, 1922-1944*, Einaudi, Turin 1989.
Cohen J.-L., *The future of architecture since 1889*, Phaidon, London 2012.
De Magistris A. (edited by), *U.R.S.S. Anni '30-'50. Paesaggi dell'utopia stalinista*, Mazzotta, Milan 1997.
Nicoloso P., *Mussolini architetto. Propaganda e paesaggio urbano nell'Italia fascista*, Einaudi, Turin 2008.
Sudjic D., *Architettura e potere. Come i ricchi e i potenti hanno dato forma al mondo*, Laterza, Rome 2011.

Ivan Fonim, Krasnye Vorota Metro station, Moscow, 1932-1935

K. Ryzhkov, A. Medvedev, Taganskaya Kolcevaya Metro station, Moscow, 1950

130

Giovanni Guerrini, Ernesto
Lapadula, Palazzo della
Civiltà italiana, Rome,
1938-1953

Marcello Piacentini, Piazza
della Vittoria, Brescia,
1927-1932

132

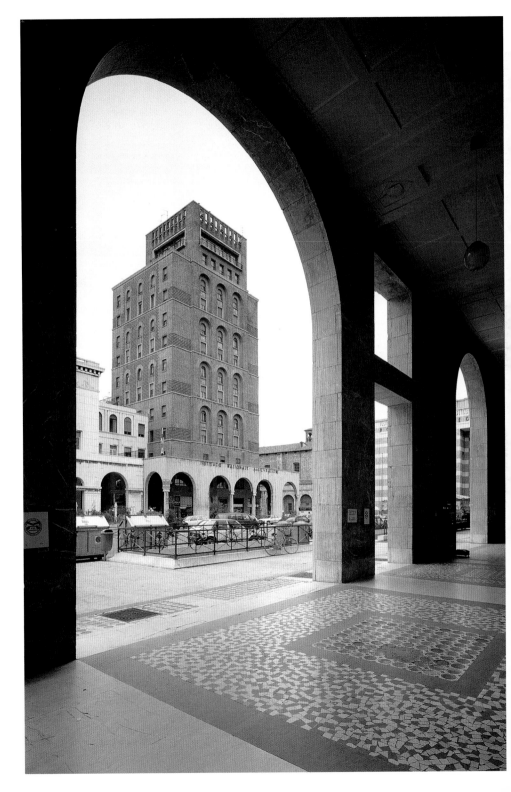

Fabio Mangone

Nordic Romanticism

Nordic Romanticism, or as it is sometimes called, National Romanticism, is an overall term describing a number of cultural currents in music, literature, painting, the applied arts and architecture which developed roughly over the period between 1885 and 1920 in central-northern Europe. The phenomenon was particularly intense and coherent in the Scandinavian countries and in Finland. Sometimes Holland has also be associated with these countries, just as far as architecture is concerned, more for evident affinities of formal language than for any genuine sharing of programmatic principles. It is more difficult to establish the position of Germany in this strand, though some recent studies consider it to have been organically involved in the phenomenon.

The unifying element of late nineteenth-century Romantic architecture lies in a particular way of looking at and drawing inspiration from the past: freeing itself from the academic styles and the stylistic revivals that had characterized nineteenth-century eclecticism, it sought, in the name of the myth of Nordic identity, to rediscover, and to draw upon with a certain degree of liberty and creativity, other traditional models, from medieval architecture to rural building forms,

often accentuating their picturesque and regional features and interpreting them in the light of a certain fantastic dimension. No full-blown theorization of Romantic architecture exists, but the shared conceptual premises lie, apart from in the emergence of the myth of a specific Nordic identity, in the basic acceptance of certain positions that developed in nineteenth-century England – in John Ruskin's crusade in favour of the "truth" of architecture, also in relation to a sincere use of materials, in the reappraisal of the world of crafts and the applied arts in the ambit of the Arts & Crafts movement, in the taste for "brick architecture" and in the passion for the medieval architecture of central-northern Italy. Many of the future protagonists of National Romanticism, from Ragnar Östberg to Martin Nyrop and Ferdinand Boberg, and likewise the Dutch architects sometimes associated with them, such as Hendrik Petrus Berlage, studied the civic and religious architecture of these regions first hand and with special interest in the course of their ritual educational tour of Italy at the end of their regular studies. Sometimes this was interpreted as the outcome of a kind of "barbaric" and Nordic *koiné*. These distant examples, and the national legacy of monuments, which were rediscovered and revalued with great intensity, gave rise to the ideal invocation of a medieval architecture; distinct from the Gothic, it was charged with the ideal connotations of building sincerity, of the expressiveness of construction and the valuing of artisanal details, often taking the form of a skilled use of traditional materials such as brick and stone, and articulated in fairly lively plani-volumetric shapes, free from any conventional schemes in obedience to the belief in individual creative freedom. Clearly distinct from the features of the contemporary phenomenon of Art Nouveau, National-Romantic Architecture did however share some of its themes, such as the attention to detail, the special interest in domestic architecture and, finally, the aspiration to produce a total artwork. It is no accident that some important Nordic buildings from the early twentieth century, for instance Eliel Saarinen's Helsinki Station, have been read by historiography as examples of Jugendstil, or alternatively, of National Romanticism.

A further common presupposition of the Romantic poetics in architecture was represented by the appeal in Scandinavia of the theories of Camillo Sitte, who suggested that the monotony and uniformity of the nineteenth-century city based on grid patterns should be countered by a picturesque urban planning strategy, which led once again to a reappraisal of the medieval period and the Italian examples of that phase. Not by chance, Nordic Romantic buildings tended to a large extent to become emergent urban landmarks, signalling nodal points, quantifying open spaces and creating points of orientation on the skyline, not just as regards important buildings of collective use, such as churches and monuments, but more common residential buildings as well. The desire to create genuine symbols of identity in the urban landscape was

particularly evident both in some civic constructions intended to be emblematic of the nation or at least of the capital – such as the City Hall of Copenhagen, designed by Nyrop, or that of Stockholm, by Östberg, or the National Museum of Helsinki, designed by the Saarinen, Gesellius and Lindgrem Group, or also, if one accepts its inclusion in the category of "Romanticism", the Amsterdam Stock Exchange, Berlage's masterpiece – and in some churches, such as Saint Michael's in Turku or Saint John's in Tampere, both the work of Lars Sonck, Engelbrekt in Stockholm, built to a design by Lars Israel Wahlman, or even the parish

Lars Israel Wahlman,
Engelbrekt Church,
Stockholm, 1914

Page 135
Hendrik Petrus Berlage,
Amsterdam Stock
Exchange, 1903

church of Kiruna designed by Gustaf
Wickman. Moreover, the neo-traditional aura
of Romanticism not rarely also informed
typologies associated with modern life in the
big cities, as in the case of the Lilla Värtan
gasometer in Stockholm, by Ferdinand
Boberg, or the telephone company building
in Helsinki by Lars Sonck, almost as if to
exorcise an age marked by powerful social
and technological changes, and by a subtle
and until then unknown development of
urbanism.

The interest in collective (civil and religious)
and industrial buildings did not exclude an
interest in housing, understood as an
experimental area for reviving the *genius loci*
in terms both of traditional materials and the
revival of vernacular constructional elements
and of the reinterpretation of folkloristic
decorative motifs. With every component of
the furnishings being carefully designed, the
house was viewed as an authentic work of
art, as demonstrated, amongst others, by
various examples in different countries, such
as: Tallom near Stockholm, designed by Lars
Israel Wahlman; the Bergöö House in
Hallsberg, minutely designed in every detail
by Ferdinand Boberg; Skogsveien near Oslo,
by Arnstein Arneberg; Villa Lasses, in
Finström, designed by Lars Sonck; and

Hvitträsk, the extraordinary house and studio
in Helsinki where the architects Saarinen,
Gesellius and Lindgren lived and worked
together.

The gradual decline of Nordic Romanticism
around the time of the Great War was linked
to the progressive rediscovery of classicism
and its establishment as a common and
normative language, in reaction precisely to
a season of marked individualism. Buildings
such as the Woodland Chapel in the South
Stockholm Cemetery, by Erik Gunnar
Asplund, bear witness to the gradualness of
the transition.

Bibliography
Davey P., *Architecture of the Arts and Crafts Move-
ments*, Rizzoli International, London 1980.
Mangone F., *Viaggi a Sud. Gli architetti nordici e l'I-
talia*, Electa-Napoli, Naples 2002.
Miller Lane B., *National Romanticism and Modern
Architecture in Germany and the Scandinavian Coun-
tries*, Cambridge University Press, New York 2000.
Tafuri M., Dal Co F., *Architettura contemporanea*,
Electa, Milan 1976.

Martin Nyrop, City Hall
of Copenhagen, 1892-1919

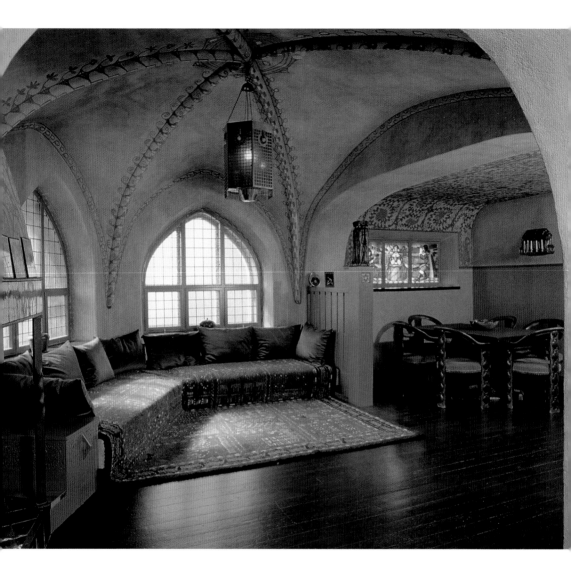

Lars Sonck, Saint John's
Church, Tampere, 1902-1907

Eliel Saarinen, Hvitträsk
House, 1901-1903

Ferdinand Boberg, Rosenbad
Building, Stockholm, 1902

138

Carl Westman, Court
House, Stockholm, 1915

Peder Vilhelm Jensen-Klint,
Grundtvig Church,
Copenhagen, 1940

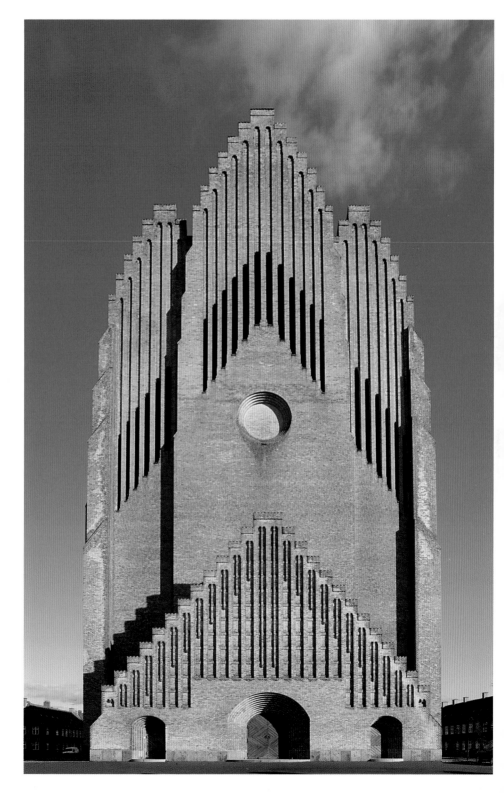

Maria Vittoria Capitanucci

Tropical Architecture Tropicalism

In a broad sense "tropical architecture" is understood to be that architecture, also contemporary, which is characterized by variegated and mutually distant idioms and forms of expression and that has reshaped the landscape and urban systems of the "tropical region", the vast belt lying between the Tropic of Cancer and the Tropic of Capricorn and which stretches from the Pacific islands, South-East Asia and Australia to India, Africa, the Caribbean and wide swathes of the Americas. While including some arid zones, the area is largely distinguished by an invariably hot and humid climate with frequent or periodic rainfall and luxuriant vegetation. Geographers speak of the "tropics" more as a family of regions falling between and near the boundaries of these parallels.

Instead, the term "tropicalism" implies a more specific meaning, indicating a geographically localized tendency, also linguistically variegated but with strong affinities in terms of results, that can be tied in with the concept of "critical regionalism" introduced into architectural debate in the early Eighties by theorists of architecture such as Kenneth Frampton, Alexander Tzonis, Liane Lefaivre and William Curtis. It is no means by chance that the latter, in his *Modern Architecture since 1900*, devotes two chapters to this phenomenon and its protagonists – "Modernity, Tradition and Identity in the Developing World" and "The Universal and the Local: Landscape, Climate and Culture" – , moving beyond the geographic limits and teasing out connotations cutting across a series of apparently irreconcilable realities. These realities featured a multifaceted galaxy of architects and buildings which, from the Fifties to the present day, had occasion to respond, in the area between the two Tropics, to the demands, impulses and articulations of the Modern idiom in the rest of the world. So

142

while the United States spoke the language of the International Style, Europe was rebuilding and focussing on the imminent end of the CIAM (International Congresses of Modern Architecture) and a critical revision of the Modern and of its diktats, with incursions both into tradition (as occurred in Italy with Gardella, Caccia Dominioni and BBPR, or in Spain with Coderch, Torroya and Sert) and into participatory involvement (as in England and Holland with Team 10 – Smithson, Candilis, Erskine – or with the MARS group), in Central and South America, but also Australia, Asia and Africa, different paths were tried out. Starting from the experience of the Modern, emphasis was placed on the traits and traditions of a specific geographic condition, but also of a political history associated with colonialism, in which the close relations with nature and pre-colonial culture were transformed into dominant themes and structural-planning challenges.

In Brazil, where the naming of the movement that arose in the field of the visual arts at the end of the Fifties originated (with the artists Hélio Oiticica, Lygia Clark, Rogério Duprat and Antonio Dias), this tendency also spread immediately to the theatre (with the playwright José Celso Martinez Corrêa) and to architecture, with prominent figures such as Lina Bo Bardi (who for Corrêa designed the well-known Oficina theatre, one of the first examples of tropicalist architecture), Lúcio Costa, Jaime Lerner, Ruy Ohtake, Giancarlo Palanti, Oscar Niemeyer, Alfonso Eduardo Reidy, Roberto Burle Marx (the great landscape artist and landscape architect), and likewise the Pritzker prizewinner Paulo Mendes da Rocha.

If the term *Tropicália* derived from an artwork by Oiticica, one of the founding concepts of the movement was anthropophagy, namely the cultural cannibalism whose original reference lay in the 1928 *Manifesto Antropófago* ("Cannibal Manifesto") by the poet Oswald de

Andrade. It was an approach that tended to be receptive to the global cultural and avant-garde universe, and without any exclusions, but at the same time it also reestablished the ties of modern "metropolitan" Brazilians with the anthropophagic Indios and with the African tradition. Such a position also tended to liberate culture from a colonial ideology. In this respect the work of Lina Bo Bardi, the Italian who chose to be Brazilian, is exemplary, starting with her Casa de Vidro (1951) near São Paulo, where she brought her Le Corbusian and Bauhaus experience into play with the extreme setting of the villa on pilotis on the edge of the jungle, but above all in her spasmodic search for inspiration through popular art, the expression of the cultural history of a place together with its natural environment, with the landscape.

Out of respect for that world Bardi would design two museums in Salvador de Bahia (the Solar do Unhao and Casa do Benin), together with the series of villas at the end of the Fifties – the Valeria Cirrel and the Casa do Chame Chame – before moving on to produce places with powerful social connotations such as the plan for the Pelourino (in Salvador) and the SESC centre in the former Pompeia factory (1977) in São Paulo. In her works, tradition, the International Style, popular art and humble materials intersected and blended into sophisticated concrete and structural techniques. She would not be the only one to work in this way in Brazil; indeed, before her the influence of Le Corbusian themes and the Modern in general had taken concrete form very early on.

Le Corbusier's plan for Rio de Janeiro dates to 1933, and the project for the Brazilian Ministry of Education building in Rio to 1936, which saw Oscar Niemeyer (with Lucio Costa, Alfonso Eduardo Reidy and others) collaborating with the Swiss master. From here the appropriation and reinterpretation of that language produced a "style" that embraced the

Boavista Bank project (1946) in Rio, the plan and the institutional buildings for Brasilia but also Villa Canoas (Niemeyer's house in Rio, dating to 1953-1954), which seems to opt for a relationship of continuity between interior and exterior, leaving it up to a sinuous roof and the intense surrounding greenery to define the hierarchies of the space and the place with the expressive force of a tropicalism that had already found expression in the Church of Saint Francis of Assisi in Pampulha (1943) and appeared, in recent times, in the Niterói Contemporary Art Museum, a space craft overlooking the bay of Rio.

To Alfonso Eduardo Reidy, who designed the Pedregulho Residential Neighbourhood in Rio, goes the sceptre for the "set" megastructure but also for what is perhaps one of the most "tropicalist" museums in Brazil, the Museum of Modern Art in Rio (1954-1958), one of the heirs of which is the Brazilian Museum of Sculpture in São Paulo by Mendes da Rocha, the undisputed master of the contemporary

scene, poetic also in a series of city residences such as the Casa Francisco Malta Cardoso, Morumbi, São Paulo (1963) or the more recent James King House, São Paulo (1980). The handing on of these influences to the rest of Latin America would be rapid. In Argentina, for example, Le Corbusier's realization of Villa Curutchet in La Plata (1946-1953) represented an occasion for exchange and influence with another great designer, Carlos Raul Villanueva, from which there would also stem the "tropicalist" designs of Amacio Williams, such as the villa for his brother, or of Raphael Graziani's EMSA building. Mexico, on the other hand, had already chosen its own path, with the incomparable work of Luis Barragàn (the San Cristóbal Estates equestrian development, Los Clubes, Mexico City 1964-1968) but also with the highly talented Ricardo Legorreta (the hotels and his studio in Lomas, 1967) and the sophisticated vaulted structural conceptions of Felix Candela (Ciba laboratories and Bacardi plant),

and through to the University of Mexico City (1953) of Enrique del Moral and Mario Pani. Venezuela responded with the sophisticated University City of Caracas designed by Carlos Raul Villanueva (1950-1959), where art, structure, public space and urban design came together in the iconic covered plaza and in the great hall, while Uruguay spoke the language of the great Eladio Dieste. In Cuba, where the influence of the United States was great and where Max Abramovitz had realized the US Embassy between 1952 and 1953, we find, a decade later, a very intriguing project strongly bound up with nature and the Caribbean tradition, the Escuela Nacional de Arte of Cuba (1961-1965), the work of the Italo-Cuban Vittorio Garatti.

The figure of Le Corbusier was once again an interesting *trade d'union* in the step towards Asia. It was the Swiss master, together with the great Louis Kahn with his Indian Institute of Management in Ahmedabad (1962-1974), more perhaps than with the iconic Parliament of Dacca, who influenced entire generations in Bangladesh, Sri Lanka and India. Here, after the plan for the city of Chandigarh (1950-1952) and the realization of government buildings, in addition to the Sanskar Kendra museum, the Mill Owners' Association headquarters and the residences in

Ahmedabad, whole generations of architects would reread Le Corbusier's legacy, respecting the features of the place and combining traditional techniques and materials. That "Western" poetics, attentive to the relationship with light, water, matter and lines, survived in the projects of Balkrishna Doshi, in his Sangath studio (1979-1981) and the Institute of Indology (1961) in Ahmedabad, but also in the Indian Institute of Management in Bangalore and in mixed-income housing in Hyderabad (1968-1971). It is evident in the visionary works of Raj Rewal (Asian Games Housing in New Delhi, 1980) and above all in the essential and geometric poetics of Charles Correa, from the exemplary Gandhi Ashram (1958-1963) to the later Kanchanjunga Tower in Mumbai (1983). There is also the work of his talented "pupil" Rahul Mehrotra, with the projects for the Campus Magic Bus and the Hewlett-Packard Campus in Bangalore, which, with a series of interesting residences, brings us to the sophisticated recent work of Studio Mumbai and of Rafiq Azam in Bangladesh.

In Sri Lanka, amongst the pioneers of a highly revisited "modernity" we find, between 1948 and 1977, Minnette de Silva, Valentine Gunasekera and Geoffrey Bawa. The latter, a prominent figure on the Sri Lankan architectural scene with his beautiful resorts (such as the Triton Hotel, 1979-1981, in Ahungalla, and the Kandalama Hotel in Dambulla, 1991-1994) and earlier works like Bridget's Montessori School in Colombo (1963-1964) and the Steel Corporation offices in Oruwela (1966-1969), point to and prefigure a "sustainable" path for a formal synthesis between traditional spaces and modern comfort.

Japan deserves separate treatment due to that nation's systematic ability to maintain its own identity in the rereading of the modern (Tadao Ando) and of technological innovations, just as, in a certain sense, happened in

Oscar Niemeyer, Villa Canoas,
Rio de Janeiro, 1953-1954

Opposite
Lina Bo Bardi, Casa de Vidro,
São Paulo, 1951

Pages 144-145
Lina Bo Bardi, Museo de Arte,
São Paulo, 1950

Lina Bo Bardi, Sesc Pompeia,
São Paulo, 1977

Oscar Niemeyer, Church of Saint Francis of Assisi, Pampulha, 1943

Oscar Niemeyer, Museo de Arte, Pampulha, 1956

Australia with figures like the Pritzker prizewinner Glenn Marcutt (Ball-Eastaway House in Glenorie, 1980-1983). The honour of representing the African response goes to the sophisticated and cultured Egyptian architect Hassan Fathy, with New Gourna Village (1946-1953), made entirely from raw earth (like the André Revereau medical centre in Mali, 1970), and various villas and mosques dotted around, certainly not by chance, between Egypt, India, Greece and Mexico. One area that still needs to be explored in depth is the Arab and Middle Eastern experience, with some remarkable cases such as Minoru Yamasaki's Dhahran Airport (1961), SOM's Jeddah Airport (1980), and likewise the contemporary National Commercial Bank by Gordon Bunshaft and the Kuwait National Assembly Building (1972) by Jørn Utzon, especially when read from the contemporary perspective of the necessity of globalization. One can still rightly speak today about "tropical architecture", understood as projects conceived for tropical climes, but certainly not of "tropicalism". Besides the great ideological struggle between modernism and traditionalism, and the conflict between regionalism, globalization and postcolonialism that shaped debates of an often powerfully social, political, economic and cultural nature in the last century, in the contemporary era the various elements distinguishing design in this geographical belt certainly seem to be held together by the great across-the-board theme of sustainability, bio-climatic control and environmental comfort. An approach to architecture, then, which requires the project to be conceived in response to the needs and opportunities of a specific region with characteristics which, in an unexpected manner, are shared by places and countries with sometimes very far-removed languages and traditions. Climate and environmental features determine architectural necessities and responses that paradoxically lead to analogous solutions between Africa and Latin America. The inhabitants of the tropics almost all share the common problem of having to deal with the extreme conditions of a hot, humid climate. Despite the vastness of the area, stretching across a very broad swathe of the planet, these countries have a common political history: they are all, or almost all, former colonies. There is therefore a common architectural legacy dating to the colonial period – individual buildings, housing types and a "historic" urban fabric – which represents a precious past with which to engage, in the same way as with older local traditions and with more recent global innovations, in order to achieve a contemporary design.

Bibliography
Bo Bardi L., *Stones Against Diamonds*, AA Publications, London 2013.
Canizaro V., *Architectural Regionalism: Collected Writings on Place, Identity, Modernity and Tradition*, Princeton Architectural Press, New York 2007.
Curtis W.J.R., *Modern Architecture since 1900*, 3rd edn., Phaidon, Oxford 1996.
De Silva M., *The Life and Work of an Asian Woman Architect*, Smart Media Production, Colombo 1998.
Dissanayake E., *Minnette De Silva, Pioneer of Modern Architecture in Ceylon*, Orientations, Hong Kong 1982.
Falvo R.M. (edited by), *Rafiq Azam. Architecture for Green Living*, Bengal Foundation, Skira, Milan 2013.
Frampton K., "Towards a Critical Regionalism: Six Points for an Architecture of Resistance", in H. Foster, *The Anti-Aesthetic: Essays on Postmodern Culture*, Bay Press, Washington 1983.
Istituto Lina Bo Bardi and P.M. Bardi (ed.), *Lina Bo Bardi*, Istituto Lina Bo Bardi and P.M. Bardi, São Paulo 1993.
Lefaivre L., Tzonis A., *Tropical Architecture: Critical Regionalism in the Age of Globalization*, Wiley-Academy, London 2001.
Mindlin H.E., *Modern Architecture in Brazil*, preface by S. Giedion, Colibris, Rio de Janeiro 1956.
Robson D., *Bawa. Geoffrey Bawa: Complete Works*, Thames & Hudson, London 2001-2004.
Veikos C., *Lina Bo Bardi: The Theory of Architectural Practice*, Routledge, London 2014.
Zeuler R.M., De Lima A., *Lina Bo Bardi*, preface by B. Bergdoll, Yale University Press 2013.

149

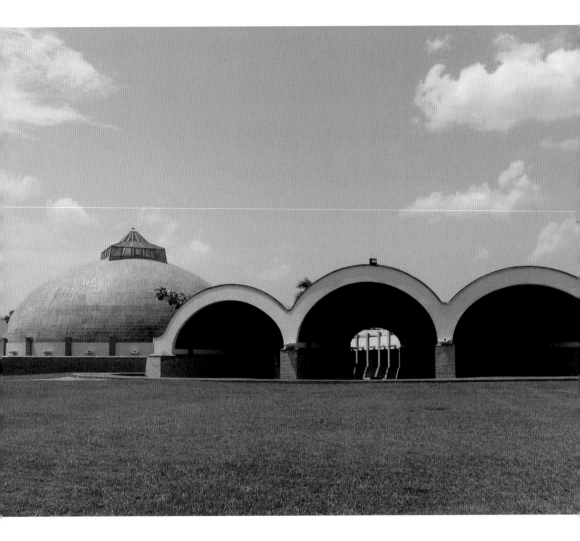

Opposite
Paulo Mendes da Rocha,
James King House,
São Paulo, 1980

Vittorio Garatti, Escuela
Nacional de Arte, Cuba,
1961-1965

151

Alessandro Benetti

New Empiricism, Bay Region Style

In the early decades of the twentieth century, while architectural criticism was committed to consecrating the achievements of the "masters" and exalting the triumph of the International Style, some very culturally sensitive places, with unusual geo-climatic characteristics, refused to align themselves with the prevailing ideology.

In the Scandinavian regions and around the San Francisco Bay, for example, modern architecture had very specific expressions that drew on the local characteristics and traditions as valuable sources of inspiration. Historiography has attributed these movements with defining the "new empiricism", an expression referring to the building of national identity in the Nordic countries to fully affirm social democracy, and the Bay Region Style, a product of the enterprising and individualistic hedonism of the sunny Californian West Coast.

After the turbulent events of the nineteenth century, which saw a series of annexations and secessions between the kingdoms of Sweden, Norway, Denmark and Finland, the Scandinavian geopolitical situation became stable around 1900: Norway declared independence from Sweden (1905) and Finland became relatively independent from the influence of the Russian Empire.

The architecture of the so-called Nordic Romanticism translated the nationalist ferment through a "reaction to the nineteenth-century historicism [...] that aspires to a simplification of language and rejects borrowing from classicism, claiming to be derived from the national tradition (Capobianco)".

This purified interpretation that "dematerialized from the mists" (Zevi) of the Gothic style, and which has become a more authentic root of Saxon architecture, characterizes the main public buildings in the works by Martin Nyrop, Lars Sonck and Ragnar Östberg.

The work of Östberg, first and foremost, had a considerable influence on Erik Gunnar Asplund and Sigurd Lewerentz, the two main designers of the subsequent generation of Swedish architects, co-authors of the cemetery south of Enskede (Stockholm, begun in 1915). Here, the Woodland Cemetery (1918-1920) launched the reflection on "classicism" as a timeless constant that preceded construction, and was further developed in the Asplund Library, Stockholm (1928). Asplund in Sweden, like Alvar Aalto in Finland, is a key figure for understanding the positively empirical attitude of Scandinavian architects toward modernism. The pavilions of the Universal Exposition of Stockholm (1930), for example, offer an interpretation of it that is both rigorous and light-hearted. Here Zevi recognized the "act of the birth of the post-rationalist movement [...] declaration of independence from Puritanism and its syntactic dogmas, a joyful invitation to a maturing of the idiom".

Of the Swedish functionalism canonized at the Exposition, Sven Markelius was its most consistent interpreter, in buildings such as the residential apartment building in Berget (Stockholm, 1929) and the villa in Nockeby (1930). On the other hand, the same Markelius was continually questioning and contextualizing the principles of modern architecture, to the extent that in 1947, his villa in Kevinge was indicated by Eric de Maré as an accomplished example of the new empiricism, praised as (yet another) alternative to the rigidity of Nordic functionalism. The quality of humanity in the villa is expressed in the humble prose and veiled vernacular style of the façades in exposed brick and natural painted wood, and totally immersed in the landscape, with a garden that blends seamlessly into the woods. Their experimentation with the new

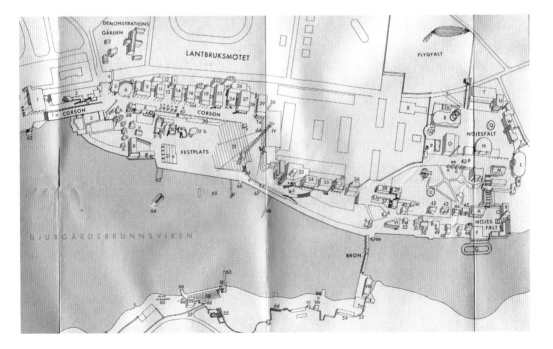

empiricism finds its terrain of choice in the residential neighbourhoods on the outskirts of the Swedish cities. Leif Reinius and Sven Backström designed and built new residential neighbourhoods in Danvikslippan (Stockholm, 1943), Gröndal (Stockholm, 1944), Rosta (rebro, 1948) and, first and foremost, in the centre of Vällingby, beginning with the master plan drawn up by Markelius himself. The satellite city of Vällingby, inaugurated in 1954, is regarded as one of the greatest achievements of twentieth century urban planning. Organized around a community centre and directly connected to Stockholm from the subway, it is the successful realization of the theory of the "ABC community" (in Swedish: A = place of work; B = homes; C = commercial centre) and for decades was the model of reference for Italian and English urban planning.

The developments in architecture in California up to the end of the nineteenth century originated from two different traditions, imported with the successive waves of colonization. The construction practices of Hispanic-Mexican origin, of which the first records date back to the sixteenth century, overlap with the mid-nineteenth century proto industrial know-how that came from the east coast of the United States.

The buildings of the first colonization provide an excellent lesson in adapting to local climatic and production conditions: the building designs, narrow and decidedly elongated (it was difficult to find long pieces of timber due to the absence of sawmills) are characterized by sloping roofs that jut out quite far with respect to the body of the building made of sun-baked brick, with the dual purpose of providing protection from heavy seasonal rains and achieving spacious shaded living areas (one of the best and most widespread examples of this type is the Ray House in Sonoma, 1846). From New

Poster of the Stockholm Exhibition, 1930

Opposite
Erik Gunnar Asplund,
Library, Stockholm, 1928

Page 153
Plan of the Stockholm
Exhibition, 1930

England, however, those frantic invaders who came with the gold rush brought with them whole buildings, prefabricated on the east coast, in the typical square plan in a wooden structure (examples of this are the terraced houses on the slopes of San Francisco, very colourful and with wide bay windows).

It was in San Francisco, at the beginning of the twentieth century, that the first local "professional" architects developed an interpretation of modernity that was descended directly (and critically) from these historic premises and extremely sensitive to the peculiar geographical environment and climate of the bay.

The so-called Bay Region Style (a term coined in 1947 by Lewis Mumford in the pages of the "New Yorker") is also and primarily the constructed interpretation of the California way of living: its main testing ground is the single family dwelling, seeking the maximum integration between domestic space and natural landscape, where the temperate climate eliminates the functional threshold between interior and exterior.

Over the course of the last century, the "bay style" experienced at least two main cycles of flowering and decline. The first cycle was launched by some designers who were not from the area, and who trained with the masters of modern architecture in less remote areas of the western world. These included Julia Morgan, Page Brown, Willis Polk, John Gale Howard and above all, Bernard Maybeck.

His building for the Out-Door Art Club (Mill Valley, 1905) is a simple classroom with elongated proportions. Its long sides open fully and confidently into the garden from a continuous sequence of glass doors. The structural beams go through the roof and to the outside, an elegant and unexpected expressive jolt that is vaguely reminiscent of Gothic architecture.

155

A student of Maybeck, William Wilson Wurster was the leading exponent of the Second Bay Tradition, which was influenced by a certain aesthetics of the modernist machine, but with a positively local interpretation of it in its choices of materials, construction methods and environments (from this point of view, the partnership between the landscape architect Thomas Church and Wurster was fundamental). Numerous single family dwellings were built by Wurster (from 1945, an associate of Theodore Bernardi and Donn Emmons) in San Francisco, including the Reynolds House (1946) and the Walters House (1951): in this last case, the irregular arrangement of the windows and particularly the suggestion of a corner bay window which soars dizzyingly over the valley are its main features.

Of the many authors who participated in this successful season, it is worth mentioning Gardner Dailey (with his Avasino Apartments, San Francisco, 1941); Joseph Esherich, designer of the Wiper House (Sausalito, 1950), the curious completion, in Bay Region style, of the stone castle left unfinished at the time by the millionaire William R. Hearst. Finally, there is Eric Mendelsohn, whose Russell House (Pacific Heights, 1952) combines the extensive band of windows in the rationalist style with the bay window and sequoia redwood exterior, exquisitely "Californian".

Bibliography
Biraghi M., *Storia dell'architettura contemporanea I*, Einaudi, Turin 2008.
Casabella, n. 232, October 1959.
Mattsson H., Wallenstein S.O., *Swedish Modernism, Architecture, Consumption and the Welfare State*, Black Dog Publishing, London 2010.
Zevi B., *Storia dell'architettura moderna*, Einaudi, Turin 1950.

Sven Markelius, House
in Kevinge, 1947

Bernard Maybeck, Out-Door
Art Club, Mill Valley, 1905

Leif Reinius and Sven
Backström, Satellite city,
Vällingby, 1954

Alessandro Benetti

Neorealism

The relevance of the use of the adjective neo-realist in the definition of a certain type of post-Second World War Italian architecture is still the subject of heated discussions, for several reasons.

On the one hand, it comes, first and foremost, from the literary and cinematic world and refers to a much broader cultural climate, in which *The Path to the Nest of Spiders* by Italo Calvino (1947) and the Oscar-winners by Vittorio De Sica (*Sciuscià*, 1946, *Bicycle Thieves*, 1949) are the most famous essays on this topic.

On the other hand, once inherited by the world of architectural criticism, the neo-realist epithet was used to indicate the work of a very small group of architects and not a particularly large group of works, largely attributable to the institutional framework of the plan, Piano Ina Casa.

Promoted by the Minister of Labour and Social Security at the time, Amintore Fanfani, and launched in 1949, the Plan provided for the construction of more than 350,000 public housing units throughout Italy, to be built over 14 years.

In this favourable context, free from the pressures of private speculation, the designers involved had the opportunity to reflect deeply on how to develop the housing, involving not only logical aspects but also, and primarily, linguistic aspects. The desire to communicate with the most disadvantaged sections of the population, at which the plan was mainly directed, contributed to the rapid abandonment of functionalist purism in favour of a more complex syntax, which, for various reasons, integrated the signs of a rediscovered vernacular architecture. These signs were shown to guarantee the possibility of reconciling contemporary living spaces with the ways of life and traditions of the inhabitants. It is true that only a few projects of quality were actually able to find this virtual correspondence between urban landscape and community: in many cases what prevails is an empty formalism, which is the major limitation of all neo-realist architecture.

Mario Ridolfi (Rome, 1904 - Marmore, 1984) and Ludovico Quaroni (Rome, 1911-1987) were the protagonists of this brief season, which was an interlude of a deep questioning of their poetics for both of them. Through neorealism, Ridolfi evolved from the personal interpretation of rationalism developed in the Thirties and Forties (think, for example, of the Post Office in Piazza Bologna in Rome, 1933-1935) towards the tormented expressionism

of his last works (such as the project for the Motel Agip in Settebagni, 1968-1969). Similarly, in a few years, Quaroni drifted towards the controversial Brutalist syntax exemplified by the Sacra Famiglia or Holy Family church in Genoa (1972).

The residences of the Case Ina in the Quartiere Italia in Terni (1948-1949, by Mario Ridolfi with Wolfgang Frankl) were simultaneously the first projects built under the plan and the inaugural experiment of the Italian neo-realist season.

The simple typological plan of the four buildings guaranteed each unit a dual east-west view and a clear division between the living and sleeping areas, with some new solutions added, and designed according to the climatic conditions of the area. For example, the considerable thickness of the structure of the buildings (12 meters) makes it possible to build rooms of a decent depth, while the arrangement of the square balconies, rotated with respect to the plane of the façade and partially set in like niches, protects them from summer heat and allows for a possible conversion to a closed home environment.

Delivered just a few months from the Quartiere Italia, the Ina Casa Complex in Cerignola (1950, Ridolfi and Frankl again) is one of the best examples of neorealist architecture.

Located on the edge of the historic centre of the Apulian village and organized around a central pine wood, the district of Via Pantanella is characterized by a great variety of types, meeting the needs of the various categories of workers that would eventually settle there. The 4-5 storey "tall buildings for white collar employees" and the "apartment blocks for labourers" (with gardens and separate accesses to each unit) are flanked by three storey terraced housing, with duplexes on the top two storeys, Ridolfi's first completed work of this type.

Here, the neorealist poetics of the Roman architect reached a high level of maturity and synthesis, approaching a "zero degree of the linguistics and technology of spontaneous architecture" (Valerio Palmieri). There are few signs of the vernacular (of all of them, the terra cotta parapets of the tall buildings, the tiles of the sloping sides of the row houses and the ubiquitous dark double shutters) overlapping with the white tufa masonry, commensurate with the clear curbs in exposed concrete. The purity of the volumes from the era of "Frederik" (Rossi and Canella) with very short overhangs and the use of external stairs in the terraced houses are some key elements that define both contemporary architecture and an architecture that is intrinsically Apulian. Again, deep in southern rural Italy, immediately after the war, the housing crisis in Matera began a heated debate involving the main exponents of the Italian cultural scene. The publication of *Christ Stopped at Eboli* by Carlo Levi (1945) helped to widely publicize the image of an archaic South, dominated by inaction, backwardness and superstition. The rupestrian neighbourhoods of the capital of Basilicata are the most striking symbol of this.

The project of Adriano Olivetti and INU (National Institute of Urban Planning) was behind the construction of the new village La Martella (starting in 1951), designed by Ludovico Quaroni with Luigi Agati, Federico Gorio, Pier Maria Lugli and Michele Valori. From the summit of a hill, the village overlooks the countryside and establishes a direct visual link with the ancient town centre, whose spontaneity and morphological richness it attempts to mimic. The urban plan, which is organic in inspiration, follows the contours and is organized around the civic centre where community services and the church of San Vincenzo de' Paoli (Quaroni again) are clustered.

Extensive use of the Lucan tufa, grouping the houses in pairs and re-proposing dwellings typical of the Sassi district, and providing incentives for locals to work on their properties, are a clear homage to local tradition. The Roman architects provided a consistent interpretation of it, basically simplistic and subtly paternalistic.

In those same years, in the very different context of the industrial North, a team of Milan designers collaborated to create the Quartiere Ina Casa in Cesate (1950-1954, by Franco Albini, Gianni Albricci, BBPR, Ignazio Gardella, Luigi Castiglioni). The results were as contradictory as they were in La Martella: the attempt to restore the aggregation style used in the Lombardy countryside, re-proposing the foundational structure of the courtyard, failed because it denied the relationship with the metropolis of a village that was now transfigured into a suburb. There is little value in the "rural" eloquence of the decidedly vertical windows, the exposed bricks of the church of San Francesco d'Assisi (Gardella, 1954-1959) and the arched doorways of the terraced houses (Gardella again): the proximity of the railway station encourages commuting into the city, and Cesate participates fully in its pace and way of life.

If it is true that the Piano Ina Casa profoundly affected the construction of the landscape in all the major Italian cities, Rome remains its undisputed capital and the main testing ground for neo-realist architecture. The tumultuous expansion into working-class suburbs was channelled into the creation of autonomous units by the studies for the Master Plan, units that were equipped with all the necessary community services and strategically located along the main throughways of the historic city.

In the Quartiere Tuscolano (1950-1960), the linear building by Saverio Muratori and Mario De Renzi combines the complexity of the urban routes and opens up in a great gateway to the street behind it, while the horizontal residential complex by Adalberto Libera brings back the patio as a semi-private space par excellence. The actual quality of the morphological solutions is suited to Tuscolano with an overall architectural language that is positively laconic, in sharp contrast to the

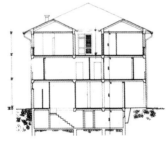

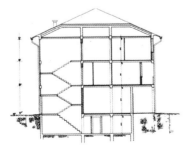

163

almost contemporary Tiburtino district.

A group enterprise guided between 1949 and 1954 by the "usual suspects" Ridolfi and Quaroni (here with Carlo Aymonino, Carlo Chiarini, Mario Fiorentino, Federico Gorio, Maurizio Lanza, Sergio Lenci, Pier Maria Lugli, Carlo Melograni, Gian Carlo Menichetti, Giulio Rinaldi and Michele Valori), the Tiburtino is the most eloquent exhibition of Italian neo-realism.

The project emphasizes the importance of the road as a structuring element for the urban fabric and the central piazza as a gathering space. On the other hand, the alterations made since the initial design – of all of them, the enlargement of the transversal axis running through the sector and the planned facilities for the downtown district that were not built – prevent the urban structure from performing its task as a binding zone between many constructed fragments and defining the conditions for developing the community that the designers had in mind.

The types of buildings proposed (such as disproportionate towers and terraced houses on the slope, both by Ridolfi) are combined in a paratactic way without a clear compositional and functional hierarchy. Here more than elsewhere, the ostentation of the vernacular signs states its final detachment from the social and cultural reality that was ponderously developing in the neighbourhood, now far from being the size of a township and instead committed to defining its role as a functional part of the contemporary city.

The "failure" of the Tiburtino was sufficient enough to push Quaroni to a profound self-criticism, which takes form in the pages of *Casabella*, in a landmark article in which he writes indignantly about the district as *Il paese dei barocchi* (*The town of the Baroque*).

This moment of awareness on the part of the Roman architect, shared by all of those involved, is in many ways common to that which affected the whole neo-realist wave. Italo Calvino said that neo-realism was also and above all the "urge to recount" produced by the "reborn freedom to speak". Having abandoned any pretence at objectivity, the writer admits, "Even though we were supposed to be concerned with content, there were never more dogged formalists than we, and never were lyric poets as effusive as those objective reporters we were supposed to be".

Bibliography
Casabella, no. 210, June-July 1956; no. 215, April-May, 1957.
Casciato M., *Neorealism in Italian Architecture*, in Williams Goldhagen S., Legault R. (edited by), *Anxious Modernism. Experimentation in post-War Architectural Culture*, CCA Montreal, MIT Press, Cambridge Mass. 2000, pp. 25-54.
Cellini F., D'Amato C., *Le architetture di Ridolfi e Frankl*, Electa, Milan 2005.
Di Biagi P. (edited by), *La grande ricostruzione. Il piano Ina-Casa e l'Italia degli anni '50*, Donzelli Editore, Rome 2001.
Ghirardo D., *Italy. Modern Architectures in History*, Reaktion Books, London 2013.
Molinari L., Scrivano P. (edited by), "Postwar Italian Architecture 1944-1960", in *2G International Architecture*, n. 15, Gustavo Gili, Barcelona 2000.
Portoghesi P., "Dal neorealismo al neoliberty", in *Comunità*, n. 65, 1958.
Tafuri M., *Storia dell'architettura italiana 1944-1985*, Einaudi, Turin 1982.

Page 161
Ludovico Quaroni
with others, Villaggio
La Martella, Matera, 1951

Page 163
Giancarlo De Carlo,
Quartiere Spine Bianche,
Matera, 1954

164

Mario Ridolfi, Towers,
Quartiere Tiburtino, Rome,
1949-1954

Mario Ridolfi, Pallotta
House, Terni, 1960-1964

Mario Ridolfi, Terrace
houses, Quartiere Tiburtino,
Rome, 1949-1954

Mario De Renzi, Saverio
Muratori, Building,
Quartiere Tuscolano, Rome,
1950-1960

Ludovico Quaroni, Mario
Ridolfi and others,
Quartiere Tiburtino, Rome,
1949-1954

167

Maria Vittoria Capitanucci

International Style

One wonders whether, in 1932, when Henry-Russell Hitchcock and Philip Johnson wrote the essay *The International Style: Architecture since 1922,* to accompany the exhibition "Modern Architecture" held in the same year at the Museum of Modern Art in New York (designed by A. Barr and curated by Johnson himself), in their lucid analysis, they could have imagined the profound impact that that language, those protagonists and those works would have on the decades to follow, in America and around the world. Early admirers of what had been envisaged in Europe since the Twenties, with the architectural and cultural revolution represented by the Modern Movement, and involved in what was taking place in the United States, first, with the timid transmigration of the European avant-garde and then, with the exodus of numerous designers and intellectuals fleeing racial and political persecution, the two critics chose to present the American public with a universe that would open up broad horizons of contemporary culture, hoping for an international architecture, free of any tradition or regionalism.

In this sense, Mies van der Rohe's work was emblematic, and with him, the Bauhaus universe that moved with him to the United States. This was a new way of seeing. It was not directed exclusively at architectural language, but was certainly fresh and exempt from historicism, although often based on the non-visible proportional classicist models and an undeniable functionalism. Above all, it was focused on design that emphasized structural research, on a different vision of the urban plan, on the use and experimentation of new materials, as well as the modern building site in the construction industry that those works brought with them. The United States, with its economic situation, could develop these aspects, appropriate them, bringing into play a new and different relationship between the client, economy and architecture.

Within a decade, distinguished members of the European Modern Movement had arrived on American soil, invited by the most prestigious universities – Mies and Hilberseimer to Chicago, Eliel Saarinen to Cranbrook, Konrad Wachsmann, Walter Gropius, Marcel Breuer and Sigfried Giedion to Harvard – also to pursue a career freely, far from the European dictatorships and war. For the teaching appointment at Harvard, then awarded to Gropius, the

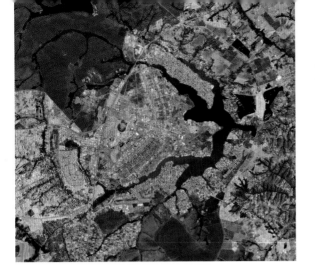

Aerial view of the city
of Brasilia

shortlist included only the Europeans Mies, Le Corbusier and Oud. It is certainly no accident that in the late Fifties in a university like Yale, where the great Louis Kahn later designed the iconic Yale Art Gallery, the dean of the faculty was Paul Rudolph. Rudolph was another undisputed leader of the International Style, as well as a client for the gallery commission, and Serge Chermayeff, long-time collaborator of Mendehlson, and the historian Vincent Scully, also taught there. These were the spokespeople for an international language that, coupled with the visionary mathematics research of engineer-poet Richard Buckminster Fuller, formed the generation of Archigram, Cedric Price, and Friedman, but also Foster and Rogers, heirs-elect of that research.

In any case, many of the personalities of those years of fervent energy, American or otherwise, become the protagonists of a trend that went well beyond the "provocations" of Hitchcock and Johnson, shifting the Modern movement to the level of a "style", or "manner", and in a sense sanctioning its long drawn-out swan song. In contrast, then, with historiography's view of the Fifties as a "season" in which an entirely American declination of the Modern

movement was evolving, follower of the original "European model" or its codification (even Manfredo Tafuri identified it, criticizing it harshly, with that place and moment in history), it is reasonable, in light of the contemporary condition, to argue that the International Style was a "plural" movement. It had a light and a life of its own that went well beyond the chronological limits (think of the influence it had on the *high tech* and *minimal* movements) and initially attributed geographies (from the U.S. to Europe and back, and then on to Central/South America and Asia). The architectural concept would not have been possible if there had not been the meeting between the board of directors of Iit and Ludwig Mies van der Rohe (and from there the entire campus and the Crown Hall), and again, between Mies and the Lamberts, the Seagram clients, and Marcel Breuer and Whitney for the museum of the same name, between Gropius/Belluschi and Pan Am airlines – with that skyscraper so reminiscent of the previous, and very much in the "International Style", Pirelli building by Gio Ponti and Pierluigi Nervi –, and certainly the meeting between Schindler or Neutra with the California bourgeoisie, resulting in "case studies on houses".

169

These experiences reflect a very specific socio-political condition, such as Roosevelt's epic New Deal, but also the years to follow that shaped the generations of Gehry and Foster. This moment was certainly not exempt from research into the "new monumentality" (from the title of a talk by Sigfried Giedion at the Symposium organized by the "Architectural Review" in 1946 in London, *The Need for a New Monumentality*), following the Great Depression and Second World War, in contrast to that expressed earlier by the European dictatorships, but that proved to be of equal communicative force and economic empowerment for the great machine of production. This was a monumentality that was not only expressed through verticality, but also, and above all, structural power and challenge, transparency, projection and recession, all elements in the lexicon of Modern architecture (think of the skyscrapers designed by Mies for Frederichstrasse, 1921) but now emphasized.

And to bear witness to how the architectural cultures mutually influenced each other, we must emphasize the contribution and suggestions from the great F.L. Wright with his "lily pad" tower for Johnson Wax, his idea of the "disappeared city" or the *Mile High Tower*, as well as the new themes, in addition to skyscrapers, and the different types that also touched the world of infrastructures, from terminals (TWA by Eero Saarinen, 1962) to bridges and complex highway systems on American soil. There was also the prominent role played by the world of engineering that in those years was closely watched by the European *entourage*. Its work was also of the highest level but focused mainly on the potential of reinforced concrete.

It is no coincidence that one of the protagonists of this period was Albert Kahn,

with his industrial structures, esteemed by Wright as well as by Mies, who used the images of the Glenn L. Martin bomber factory in Baltimore (1937) as a background for a montage of his project, as did numerous Italians, such as Nervi, Morandi, Musmeci, De Miranda, BBPR, Zanuso, Mangiarotti, Morassutti, and Latis. After the war, they were ready for a look at America and its training, as was the case with Pietro Belluschi, Mario Salvadori and Pierluigi Nervi, who, in April of 1956 made a tour of several American universities: Raleigh, Columbia, Princeton, and Harvard. At the end of the Fifties, he had commissions such as that for the bus terminal in Manhattan (1958-1962), and the Athletic Field House for Dartmouth College in New Hampshire (1960-1961). In these terms, there was a slender connection between the United States and Europe, starting with the iconic buildings of those times, such as the well-known residential projects on the West Coast by Richard Neutra, Charles Eames, J.R. Davidson, Raphael Soriano, Craig Ellwood, Pierre Koenig, A. Quincy Jones, and Fredrick Emmons, but especially the Lever House by Gordon Bunshaft (partner in the legendary studio Skidmore Owings & Merrill), the IBM offices in Rochester by Eero Saarinen, the Inland Steel Building by Bruce Graham but also the best known, the headquarters of the United Nations in New York (where an international team of architects from Niemeyer to Le Corbusier was involved). Its European counterpoint, in 1952, was the UNESCO headquarters in Paris, where, not surprisingly, we find Marcel Breuer, Bernard Zehrfuss and Pier Luigi Nervi, with advice from the CIAM (Congrès internationaux d'architecture moderne), in the persons of Lucio Costa, Walter Gropius, Le Corbusier, Ernesto Nathan Rogers, and Sven Markelius. The substantial role played by this important

170

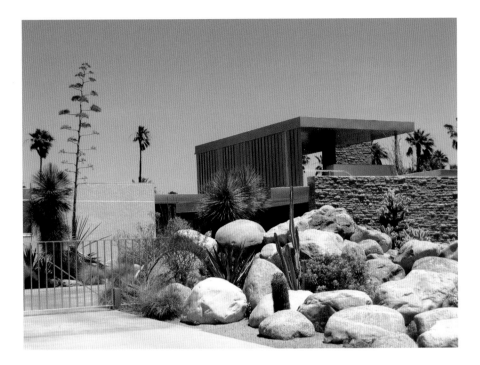

international institution, even after 1949 with the Congress of Bergamo and then until 1959 with the final Otterlo Congress, in the spread of modern architectural thought was seen on several occasions. Kenneth Frampton was one of the first to emphasize, in the absolute diversity of professional training, the similarity between the work of the "Californians" and that of the Dutch group Opbouw, the Czech 13, the British Tecton and Mars, the Spaniards of Gatepac, the South Africans of the Transvaal Group and the Brazilians of Costa and Niemeyer. A "universal" mapping of the International Style was thereby redefined, and deserves a legitimate place alongside the structural research of the great European "builders". But there was also the defining of an entirely contemporary line of research that led to Australia (Utzon) and, even more recently, to the Far and Middle East (Isozaki, Tange, Pei).

Richard Neutra, Kaufmann House, Palm Springs, 1946

Bibliography
Biraghi M. (edited by), *Reyner Banham, Architettura della seconda età della macchina: scritti 1955-1988*, Electa, Milan 2004.
Desideri P., Mammarella A., *International Style?*, Meltemi, Rome 2004.
Frampton K., *Storia dell'architettura moderna*, Zanichelli, Bologna 1981.
Giedion S., *Mechanization Takes Command: a contribution to anonymous history*, Oxford University Press 1948.
Hitchcock H.-R., Johnson P., *The International Style Architecture since 1922*, MoMA, New York 1932.
Scrivano P., *Storia di un'idea di architettura moderna: Henry-Russell Hitchcock e l'international style*, F. Angeli, Milan 2001.

Walter Gropius, Pan Am
Building, New York,
1960-1963

Opposite
Ludwig Mies van der Rohe,
Seagram Building, New York,
1958

Page 174
Oscar Niemeyer, National
Congress of Brazil, Brasilia,
1960

Oscar Niemeyer, Cathedral,
Brasilia, 1970

Page 175
Arne Jacobsen, SAS
Building, Copenhagen,
1956-1960

Anna Barbara

Organic Architecture

The first official definition of "organic architecture" dates back to 1939, with the title of a book by the architect Frank Lloyd Wright. More than an architectural style or season, it is an approach to design that has officially spanned the history and geography of architecture for over a century. Because of its vastness, it has encompassed many different types of designers and many different architectural traits. In some cases, its complexity even generates confusion inasmuch as some architects embraced organic architecture for just one part of their lives and not as a faith to the bitter end. The theoretical centre of organic architecture is the balance between nature, technology, building and the idea that architecture is a single organism, at one with the environment and its inhabitants. Organic architecture was mainly inhabited by communities that subscribed to its theories as their own, capable of guiding not only spatial choices, but also existential and social choices. A cornerstone of organic architecture is the participation of the senses in the architectural design, using them not for design scenic purposes, but as a tool to pursue a profound coherence in the design and a strong sense of place.
One reference to organic architecture is the work of Rudolf Steiner, founder of the worldwide Anthroposophy movement. The movement built two buildings that summarize the idea of oneness between man and nature. In different eras, but with the same concept, Steiner designed *Goetheanum*, first in wood, which was destroyed by fire (1913-1922), then in concrete. This was completed after his death in 1928. The headquarters for the movement was used to host events, conferences and meetings, but also recounted the fluid nature of space, dynamism, and above all the tension engendered by the elements in a state of transition from the invisible to the visible, capable of formulating balances in energy.
The key figure for organic architecture is F.L. Wright. In his first architectural period, that of the prairie houses, the architect attempted to summarize the key elements of this architecture:
- fluid relationship between air and light that must move smoothly through space;
- strongly sliding horizontal planes so as to slide the architecture in nature and vice versa;
- eliminate the idea of circumscribed and delimited rooms to ensure an opening into the spaces;
- use windows as permeable openings;

- use a limited quantity of materials and establish a relationship between the material and the architecture's identity;
- integrate systems and furnishings.

The residences built by F.L. Wright in Oak Park are a synthesis of these basic premises. Robie House, designed (1908-1910) for the 27-year-old Mr. Robie, extends over two bands that slip over one another both in the plan and in the section where the deep overhangs of the ceiling allow the light to slide into the open interior spaces, open but with distinctions in volume through recesses in the roof and material lines. The architectural choices are also the synthesis of a vision of society and the family, as well as the relationship between the American bourgeoisie and nature through the use of technology.

The most famous organic design by F.L. Wright is *Fallingwater* – the house over the waterfall – which Wright designed in 1935 for the Kaufmann family. Rarely in the history of architecture has it been so difficult to separate nature from architecture, inasmuch as one is blended with the other, penetrating each other. The house was built with the same stone as that of the waterfall, just as the rushing sound of the water and the colour of moss are ingredients shared by the landscape and the building.

The organic research also continued into F.L. Wright's later career, particularly at Taliesin West, where the architect resided during the winter and where he had established a campus of architecture. The Taliesin project was the statement that architecture is an evolving organism, and that it has continuity with its context and materials and the resident community that is continually transforming.

There were heirs to Wright's organicism throughout the world. One of his collaborators for a short, but important period of his life was Richard Neutra, who understood Wright's organic language more than others. It was not so much a case of style, but rather a design approach where the elements of nature and architectural elements had equal weight. Neutra believed that architecture should improve the lives of its inhabitants, and that the relationship with nature should be cultivated and designed in constant balance: light, air and ventilation, water and sun, but also the arrangement of the indoor and outdoor spaces into a single composition without fractures. Nature is central to the genesis of Neutra's works, as a context and a constructive element. Neutra's architecture had certain constants: huge windows that open to the view of the landscape, but also for cooling the environment, thinner ceilings and overhangs for shelter from the sun and supported by *spider legs* or slender pillars, curtains and adjustable slats for the sun, pools of water to provide reflection. The exterior landscape is consistent with the interior, but also with the physiological and psychological elements of its residents. For Neutra, architecture interacts with the perceptions and from this sensory experience comes a greater organicity.

Alvar Aalto, widely regarded as one of the masters of the Modern Movement, designed organic architecture with great care. However, because he was a Finnish designer, it is impossible not to take into consideration the special attention inherent in the Nordic cultures towards the relationship between architecture and nature, and a great ability to integrate a building with its environment. Therefore, Aalto's works are organic in an environment where there is already an awareness in regard to the use of materials, a precise relationship with the natural light, the curved forms (but not necessarily) that connect the architecture to the landscape. A prime example is the Viipuri Library (1927-1935) in which the details

177

show this organic relationship between the interiors, architectural form and the surrounding environment. This can be seen in the cones of light that are used to make indirect natural light to illuminate the reading rooms or a section of the conference room, with a corrugated ceiling, in wood, that defines a harmonic and acoustic section capable of ensuring (though of no great height) perfect sound.

With a leap in time and space, organic architecture arrived in the Sixties in Italy, where Bruno Zevi, with his theoretical writings and the magazine *Architettura cronaca e storia* created a fundamental critical and controversial tool for the diffusion of the organic culture after the Second World War. The work that best conveys organic architecture in Italy is a church, Chiesa dell'autostrada (San Giovanni Battista) by

Giovanni Michelucci, 1960. This controversial work summarizes the expressive and moral tensions that underlie the architect's effort to synthesize the architectural composition with the structures and the environment. The relationship with light, the surfaces, the materials and the forms can be considered organic, although some brutalist variations can be found there, such as the pattern on the concrete forms. Michelucci avoided classifications and one of his most famous works denounced the banality of slotting the masters and their unique experimental research into theoretical categories.

There is an equally volatile strength in the work of Paolo Soleri, who in the late Sixties decided to found the city of Arcosanti in the Arizona desert. It is, first and foremost, a concrete utopia, built on the basis of "arcology", in other words, the idea of urban

scale construction with a high population density, capable of having an internal form of ecology. Arcosanti has been a work-in-progress since 1971 and has been uninterruptedly supported by active volunteers since then. Soleri is another "descendant" of Wright and his Taliesin West experiment, where once again nature is the matrix for architecture, devoid of formalism. It is nature that suggests, first and foremost, organic behaviours that can generate forms and spaces. The organic dimension is inherent in the vision, but also in the production that uses poor and elementary techniques to create domes, building mounds of earth in the shape of half-spheres to empty them from the inside later on. But its cosmological design is also organic, as is the relationship between private and public space, a spatial hybrid and continuum that gives strength to the architectural and urban organism as an inseparable whole.

Bibliography
Curtis W.J.R., *L'architettura moderna del Novecento*, Bruno Mondadori, Milan 1999.
Wright F.L., *Architettura organica*, Muggiani Tipografo editore, Milan 1945.
Zevi B., *Verso un'architettura organica*, Einaudi, Turin 1945.

Frank Lloyd Wright, Taliesin West, Scottsdale, 1937

Opposite
Rudolf Steiner, Goethenaum, Dornach, 1928

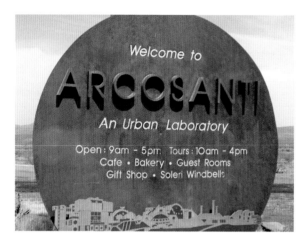

Paolo Soleri, Arcosanti, 1971

181

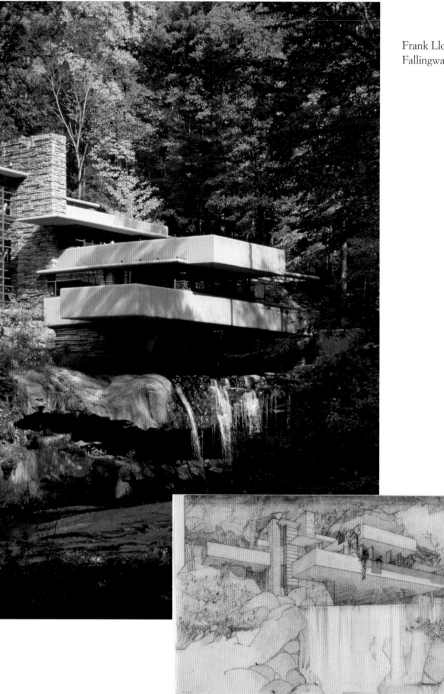

Frank Lloyd Wright,
Fallingwater, Mill Run, 1935

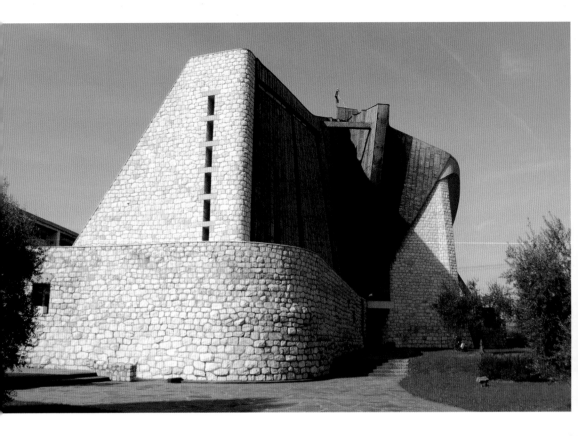

Giovanni Michelucci,
San Giovanni Battista
Church, Autostrada del Sole,
Campi Bisenzio, 1960

183

Luca Molinari

New Italian Design, Neo Liberty

In the first months of 1950, Ernesto Nathan Rogers, the former editor of the magazine *Domus* and an influential member on the management board of CIAM, was asked by the English magazine *The Architects' Journal* to write an essay about post-war Italian architecture. The features he discussed are particularly significant: "In these, as in other projects, can be seen the particular style of Italian architecture which, in the midst of other present-day architectures, has retained unmistakable characteristics. [...] The evolution through which Italian architectural style has passed during the last thirty years is linked with large scale transformations of architecture in other countries. From the more rigid forms of early rationalism, architecture is moulding for itself a more mobile physiognomy which is faithful to the technical exigencies and to the various circumstances of human life. [Italian Architecture] it is also the concrete

expression of the humanistic approach to architecture – that is to say of architecture's unity and universal vision linking the activities of contemporary architects to the deepest origins of our traditions."

A year later Alberico Belgioioso and Franco Albini were called upon, as members of the CIAM, to organize an exhibition about contemporary Italian architecture at the RIBA in London. The event was significant because it was the first foreign exhibition devoted to the nation's architecture since the end of the war. The selection, comprising a total of fifty panels, covered the work of Sant'Elia, Terragni and Lingeri, Pagano, Persico and Nizzoli, BBPR, Gardella, Albini, Bottoni, Mucchi, De Carlo, Menghi, Zanuso, Gandolfi, Cerutti, Marescotti and other Italian architects associated with the Italian CIAM circuit and the MSA (Movement for Architectural Studies).

Both the exhibition and Rogers's article

displayed some of the significant characteristics of what we can define as the New Italian Design of the post-war period, a cultural and stylistic phenomenon that was quite independent from the modernist work being done in the rest of Europe, and which would strongly mark the identity of Italian architectural culture at least until the first half of the Sixties.

Above all, both of these experiences clearly indicated a strong continuity with Italian rationalism, and at the same time established a progressive distance from the formal "rigidity" of European functionalism, in the name of a strongly "humanistic" character which, just a few years later, would turn into a sharp attention for the historic context and its environmental traits. This cultural line was fully expressed by the magazine *Casabella*, edited from 1953 by Ernesto N. Rogers and to which the new editor added the word "continuità" ("continuity"); for a decade it forcefully represented the independent traits of an Italian-style modernity alternative to an interpretation of the modern European language more closely aligned with the "fathers" of the Modern Movement and subject to a stylistic formalism which was impoverishing the more experimental features.

What Italian architecture expressed with increasing clarity after 1945 was a process of individual redefinition of the lessons of the Modern, which gave form to a unique experience in the European context and responded to what Alfred Roth, in his important book *La Nouvelle Architecture* (1939), identified as the emergence of national traits within an overly universalistic vision of the early Modern Movement. Besides this, what should not be underestimated is that the original nature of post-war Italian architecture also represented the anomaly of the economic and social modernity of a country which had only got

Cover of *Domus* no. 267, 1952, with the façade of the house in Viale Gorizia, Milan, by Marco Zanuso

Cover of *Casabella Continuità* no. 287, 1964

185

into step with the more developed and industrial Europe since the Twenties. From the second half of the Fifties, in particular, Italy experienced a very strong economic boom in terms of its domestic consumption habits and the production of goods. This stimulated a demand for new spaces and objects representing this fever of modernity, which seemed to be sweeping across society, definitively changing the imagination and destiny of the nation.

It would however be limiting to regard New Italian Design as a simple expression of a composite inquiry in the field of architecture, because research and industrial production in general was looking increasingly to the inhabited environment in its entirety. The motto of Walter Gropius, "from the spoon to the city", was interpreted in an Italian key by combining the aspirations of a nascent national design industry with an ideal of widespread quality, the humanity and domestic warmth of dwelt environments, and a craft attention to building detail that would generate a series of unique experiences throughout Europe. This rich and fragmentary condition was clearly represented by a series of publishing initiatives that signalled a great intellectual vitality and the inherent need felt by Italian design culture to always combine design and theoretical thinking. If two historic publications like *Casabella-continuità*, edited by Ernesto N. Rogers, and *Domus*, run by its founder Gio Ponti, represented the line of continuity with the modern experiences of

Gio Ponti, Superleggera
chair, 1955

Page 186
BBPR, Olivetti shop in Fifth
Avenue, New York, 1954

the Thirties, the immediate post-war period saw the establishment first of *Metron* and then *Architettura, cronaca e storia*, both Bruno Zevi's brainchildren, *Urbanistica* and *Zodiac*, which were strongly influenced by the presence of Adriano Olivetti, and *Il disegno industriale*, founded by Alberto Rosselli, Ponti's pupil and partner.

All these experiences moved in different and often mutually contradictory ways in the channel of modern European culture, interpreting it and, at the same time, widening its critical and problematic level, often finding an important experimental laboratory both in the Milan Triennale and in the rooms of the IUAV of Venice. It was no surprise, then, to see a polemic being started in *The Architectural Review* by the English critic Reyner Banham about the "betrayal" of modern Italian architecture, echoed just a few years later by the heated discussion at the last CIAM congress in Otterlo in 1959,

when Rogers and the BBPR presented the Velasca Tower, which had just been completed in Milan.

Both discussions were generated by the observation of a distance, linguistic more than conceptual, between the Italian rationalist works of the Thirties and the stylistic and cultural complexity of the many post-war experiences.

In the Otterlo congress alone, the Italians forming part of CIAM presented the new Olivetti canteen of Ignazio Gardella, who gave expression to an organic dimension of the communal space; the council housing project in Matera by the young Giancarlo De Carlo, a reflection on the material and neo-realist dimension of traditional materials; and the Velasca Tower, a genuine ideological manifesto of "continuity" and of an alternative idea of modernity within historic city centres. Comparing and viewing these works in conjunction with the community experience

of Adriano Olivetti in Ivrea, with the reflections on the dwelling space by Luigi Caccia Dominioni, Franco Albini, Figini and Pollini, Ludovico Magistretti, Mario Ridolfi, Monaco and Luccichenti and Adalberto Libera between Milan and Rome, with the neo-Liberty restlessness represented by the Turin architects Gabetti and Isola, by Gae Aulenti and the Gregotti-Stoppino-Meneghetti Studio, with Carlo Scarpa's work on exhibition spaces, with Gio Ponti's reflections on a domesticated and Mediterranean modernity, with the experiments in organic architecture in Florence and Rome, with the investigation into the form of the city conducted by Ludovico Quaroni, Giovanni Astengo and Giancarlo De Carlo, and with the emergence of industrial design with the Castiglioni brothers, Ettore Sottsass Jr, Marco Zanuso, Bruno Munari, Vico Magistretti, Danese, Azucena, De Padova, Arflex, Kartell, Brionvega and Zanotta, gives an idea of the novelty and complexity of New Italian Design in an intense period coinciding with the explosion of the economic boom and lasting until the emergence of a new problematic and antagonistic phase in the middle of the Sixties.

The closure of *Casabella-continuità* in 1964 might be taken as one of the end dates of this phase. This was likewise indicated by the generational change that took place in the curatorship of the 1963 Triennale, which saw the significant presence of Vittorio Gregotti, Gae Aulenti, Aldo Rossi and Umberto Eco, marking, in the key words and the visual universe, a change of paradigm, bringing us closer to a more critical dimension of the concept of modernity.

Bibliography
Dal Co F. (edited by), *Storia dell'architettura italiana. Il secondo Novecento*, Electa, Milan 1997.
Feiersinger M. e W., *ITALOMODERN Architektur in Oberitalien 1946-1976*, exh. cat., Innsbruck, 2011, Springer, Wien 2012.
Ghirardo D., *Italy. Modern Architectures in History*, Reaktion Books, London 2013.
Kidder Smith G.E., *Italia costruisce*, Comunità, Milan 1955.
Molinari L., Scrivano P. (edited by), "Postwar Italian Architecture 1944-1960", *2G International Architecture*, n. 15, Gustavo Gili, Barcelona 2000.
Tafuri M., *Storia dell'architettura italiana 1944-1985*, Einaudi, Turin 1982.

Roberto Gabetti and Aimaro
Isola, La Bottega d'Erasmo,
Turin, 1956

Opposite
Vico Magistretti, Building
in Milan, 1969-1971

189

Luigi Caccia Dominioni,
Building in Milan, 1958-1963

Gio Ponti, Pierluigi Nervi
and others, Pirelli Tower,
Milan, 1958

190

191

Ignazio Gardella, House at
Zattere, Venice, 1953-1958

Carlo Scarpa, Gipsoteca
Canoviana, Possagno, 1957

192

Franco Albini, Palazzo Rosso
Museum, Genoa, 1953-1961

BBPR, Velasca Tower, Milan,
1948-1958

195

Chiara Ingrosso

Team 10

Team X or Team 10 was an international group of architects united by the objective of surpassing the formalism and abstraction inherent in functionalism stigmatized by the classic image of the Modern Movement, to bring architecture closer to the intangible human needs and desires. It was an informal network that united several architects who, in some cases, had worked together drafting projects and had exchanged views through regular meetings, publications, and educational workshops.

The group began to form in the early Fifties, and particularly from the time of the CIAM meeting in 1952 in Sigtuna, Sweden. It was partially formalized in 1954 in the Netherlands, at Doorn, during the organizational meetings for the CIAM X that took place until 1956. The Team 10 meetings continued to take place even after the CIAM conferences had ceased, marked by the congress in Otterlo in 1959. They took place on a regular basis until 1981 (the year of the death of Jaap Bakema).

From the time of its establishment, Team 10 was openly opposed to CIAM's rigid organization and what it represented. In particular, the birth of the group marked the explosion of a generational conflict that began at the Congress of Modern Architecture in Aix-en-Provence (1953). On this occasion, the younger architects presented a series of studies and projects that were openly at odds with the analytical and functional method proposed by the Athens Charter (1943), employing an exhibition method that questioned CIAM's grid, presented by the Ascoral (Assemblée de constructors pour une rénovation architecturale) at the CIAM in Bergamo in 1949. The Urban Re-Identification Grid by the British couple Peter and Alison Smithson, with their project for the Golden Lane housing complex in London (1952), together with Habitat du plus grand nombre Grig of the Gamma Group (Groupe d'Architectes Modernes Marocains), illustrated by the Carrières Centrale project in Casablanca (1953) by ATBAT (Atelier des Bâtisseurs), showed an approach that advocated the quality of the architecture and the city, with a focus on community routines, daily life, street life, and children.

In 1954, under the direction of Jaap Bakema and at the initiative of Sandy van Ginkel, a meeting in Doorn for the preparation of the Tenth International Congress was announced, and its theme was to be the habitat. During the meeting, a manifesto was

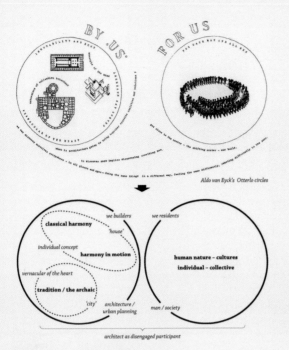

Aldo van Eyck's Otterlo circles

we builders   we residents

classical harmony

'house'

individual concept

harmony in motion

vernacular of the heart

tradition / the archaic

'city'   architecture / urban planning

human nature – cultures

individual – collective

man / society

architect as disengaged participant

Aldo van Eyck, *Otterlo Circles*, 1959

Aldo van Eyck, Playground in Laurierstraat, Amsterdam, 1955-1960

drafted in which the close connection between architecture and the social and anthropological fields was reaffirmed. The new planning criteria was to take into consideration the characteristics of the community, the environment and its individual character and the CIAM grid needed to be modified to become a more qualitative analysis tool.

In the same year, further meetings were announced. At the meeting in Paris, in particular, the CIAM X Committee was appointed, with the mission of organizing the CIAM X. On this occasion, the term "Team 10" appeared for the first time in a document of the Algerian delegation that included Candilis.

The tenth congress, held in Dubrovnik in 1956, is considered by many of its members to be the last CIAM meeting. Here, with so many founding members absent, Team 10 broke away as an independent group and opposed the committee made up of the older generations.

Team 10 presented a series of grids. The Smithsons analysed the concept of the 'cluster' using the diagram "Scale of Association house-street-district-city" (which clearly refers to Patrick Geddes' "Valley Section"). Aldo van Eyck exhibited two grids: *Lost Identity Grid* and *Nagele Grid*. In the first grid, he presented his designs for the playgrounds built in Amsterdam on sites damaged by bombing. In the second he presented his project for the Nagel village in the Noordoostpolder. The tables, which also recall the contemporary art works by Cobra and Experimental Group, were fully in line with the discussions conducted by Team 10 on research into a study methodology that could take into account real problems, occasionally minute ones, ordinary, but also poetic, that would have to be the basis of the design choices.

The wave of renewal also led to changes in the organization of the congresses, to the point that it was decided to do away with division into national delegations, do away with a chairman and, finally, to eliminate the grid as a method of exhibiting projects. The congress held in Otterlo in the Netherlands in 1959 officially formalized the end of the CIAM meetings. The meetings were then organized according to the new informal rules that later characterized the Team 10 meetings that followed. Here, Van Eyck presented his project for the orphanage in Amsterdam (1955-1960) and the Smithsons presented their work for the Haupststadt Berlin competition (1957-1958), for the post-war reconstruction of the capital.

Alison and Peter Smithson, Golden Lane, London, 1952

Alison and Peter Smithson, *Urban Re-Identification Grid*, Ciam 9, 1953

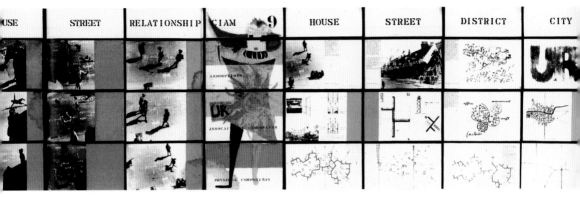

The members of first Team 10 group included some of those who had signed the manifesto in Doorn: Jaap Bakema, George Candilis, Rolf Gutmann and Peter Smithson. Except for Peter Smithson, who did not attend his first CIAM meeting until 1953, all members of the group had participated in their national delegations at the CIAM meetings after the war, also making important contributions.

Joining the group later were Bill and Gill Howell, Aldo van Eyck, Sandy van Ginkel, Alison Smithson, John Voelcker, Shadrach Woods and Giancarlo De Carlo, who officially took part in Team 10 from the end of the CIAM meetings. However, accurately defining exactly who was in the group proves to be somewhat complex as its membership changed from year to year and its meetings were attended by many architects, including: José Coderch, Ralph Erskine, Oswald Mathias Ungers, Rolf Gutmann, Oskar Hanse, Charles Polonyi, Reima Pietilä and others.

With the end of the CIAM conferences, a new phase began for Team 10. The first meeting of the "Team 10 out of CIAM" was organized in 1960 by Candilis-Josic-Woods in the South of France, in Bagnols-sur-Cèze, where the group was working on an important expansion plan. The purpose of the meeting was to start with the project and discuss some broader topics such as the role of the architect in contemporary society, the city-region relationship, trends in contemporary architecture, and so on. Subsequent meetings followed the same model; an architect invited other members of the group to the location where he had designed and built or was completing a project which would trigger the discussion. The meetings included the one in Urbino (1966), organized by Giancarlo De Carlo during the project for the Collegio del Colle (1962-1966), the one in Toulouse-Le Mirail (1971), convened by Candilis with his expansion project and dedicated to a specific theme, "repetition", the meeting on "the matrix" in Berlin (1973), where Candilis-Josic-Woods with Manfred Schiedhelm had designed the Free University (1963-73), the meeting in Rotterdam (1974) in which it was possible to see the projects designed by Van Eyck (the Pastoor Van Ars church, 1964-1969) and Van den Broek-Bakema (Terneuzen Town Hall, 1963-1972), and the meeting in Spoleto (1976) on the occasion of the completion of the Villaggio Matteotti in Terni designed by De Carlo (1976).

During the Sixties, the members of the group were involved in various projects that addressed the new issues that had arisen in a historical moment characterized by the transition from post-war construction to the establishment of the welfare state: the large numbers (and the mega-structures), the infrastructures, the expansion plans for consolidated cities, and the university campuses. At the end of the Sixties there was an internal crisis for organizational reasons, but also a crisis of content, which exploded in the conference organized by De Carlo in Urbino in 1966. This led to the group questioning its identity. Added to this was the criticism by students at the inauguration of the Milan Triennale in 1968 dedicated to "The Large Number", organized by Team 10.

In the Seventies, the meetings became even more informal and the group more restricted, almost like a family. The meetings were held to discuss projects and always provided an opportunity to think about new issues. In those years, many of the Team 10 members, including De Carlo, Van Eyck, Bakema, Erskine, had the opportunity to design low-cost housing that involved, for example, taking a stance with respect to the role of the participation of the inhabitants or urban renewal.

With the death of Bakema the meetings came to an end, but many of the architects of the Team 10 "family" stayed in touch individually and worked together for workshops. The most emblematic case is that of ILAUD (International Laboratory of Architecture and Urban Design) founded by De Carlo in 1976. ILAUD brought together students and faculty professors as well as universities from different countries. It was attended at various times by Peter Smithson, Bakema, Van Eyck, Candilis, and Erskine. Up until 1991, De Carlo's workshops openly carried on the legacy of Team 10's line of thought and some of its themes.

Bibliography
Risselada M., Van den Heuvel D. (edited by), *Team 10 1953-81. In Search of a Utopia of the Present*, NAI Publ., Rotterdam 2006.Smithson A. (edited by), *Team X Primer*, London 1968.
Smithson A., *Team X out of Ciam*, London 1982.
Smithson A. (edited by), *Team X Meetings 1953-1984*, New York 1991.
Stanek L. (edited by), *Team 10 East: Revisionist Architecture in Real Existing Modernism*, Books n. 9, Museum Modern Art Warsaw 2014.
Various Authors, *Ciam/ Team 10 The English Context*, Faculty of Architecture TU, Delft 2002.
Various Authors, *Team 10, Keeping the Language of Modern Architecture alive*, Faculty of Architecture

200

George Candilis, Alexis Josic,
Shadrach Woods,
Freie Universität, Berlin,
1963-1975

George Candilis, Alexis Josic,
Shadrach Woods,
Freie Universität, Berlin,
1963-1975

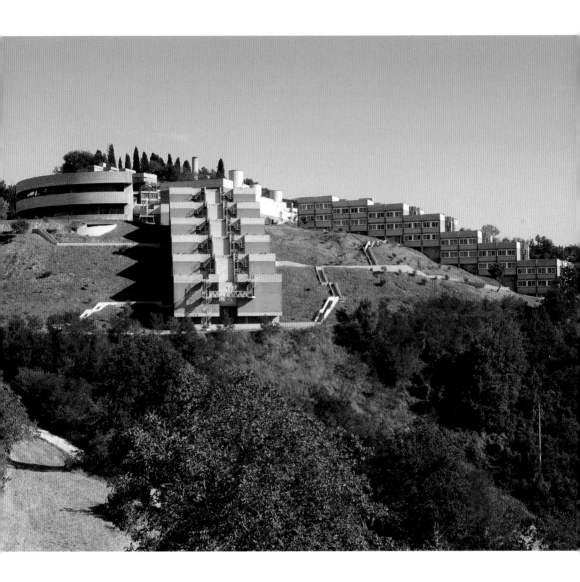

Giancarlo De Carlo,
University college on the Colle
dei cappuccini, Urbino, 1962-
1966

203

Luca Molinari

Brutalism

There is still no consensus on a historiographical clarification of the authorship of the term "brutalism". Kenneth Frampton exemplifies this in his *History of Modern Architecture.* Here he highlights the presence of comments by Hans Asplund about a work built in Sweden in 1950, by the critic Reyner in "The Architectural Review" about a small house designed by the Smithsons in Soho in 1953, or the Art Brut experiment promoted in 1947 in Paris by Jean Dubuffet.

But the issue of the historiographical definition of what New Brutalism was and does represent for the modernist architectural culture in the post-war period is not related solely to circumscribing the times, protagonists, works and influences that this movement has generated since the mid-Fifties, but to help in making the public aware of a number of modern "monuments" that still represent today a generous, experimental and problematic attempt to shape a different modernity, capable of interpreting the profound metamorphosis that swept the West following the war. The brutal architecture of reinforced concrete, brutal because it is visible, a widespread and proudly modern industrial product, partially corresponds to the public architecture of the welfare state that we can now begin to interpret in all its richness and complexity as one of the most important and influential social and design phenomena in both the Western bloc and the Soviet Union after World War II.

This different perspective could give us a new insight into the whole phenomenon of brutalism which could then be divided into two parts: the historically limited experience of the New British Brutalism related to the comments of the critic Reyner Banham between 1952 and 1966, the year in which his book *The New Brutalism: Ethic or Aesthetic?* was published, and a large part of the civil public architecture built between the late Fifties and the end of the Sixties that took its language and most basic poetic materials from brutalism.

The central figure of Le Corbusier is still there in the background, and the oft-quoted line from Banham again, *"L'architecture c'est, avec des matériels brutes établir des rapports émouvants"*. It indicated the need to go back to seeking the truth through the purity and the primal force of the material potentially expressed in the brutal cement work of the Unité d'habitation in Marseilles and many of Le Corbusier's works following the Second World War. It had a powerful effect on the hunger for truth expressed by the younger modernist generation in reaction to the aestheticisation expressed by the International Style.

But first and foremost, post-World War II England, a complex social and cultural environment that so well represented the tension of a country that was victorious, but marked by a severe economic crisis and the deep wounds of the war that had just ended, during the Fifties produced a series of artistic phenomena very different from each other. They ranged between the subversive and restless impulses of Banham, militant critic of the magazine "The Architectural Review", the peaceful return to a modernist order, that looked to the reassuring northern New Empiricism, and sophisticated experiments of the Cambridge School that was re-interpreting the legacy of Mies van der Rohe, and found in Wittkower's book *The Architectural Principles in the Age of Humanism* an ideal reference to his action in the many public works built in the country.

In this England, the concerns of the new generation of modernist architects expressed after the war ended found, in part, a solution in the New Brutalism, with its call for construction ethics, and in the emergence of an anti-stylistic vision of modern architecture. The publication in the early Fifties of the secondary school of Hunstanton and the house in Soho, two projects by Alison and Peter Smithson which were immediately indicated by Banham as designed as the turning-point within the British pompousness, marked the beginning of the brutalist season in Europe.

In his seminal essay entitled *The New Brutalism* published in December 1955 in "The Architectural Review", the British critic outlined the basic features of the new movement, beginning with two works by the Smithsons, citing them for the ability to decisively return to the roots of the Modern

Reyner Banham

The New Brutalism

Movement. They rework the lesson of Mies van der Rohe and Le Corbusier in their choice of materials (exposed concrete) and construction details taken to the limit of visual and functional essentiality, turning them into two bodies that represent a moral and poetic reaction capable of looking clearly at the "truth of the material" and "honesty of construction".

Following an interpretation of brutalism as a critical action on the British reality, Banham called for a necessary "parallel between life and art". This was well reflected in the Smithson's relationship in the Independent Group, a collective that brought together British designers with the artist David Paolozzi, who had trained in Paris with Dubuffet, and the photographer Nigel Henderson, who during the Fifties produced a series of exhibitions and events that were crucial to the modernist British cultural scene.

"Parallel of Life and Art", an exhibition at the Institute of Contemporary Arts in London in 1953 and "This is Tomorrow" at the Whitechapel Art Gallery in 1956, were the two central events for the Independent

Group. They had intense polemical and critical support from Reyner Banham. In both events two imaginary opposites that perfectly represented England and the Western world at this stage were blended and compared: the living memory of the painful war that had just ended and the emerging consumer society represented by those objects of desire that were progressively populating the new domestic landscape, anticipating a pop sensibility that would explode in just a few years.

In the same period, the young Stirling and Gowan aligned themselves with the New Brutalist poetics with a series of works that took a lesson from the last Le Corbusier. It opened up a conceptual and stylistic front that became very important for England in the decades to come. With the urbanization of Ham Common in 1958, these architects began with the Maison Jaoul by Le Corbusier, reinterpreting the relationship between the simple and rough concrete structure and brick. But it was then with two public works, the Engineering Laboratory at the University of Leicester in 1959 and the Faculty of History at Cambridge in 1964, that the two architects made a further conceptual and formal leap. The lessons of Le Corbusier and Aalto were reinterpreted in a problematic way, including elements from the industrial world and using a spatial and formal language that reinterpreted the logic of the "machine for living" in a contemporary and less illusory way.

The short season of the Anglo-Saxon New Brutalism seemed to have finally waned. Though in these years the brutal use of reinforced concrete and a modernist neo-monumental approach seemed to take shape in English cities thanks to a new generation of designers such as Denys Lasdun, Colquhoun, Howell and Killick, Colin St. John Wilson and Leslie Martin.

In 1966, Reyner Banham published the book *The New Brutalism: Ethic or aesthetic?*, in which he sought to assess the brutalist experience from its origins to its international development, raising the question of a gradual shift in the experiences from its strong ethical tension to its being a diffused and consumed language in its critical dimension.

In addition to the early works of Smithson and Stirling-Gowan were the many works of public housing, the English *new towns*, residential experiments by Atelier 5 in Switzerland, the powerful and celebrated brutalist project Istituto Marchiondi by Vittoriano Viganò in Milan, the first works by Paul Rudolph and Kikutake, or the fringe structuralist evolution of the Dutch Team 10 with works by Van den Broek & Bakema or Aldo van Eyck. These indicated a process of magmatic and problematic self-reform that crossed the Modern Movement and its new generations during the Fifties, in the illusory attempt to seek answers in the materials that originated in its recent history, confirming a pride in modernity that was already being challenged by the emergence of the contiguous radical experiments.

Bibliography
Banham R., "Parallel of Life and Art", in *The Architectural Review*, October 1953, pp. 259-261.
Banham R., "The New Brutalism", in *The Architectural Review*, December 1955, pp. 355-361.
Banham R., *The new Brutalism Ethic or Aesthetic?*, The Architectural Press, London 1966.
Berman A. (edited by), *Jim Stirling and the Red Trilogy. Three Radical Buildings*, Frances Lincoln, London 2010.
Clement A., *Brutalism: Post-war British Architecture*, The Crowood Press, Ramsbury 2011.
Colomina B., *Domesticity at War*, MIT Press, Cambridge Mass. 2007.
Fleming J., Honour H., Pevsner N., *The Penguin Dictionary of Architecture*, Penguin Books, London 1966.
Pedio R., "Il nuovo Istituto Marchiondi a Milano. Brutalismo in funzione di libertà", in *Architettura, cronaca e storia*, n. 40, February 1959, p. 683-689.
"Psychiatric Institute in Milan", in *The Architectural Review*, n. 771, May 1961, pp. 304-307.

Risselada M., Van den Heuvel D. (edited by), *Alison and Peter Smithson, from the house of the Future to a house of today*, 010 Publishers, Rotterdam 2004.
Robbins D. (edited by), *The Indipendent Group: Postwar Britain and the Aesthetics of plenty*, MIT Press, Cambridge Mass. 1990.
Smithson A., Smithson P., *The Charged Void: Architecture*, The Monacelli Press, New York 2001.
Van den Heuvel D., *Alison and Peter Smithson, a Brutalist story*, Faculty of Architecture TU, Delft 2013.

Alison and Peter Smithson, Smithdon High School, Hunstanton, 1949-1954

Page 205
Reyner Banham, *The New Brutalism*, London, 1955

Alison and Peter Smithson,
The Economist Building,
London, 1959-1965

Vittoriano Viganò, Istituto
Marchiondi, Milan, 1957

Luca Molinari

Radical Architecture

Even today, starting with the exhibition "Radicals", curated in 1996 by Gianni Pettena at the Venice Biennale's Sixth International Architecture Exhibition, which marked the start of a long period of research and studies on international radicalism, it is difficult to clearly establish the roles and exchanges that occurred with the first generation of truly globalized designers, artists and theorists who changed the way we look at, think about and give shape to postmodern design.

As Pettena writes, "The long experimentation period, which began in the Sixties actually put an end to the idea of 'classical modernity'. The desire was to go beyond architecture, that is, to refine new languages and energies for projects intended for an 'Invisible City', a city without architecture as it was traditionally understood, but designed for the future based on the sensibility and insights of the present".

The term "radical" today is attributed to the critic Germano Celant, who introduced it in a 1970 essay for the first time to describe a cultural and conceptual attitude toward a different and alternative way of doing and thinking about architecture. It is no coincidence that this term arises precisely in the historical phase that established an interesting watershed between a first phase of the explosive climate of protest that was spreading throughout the Western world during the 1960s, and an even more critical dimension of the very idea of modernity that contaminated a new interpretation of the idea of the metropolis and landscape, and that would inevitably come up against the global energy crisis of 1973, establishing a crucial discriminating factor for interpreting this movement's fate.

Nor should we forget the profound revival on the part of this generation of designers, stemming from the direct comparison with the other visual arts that in those years were revolutionizing keywords, tools, and communication methods, by introducing a conceptual dimension that was previously non-existent and eventually became a central element in making art. The global explosion of Pop Art and the first, basic experiments in Land Art became central to the way designers would interpret and design reality in this phase.

In addition to this, another central element was the onset of the political and participatory dimension within the design culture. From individual commitment, practice became shared and diffused,

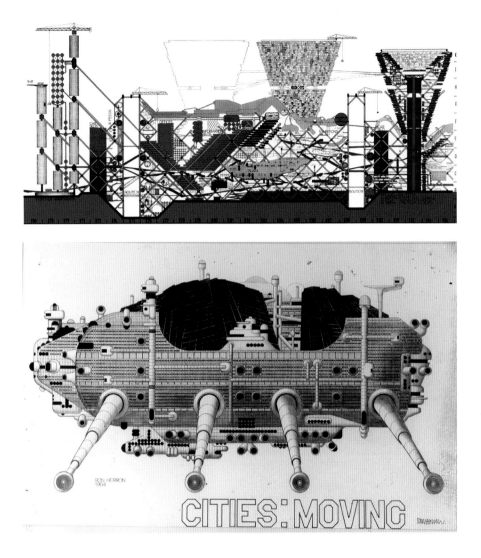

Archigram, *Plug-in City*,
1964

Ron Herron (Archigram),
Walking City, 1964

Page 213
Superarchitettura, poster,
1967

marking another pivotal moment in design practice activated by these authors, in most cases, veritable collectives based on the historic avant-garde model.

The first mature experiments in what could be called, in retrospect, radical architecture, in England were being carried out by the publishing and design group Archigram, a collective made up of Peter Cook (1927), Warren Chalk (1930), Ron Herron (1930), Dennis Crompton (1935), David Greene (1937) and Michael Webb (1937), named after the magazine published for the first time in 1961.

Archigram was never a structured group but rather a collective of authors who collaborated together, from time to time signing the various proposals that over that decade were to have a decisive impact on the international architectural culture. It is no coincidence that this experiment began in England, where New Brutalism and the Independent Group had introduced a new aesthetics of the everyday and the idea of criticism of the present and modernity, stimulated by critical texts by Reyner Banham. Banham also supported "The Living City", the first major exhibition curated by Archigram in 1963. This was followed by, in the next few years, the project-matrix Plug-in-City by Peter Cook (1964), Walking City by Ron Herron (1964) and Living Pods designed by David Greene from 1966.

In these works, which, on the one hand, call into question the way of visually representing the design with a flamboyant pop aesthetics, and, on the other hand, call into question the traditional imagery of the city by including unsettling content and the idea of an absolute mobility of the urban body, its physical and electronic connectivity, an idea of an unstable and fluid community, a transfer of the idea of architecture as a "machine for living" to a new mechanized and encompassing anthropic landscape.

The influence of Cedric Price, the British designer and theorist, the inventor of the Fun Palace in 1961, a huge entertainment palace that could be disassembled and transported on rails from one city to another for a specified time, was crucial in reinterpreting Le Corbusier's experiments and, with this, the experiments on form by the new engineering of Konrad Wachsmann and Buckminster Fuller.

The mentoring role became even more crucial when Price and some members of Archigram were asked to teach at the AA in London in the late Sixties, where a new generation of architects was trained, including Rem Koolhaas, Elia Zenghelis, Bernard Tschumi and Zaha Hadid.

In the early Sixties, in addition to Japanese Metabolism, a number of groups worked from the Austrian *Manifesto of Absolute Architecture,* the brainchild of Hans Hollein and Walter Pichler in 1962. It declared liberation from the modern functionalist cage in the name of a quest for autonomy and absolute purity that would transform everything inhabited and lived-in into architecture.

The absolutist images and theoretical writings of Raimund Abraham in the early Sixties, the visual provocations by Hollein, the temporary inflatable architectures by Haus-Rucker-Co and Coop Himmelb(l)au made up one of the most vital and corrosive European approaches. They played a leading role in the experiments that, starting in the mid-60s, began in Italy and became one of the major areas of research and influence on the international radical scene. In fact, a small exhibition held in Pistoia in 1966 and entitled "Superarchitettura" officially opened the season with two newborn Italian radical groups from Florence: Archizoom with Andrea Branzi, Gilberto Corretti, Paolo Deganello and Massimo Morozzi, and Superstudio, made up

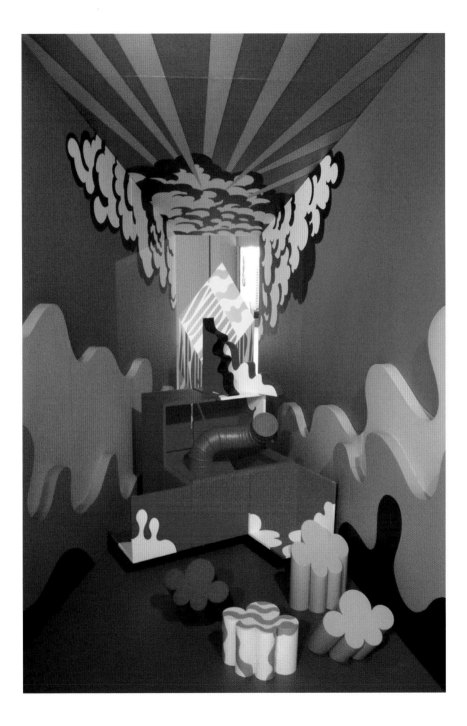

213

"The ultimate aim of modern architecture is the elimination of architecture itself"

Archizoom Associati

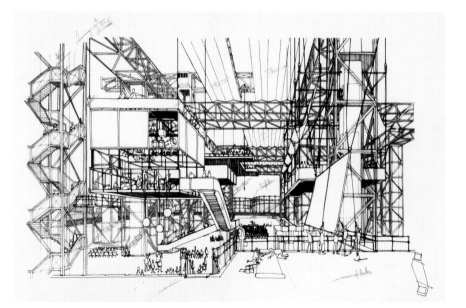

Cedric Price, *Fun Palace*, 1961

Superstudio, *Monumento
continuo nella Palude*, 1969

of Adolfo Natalini, Cristiano Toraldo di Francia, Roberto Magris, Piero Frassinelli and Alessandro Magris.

This small, colourful exhibition brought to Italy the virus of a powerful change from the symbolic and visual point of view, calling into question a new urban imagery based on the American pop experience, a subtle critique of consumer society through the design of paradoxical objects and a new narrative mode in which the representation took on an unprecedented ideological and conceptual value for the Italian architectural culture.

It is no coincidence that both Superstudio, Archizoom and other protagonists of the Italian radical movement such as UFO (1967), Zziggurat (1969), 9999 (1969) and Gianni Pettena (1970) were born in Florence, the crossroads of the first American universities that had established their Italian headquarters here, the first truly international bookstore that imported American pop scene materials, and site of the flood of 1966 which was such an important experience for the students of the early Sixties.

Unlike their British colleagues, the Italian radicals' work is positioned on a different scale. It took an original approach to the relationship between the image of the design and the theoretical development typical of the national architectural culture, as with the series of "Monumento Continuo

Hans Hollein, Project (unrealized) of the city in the form of aircraft carrier in a landscape, 1964, New York, The Museum of Modern Art

Archizoom, "No stop city", in *Domus* n. 496, 1971

(Continuous Monument)" (1969) and "Dodici Città Ideali (Twelve Ideal Cities)" by Superstudio, with the theoretical images of "No-Stop City" by Archizoom (1970), "L'anarchitetto (The anarchitect)" by Gianni Pettena and the communication and city experiments by Ugo La Pietra.

In addition to this, household items designed for Poltronova, Gufram, Danese and Arflex by Superstudio, Archizoom and Gruppo Strum, as well as by Ettore Sottsass jr. and Enzo Mari, initially began as a form of anti-design thanks to a paradoxical and ironic use of form and the new industrial materials. But together they began a radical reform of the way design is conceived and executed, with the experiments of the 1970s by Memphis and Alchimia.

The complex relationship between the various arts and a different form of design seen as a collective urban experience also found another interesting outlet in the series of discotheques designed for those years.

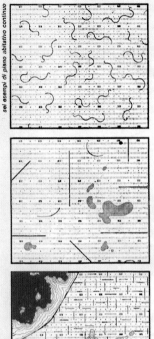

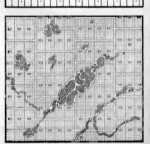

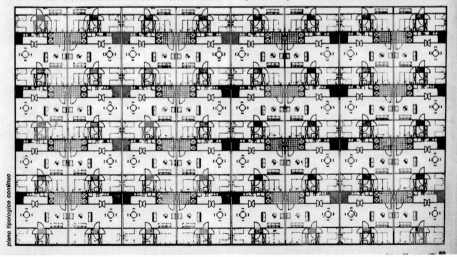

sei esempi di piano abitativo continuo

paesaggio interno — interior landscape

piano tipologico continuo

« Non esiste oggi alcun dubbio nel riconoscere nel fenomeno urbano il punto più debole dell'intero sistema industriale.

La metropoli, tradizionale « scena madre del Progresso », è oggi di fatto il settore più arretrato e confuso della realtà del Capitale; e tutto questo ad un tale livello che viene da domandarsi se la città moderna, più che un problema non risolto, non sia un fenomeno storico oggettivamente superato.

Bisogna cioè capire se il Capitale si pone ancora oggi, come un secolo fa, il problema della gestione della propria immagine e del proprio funzionamento al livello della forma urbana, o se piuttosto le trasformazioni avvenute ed in atto non hanno trasferito la sua realtà su di un'altra scala, trasformando il concetto stesso di città.

In questo momento dunque il problema non è più quello di immaginare una metropoli più umana e più ordinata, ma piuttosto quello di capire profondamente le leggi oggettive che presiedono al configurarsi del fenomeno urbano-architettonico, demistificando la complessa ideologia che ne accompagna il dibattito e ne condiziona la forma.

Il mito naturalistico della libera concorrenza poneva la città degli scambi e del commercio a garantire le condizioni ideali del mercato, realizzando l'equilibrio naturale tra gli opposti interessi, nel quadro generale della raggiunta armonia tra tecnica e natura.

Oggi l'uso dei medium elettronici sostituisce la prassi urbana diretta: l'induzione artificiale al consumo permette una ben più profonda infiltrazione nella realtà sociale che non i fragili canali di informazione della città.

La metropoli cessa di essere un « luogo » per divenire una « condizione »; è proprio tale condizione infatti che viene fatta circolare in maniera omogenea nel fenomeno sociale attraverso i Consumi.

La dimensione futura della Metropoli coincide con quella del Mercato stesso.

La metropoli come concentrazione intensiva corrisponde alla fase ormai superata della accumulazione spontanea del Capitale.

In una società programmata infatti la gestione degli interessi non ha più necessità di organizzarsi sul luogo stesso degli scambi.

La totale disponibilità del territorio e la sua totale penetrabilità elimina la città-capolinea e permette l'organizzazione di una maglia progressiva di organismi di controllo su di esso.

Nella ideologia borghese equilibrio ecologico e giustizia sociale diventano parti di una stessa battaglia: la città fornisce con la propria immagine la verifica formale di tale equilibrio.

Nel Piano Urbanistico dunque viene ricercata la non impossibile armonia tra l'Interesse Generale e quello Particolare: tali categorie però vengono

Paola Navone
Bruno Orlandoni

architettura "radicale"

documenti di
casabella

Paola Navone, Bruno Orlandoni, "Architettura 'radicale'", *Documenti di Casabella*, 1974

Pages 220-221
Ant Farm and others, Cadillac Ranch, Texas, 1974

The Piper Pluri Club created by Pietro Derossi (1966), the Space Electronic by the 9999 and Mach2 by Superstudio in Florence (1969), Bang Bang by Ugo La Pietra in Milan, were some of the places where experimental art, electronic music, performance and architecture came together in an experimental and open space that interpreted the profound social and cultural change European society was undergoing in those years.

Between the late Sixties and early Seventies, there were three public events that enshrined the height of the international radical culture. Together, they were at the edge of the profound economic and social change represented by the energy crisis of 1973.

The first was the Triennale in 1968 dedicated to the topic of "Grande numero (Large numbers)" and curated by Giancarlo de Carlo. De Carlo tried to start a dialogue between Team 10 and Archigram, Superstudio, Arata Isozaki and UFO. Paradoxically, the exhibition with the strongest subversive content of this phase of Italian culture was occupied by students and workers, and in fact never saw the light of day.

The second was the Expo in Osaka in 1970, the height of splendour for the Metabolist movement. The last example was the great "Italy the New Domestic Landscape" exhibition, curated by Emilio Ambasz at the MOMA in 1972. There, the most political and visionary generations of Italian designers represented by Ettore Sottsass jr., Superstudio, Archizoom, Gaetano Pesce, Mario Bellini, Marco Zanuso and Richard Sapper, Alberto Rosselli, 9999 and Gruppo Strum, were asked to produce a number of home environments in which design, electronics, and the new media would define the radical critical framework for the contemporary mass societies of the world.

The United States became the last of the great radical culture frontiers, after the early Sixties, when the Pop culture and the Beat Generation had nourished the imaginations of the younger generations in Europe and Asia.

Ambasz's experiences as a curator at MoMA from 1969 to 1976, but primarily the research by Ant Farm from 1968, and Site from the early Seventies, created a further shift in the scale of interest to the landscape as the last setting of the crisis of modernity encountering contemporary experiments in land art.

The magazine *Casabella* managed by Alessandro Mendini between 1970 and 1976, which later merged with the magazine *Modo* in 1977, became the last significant attempt to conceptualize this highly complex and heterogeneous experience. In fact, it became the swan song of a phenomenon that continues to profoundly influence our culture even today.

Bibliography
Ambasz E. (edited by), *Italy: The New Domestic Landscape*, Moma, New York; Centro Di, Florence 1972.
Branzi A., *Una generazione esagerata*, Baldini e Castoldi, Milan 2014.
Colomina B., Buckley C. (edited by), *Clip, Stamp, Fold. The Radical Architecture of Little Magazines 196X to 197X*, Actar, Barcelona 2010.
Navone P., Orlandoni B., "Architettura radicale", *Documenti di Casabella*, Milan 1974.
Pettena G. (edited by), *Radicals. Architettura e design 1960-1975*, Il ventilabro, Florence 1996.
Schrijver L., *Radical Games. Popping the Bubble of 1960's Architecture*, Nai Publishers, Rotterdam 2009.

Luca Molinari

Metabolism

The short season of Japanese Metabolism, officially founded in 1960 and over by the early Seventies, was a movement that represented the first real attempt to give mature and independent form to an idea of alternative modernity, with respect to what was happening in the same period in the Western world. Together, it defines an original imagery for the economic and social boom that the Asian country was experiencing during the Sixties.

A central and charismatic figure in the progressive definition of this experience was undoubtedly Kenzo Tange, the father of modernity in post-Second World War Japan, a member of CIAM and close friend of Le Corbusier. He had the ability to rework visual and brutalist thought into a series of works, such as the Memorial of Hiroshima complex, which was to define a Japanese way to modernity.

His teaching activity, with the creation of the Tange Lab at Tokyo University immediately after the end of the war, became the nucleus of an experimental laboratory that brought together such authors as Fumihiko Maki, Kisho Kurokawa and Arata Isozaki, some of the best talents of the new Japanese architecture and future members of the Metabolism group, decisively leading the research and studies.

Tange's political and cultural role at this stage was crucial. As an invitee to the CIAM congresses from 1952 onward, the Japanese designer became the *trait d'union* between the on-going debate in Europe on the fate of the Modern Movement and the Japan that was slowly emerging from the trauma of war, seeking its own original way between the call to tradition and the modernist Western and Soviet forces. In addition to this, Tange was the main instigator of the modern national culture through intensive exchanges and meetings with most original and innovative authors of the new generations. He was also the person behind controversial public action to establish an anti-academic and problematic approach for the reconstruction of the cities destroyed by the war.

A series of writings by Tange are dedicated to the Palace of Katsura and the shrine of Ise. Both published in the early Sixties, these interpreted tradition as an innovative and lively path for Japanese architectural culture, a culture that was to have the capability of interacting with modernity, a characteristic that could be found in all members of the Metabolism group.

The official foundation of the Metabolism

movement dates to the World Design Conference held in Tokyo in 1960. Tange was one of the undisputed promoters of this initiative, which was also animated by Jean Prouvé, Paul Rudolph, Alison and Peter Smithson, Louis Kahn and Ralph Erskine as well as many young Japanese authors such as Masato Otaka, secretary of the initiative, Fumihiko Maki and Kiyonori Kikutake, who had recently unveiled his Sky House, one of the manifestos of the new Japanese architecture.

At the entrance to the congress a group of young architects, led by Noboru Kawazoe, a leading critic and editor of the magazine *Shinkenchiku*, distributed a small book entitled *Metabolism 1960*, a volume presenting the work of Kikutake, Kawazoe, Maki, Ohtaka and Kurokawa, making this term public for the first time.

And as Kawazoe himself explained in an interview, "The catalyst was Marx again. In those years I was using the term *shinchintaisha* a lot, which means 'regeneration' or 'exchanging the old for the new'. I was trying something new that we could launch for the Design Conference in Japanese and the same term is used in

biology as 'metabolism'". The goal of this group of young architects was to establish a strong break with the situation of that time and to implement a strategy that involved a radical regeneration in the terms used and the visual imagery that represented them.

The Sky House and the water towers by Kikutake, the Space City and the Wall City by Kurokawa, the reflections on the new concept of urban form by Maki's group introduced a system of materials and keywords for the architecture that sought a fusion between a re-interpretation of some fundamental characteristics of traditional architecture with the pressures and stimuli that the new Japanese society was producing at this stage.

All these works involved a change in scale to a metropolitan dimension that was tied to the debate taking place in Europe and within Team 10, regarding mega-structures. Together, they were inspired by a different imagery, bound to an organic and complex vision of reality as well as a pop imagery that was inspired by the conquest of space and apocalyptic nuclear world.

One of the designs that best handled the large-scale metropolitan project was by Tange and his laboratory for Tokyo Bay introduced in 1960. It sought to meet the needs of a quickly growing population, and providing land and homes at low cost. The proposal is for a linear city built on water, along an 80 km central spine that can accommodate 5 million new residents. All the buildings for production and commerce are situated on a central double highway, and are capable of giving employment to more than 1.5 million people. The residential system is positioned on two sides and relies on a system of bridges and causeways for progressive growth. The metaphor of an animal's spine as a system for Tokyo's new urban development plan became the central image for other urban plans conceived by Tange in this period, generating a powerful and visionary image that was to have a strong impact on the debate in Japan and the rest of the world in this period.

In those years, all architects related to the Metabolist movement produced some of their most innovative and open-minded works, working on series of common elements that characterized their work. All the designs were distinguished by their very sophisticated use of "modern" materials such as concrete, plastic materials and any cutting-edge solutions that industrial production could provide.

The possibility of making housing cells and modules that could be easily attached was combined with the building of new artificial surfaces, raised above the ground or floating on the water, much like the quest to find ways to colonize outer space. The idea of the quasi-organic proliferation of these complex new urban forms was very strongly related to central vertical nuclei and cells capable of growing both vertically and horizontally, giving body to works that in those years were unprecedented on the international scene.

The capsule housing by Kurokawa built in Tokyo and Osaka in the Seventies, the designs for the Helix City by Kurokawa, 1961, the Tetra Project by Kikutake, the Clusters in the Air by Isozaki in 1962, and the vast number of cities for water by Kikutake since 1959, are just some of the experiments and buildings that were revolutionizing the architectural and artistic Japanese and international imagination, placing this generation of authors at the centre of international debate for the first time. One of the most important moments in this particular experience corresponded with the Expo 1970 in Japan, which expressed all the wealth and the power generated by the economic and technological boom of the

Sixties, turning Japan into a new world power.

The theme "Progress and Harmony of Humanity" was the high point of this historical phase just before the great oil crisis generated an unexpected recession. The general plan was designed by Tange, who called on Kikutake to design the great tower for the Expo, and Otaka and Ekuan for the transport and the design of public spaces. Kurokawa won competitions for two large pavilions built with suspended cells and modules, and Isozaki worked with Tange on the design of the large central monumental roof, the real heart of the Exposition. The considerable public and private economic resources allowed the Metabolist designers to give shape to some of the most visionary and powerful works imaginable, creating a unique artificial landscape that attracted 64 million visitors in six months. For the same Expo, architects such as Archigram, Giancarlo De Carlo, Yona Friedman, Moshe Safdie and Hans Hollein were called to work on the great "Mid Air Exhibition" curated by Kawazoe. It was the ideal link between Team 10, some of best radical Western experiences and Japanese Metabolism, one of the most challenging and subversive groups in the international architectural culture of the Sixties.

Bibliography
Frampton K., *Storia dell'architettura moderna*, Zanichelli, Bologna 1993.
Koolhaas R., Obrist H.U., *Project Japan. Metabolism Talks*, Taschen, Cologne 2009.
Zhongjie Lin, *Kenzo Tange and the Metabolist Movement: Urban Utopias of Modern Japan*, Routledge, New York 2010.

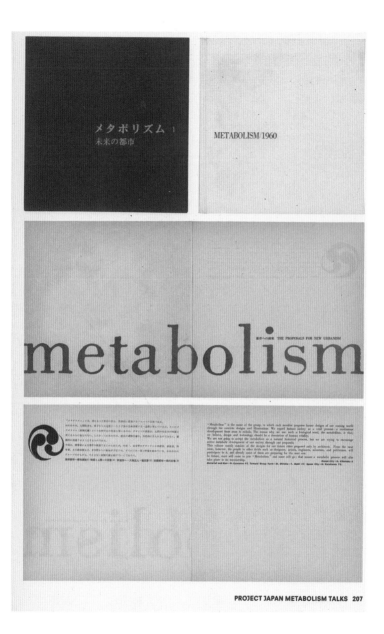

Cover of *Metabolism*, 1960

Page 223
Kenzo Tange, Plan for Tokyo
Bay, 1960

Kyionori Kikutake, Sky House,
Tokyo, 1958

Arata Isozaki, City in the Air,
1961

Kisho Kurokawa, Capsule
Tower, Tokyo, 1972

228

Valerio Paolo Mosco

Five Architects

To understand the architecture of Richard Meier (1934), Peter Eisenman (1932), John Hejduk (1929-2000), Michael Graves (1934) and Charles Gwathmey (1938-2009), who were somewhat accurately classified as *Five Architects*, or *The New York Five*, it is necessary to refer to the notion of mannerism. The term *mannerism* was coined by Giorgio Vasari, who asserted that the artists of his era, the late Renaissance, distinguished themselves for having abandoned the direct representation of nature to turn their attention to the great masters. In other words, they had begun to paint "in the manner of" Raphael or Leonardo.

In the Sixties, in the New York that was ever more enmeshed in the epic European avant-garde, several architects began to look again at the great masters of the Modern Movement, primarily Le Corbusier and more precisely, its purist season in the 1920s. The mannerist choice of the Five had a precise historical motive. In the early Sixties, the modern tradition had begun to weaken in the United States. Architecture appeared to be resting on the styles of Mies in a more facile and commercial way. It was no coincidence, therefore, that at this time, Louis Kahn's star was beginning to shine.

He vehemently proposed a return to authorship, and making this return by appealing to history. The Five, like Kahn, proposed a return to authorship and history, although for them history would not be the ancestral one of Kahn, but rather that of the avant-garde.

The appeal of the Five to return to authorship is radical. For them architecture had to return to being an autonomous discipline. It had to, in Tafuri's words, "pour itself into itself", also amending those social issues that had characterized the Modern Movement. The movement was born in 1969, when in a meeting held at the Museum of Modern Art in New York, critic Kenneth Frampton presented the work of the five architects, pointing out the similarities but not without a stretch. In 1972, the conference was followed by the publication of the volume *Five Architects*, with texts by the elite from the world of international criticism: Arthur Drexler, Kenneth Frampton and Colin Rowe.

A key figure to understand the architecture of the Five is Colin Rowe, who not coincidentally was Eisenman's teacher. In the early 1950s, Rowe had begun the work of historicizing the avant-garde. His method involved placing classical architecture in relation to modernism with what Rowe himself called *parti*. The *parti* is the main configurational diagram, in which the architecture takes its shape through the compositional process. Richard Meier, John Hejduk and particularly Peter Eisenman, took this analytical method to an extreme, a method that owes much to the spirit of the Sixties, full of semiological studies and conceptual art. Rafael Moneo calls this structuralist approach "architecture of the *process*", or a way of constructing form that is devoid of any *a priori* ideas, capable of giving life to an "intransitive" architecture, to use the expression of that period, whose motivations lie in its making, in its process. Peter Eisenman was the ultimate proponent of the architecture of the *process*. Early in his career (1967-1979), he built a series of homes that are veritable purist sculptures named in sequence after prime numbers from 1 to 9. In them, an exasperation of the purest language creates a redundant game between floors, columns and beams no longer regarded as construction elements, but as verbal phrases of a purely abstract composition. Ultimately, the method that Eisenman uses, and that he says to have learned from Giuseppe Terragni, is that of applying a series of elementary compositional acts to an initial elementary *parti:* looping, overturning, alliterating, rotating, subtracting, to the point of arriving at a meaningful form, inasmuch as it is completely autonomous. Eisenman provocatively called this architecture *cardboard architecture.* Roland Barthes, one of the most influential semioticians of the time, precisely in the same years in which Eisenman was making his case, wrote a book with the meaningful title, *The Pleasure of the Text.* Eisenman's houses seem to be the architectural personification of the pleasure of the text: in fact, they should be valued for the intellectual pleasure that they instil: a tautological pleasure, which refers to itself and nothing more.

In the Eighties, Eisenman's architecture

"Terragni does not exist. I invented Terragni. Terragni's me"

Peter Eisenmann

changed, moving away from analytical composition and becoming more drawn to the tectonic relationship with the land and the memory of ruins. The moment of transition came with the project for Cannaregio in Venice (1978). On this new course, Eisenman designed some very interesting projects, such as the Max Reinhardt skyscraper in Berlin (1992) and the building for Checkpoint Charlie again in Berlin (1980), but when it was built, the designs highlighted a falling off that demonstrated the limits of conceptual architecture (Wexner Center for the Arts in Columbus, Ohio in 1989 and the City of Culture in Santiago de Compostela in 1999). Most probably, Eisenman's masterpiece is not a work of architecture, but a sculpture: the Memorial to the Murdered Jews of Europe in Berlin (2005), which best summarizes the old and new course of its author.

Richard Meier did not arrive at the radicalism of Peter Eisenman. From the purism of Le Corbusier, he took what was functional and already in the Sixties began to shape his architecture on a *parti* which ultimately corresponded to that of the internal spaces. His first houses (the Smith House, 1965, and the Saltzman House, 1967) are much

more spectacular than those of Eisenman, and less conceptual, but also less interesting. More convincing is Meier's neo-functionalism in public buildings such as the Atheneum in New Harmony, Indiana (1975-1979) and the Museum of Decorative Arts in Frankfurt (1979-1985). In the Eighties Meier consolidated his language, making it more and more like itself, as if any evolution were forbidden. Nonetheless, Meier, one of the Five, won the Pritzker Prize in 1984 and built one of the largest museums in the world, the Getty Center in Los Angeles (1984-1997): a work in which one can clearly see the fatigue of an artistic adventure that over time has translated mannerism into a style.

Michael Graves is the most aesthetic of the five New York architects. In his reinterpretation of purism there is no will to a system. After collaborating with Eisenman, he designed the Hanselmann House (1967-1970), followed by the Snyderman House (1971-1972), both in Fort Wayne, Indiana. His attraction to iconicity led him, at the end of the Seventies, to espouse the postmodern cause, for which he designed a building that was to become the symbol of a style that contrasted the iconographic program of the New York Five: The

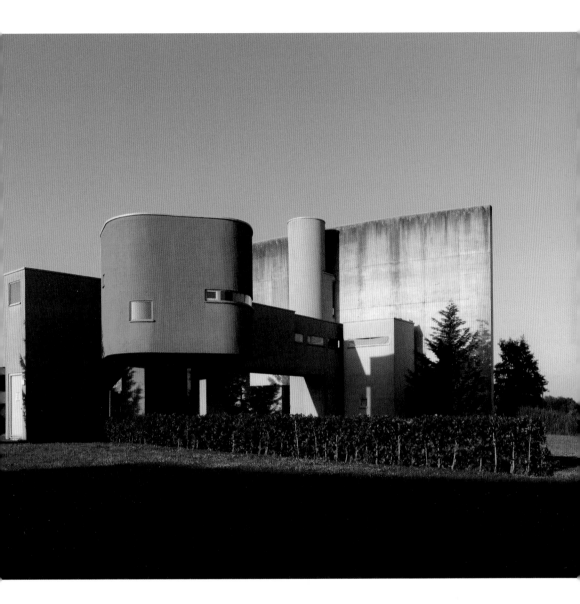

John Hejduk, Wall House
#2, Groningen, 1973-2001

Page 231
Peter Eisenman, House VI,
Cornwall, 1975

Humana Building in Louisville (1986). Another exception can be made for John Hejduk (1929-2000). With Eisenman, he was the one who emphasized the autonomy of the language to the point of losing interest in building the design. In the plans for One-Half House (1966) and House X (1966) he began with simple shapes that became meaningful through graphic hyperbole, like the very extensive walkway of House X. Hejduk's mannerism led him to make extreme choices, such as that of making an architectural work extrude from an avant-garde painting, as in the case of Diamond House (1967-1968), whose *parti* comes from the famous painting by Piet Mondrian, *Victory Boogie-Woogie*. This was followed by other significant projects, such as the Wall House (1971-1972) and the Bye House (1973). With the lyrical project 13 Watchtowers of Cannaregio (1978), Hejduk began to abandon radical abstraction, to discover an iconic and corporal dimension to architecture that owes much to Christian iconography.

Bibliography
Eisenman P., *Eisenman Inside Out: Selected Writings, 1963-1988*, Yale University Press, New Haven 2004.
Frampton K., *Five North American Architects: an Anthology by Kenneth Frampton,* Lars Müller Publisher, Zurich 2012.
Tafuri M., *Five Architects NY*, Officina Edizioni, Rome 1976-1983.
Various Authors, *Five Architects NY: Eisenman, Hejduk, Graves, Charles Gwathmey, Meier*, exh. cat., Museum of Modern Art, Witterbon, New York 1972.
Various Authors, *Five Architects*, Oxford University Press, New York 1997.

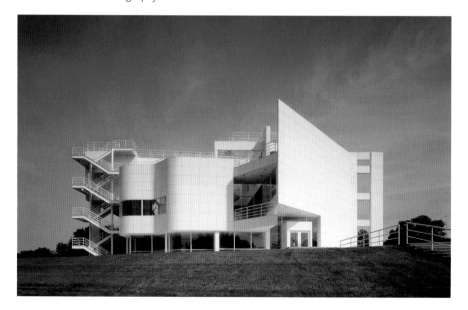

Richard Meier, Douglas
House, Harbor Springs,
1971-1973

Opposite
Richard Meier, New
Harmony's Atheneum, 1979

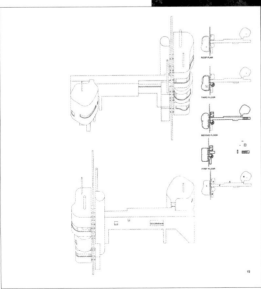

John Hejduk, Bye House,
1973

Richard Meier, Getty Center,
Los Angeles, 1997

236

Federico Ferrari

High Tech

If the technological image has always been one of the favourite forms of expression of twentieth century architects – at least from the time of the historical avant-garde onward – what are the specific features of the so-called *high tech* architecture?

The term appeared for the first time in 1978. In that year, *High tech: The Industrial Style and Source Book for the Home* by Joan Kron and Suzanne Slesin, was published. The two American critics set out to describe the process of appropriation on the part of designers, architects and private individuals, of a series of objects created in the industrial sector and then converted for domestic use: lighting equipment for industrial kitchens or countertops, metal shelving, etc. The cases presented in this volume are primarily concerned with interior design projects that make extensive use of high-tech components. According to a somewhat different meaning, the term *high tech* then went on to define an architectural style with a strong technological aspect. And it was in the UK that this category was particularly successful.

The notion of expressionism is not coincidental: it indicates the spectacularization of a language derived from industrial engineering, structural or design elements. Nor is it a coincidence that the U.K. was the birthplace and workplace for most of the major protagonists of *high tech*: these include Norman Foster, Richard Rogers, Nicholas Grimshaw and Michael Hopkins. From the writings of Reyner Banham to the provocations of the Archigram, and the works designed by James Stirling in the Fifties and Sixties – the Faculty of Engineering of Leicester is perhaps one of its most influential schools – the English architectural *milieu* appears to be particularly receptive to this type of language.

Bearing witness to its strong ties to the "brutalist" image, some of the features of *high tech* architecture were already reflected in various works from the late Sixties, including *The John Hancock Center* (1965-1969) in Som. But it is perhaps the building for the main offices of Willis, Faber & Dumas (1970-1975) by Norman Foster that first synthesized the specific features of a new mode of expression. The single-span truss structure, the escalators in the central *hall*, the smooth, sinuous *curtain wall*, which serves to show off the bearing structure: everything contributes, together with extremely sophisticated details, to giving the

238

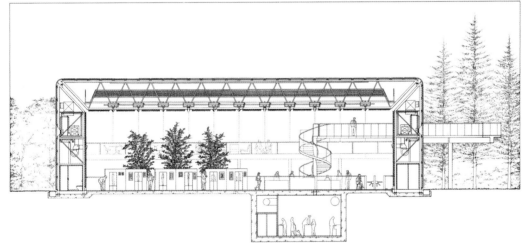

Foster + Partners, Sainsbury
Centre for Visual Arts,
Norwich, 1974-1978

Foster + Partners, Sainsbury
Centre for Visual Arts
(disegno), Norwich, 1974-1978

239

technological aspect a prominent role from an expressive point of view. The building has some features that became constant in the *high tech* architecture of the years to follow: metal structures, whether steel or other alloys, and aluminium siding, painted in various ways or not, in stainless steel or glass. From a planimetric point of view, there are large lights and interior spaces generically ascribed to the category of the *open space*. Despite the fact that on the side façades, the theme of the truss dominates once again, another work by Foster, the Sainsbury Centre for the Visual Arts (1974-1979), confirms the English architect's predilection for the theme of the reflective or translucent covering.

In these early examples, it is already possible to see that disenchanted and optimistic relationship with modernity that is the true hallmark of *high tech*, especially during the Eighties. Once the ethical and social torment had ceased, the spectacularization of technology better embodied some of the values of the emerging Thatcherite England, values that would globally shape the growing optimism of the new neo-liberal world order.

The PA Technology research center (1982-1984) by R. Rogers is representative of an approach that gives the structure, rather than the covering, a pre-eminent role of formal characterization. In fact, to confirm the substantial ambiguity, two different trends coexist in *high tech*: the architect fascinated by the aesthetics and the engineer influenced by industrial processes. Rogers may belong partly to this second category, which rightfully belonged to other figures, such as Michael Hopkins and his project for the Schlumberger Cambridge Research (1984-1985), a work that showed his engineering virtuosity. His is an architecture that spectacularizes its structural elements and makes extensive use of synthetic membranes. These are tensile structures, consistent with other experiments carried out during the Sixties. A paradigmatic example of this is the stadium in Munich (1971-1972) designed by Frei Paul Otto* and Günther Behnisch. Renzo Piano, working closely with Rogers on the Centre Pompidou – another building that in certain aspects owes something to *high tech* architecture – a number of times declared his debt to the work of the German architect and engineer. However for Rogers, while confirming his preference for an engineering rigour that goes back to Richard Buckminster Fuller and Jean Prouvé as further fundamental sources of *high tech* inspiration, there is no denying a certain formalism in some of his works.

In the very famous project for Lloyds of London (1978-1986) the citation of the Crystal Palace by Joseph Paxton is obvious. The structural element, the great vaulted ceiling in painted steel, becomes an "image" of the building, embodying simultaneously the glorification of progress and the celebration of memory. In the same years, Norman Foster completed the Hong Kong headquarters of HSBC (1978-1985). Unlike Lloyds, the plan's design elements do not play an expressive role here, but in this case too, the exhibited structure "composes" the two main façades: the cross-shaped element typical of the truss structure, magnified and made monumental, not only characterizes the outside of the building, but also dominates the large central well of light, crossed diagonally by the escalators. These two works by Rogers and Foster, icons of early *high tech* and not coincidentally built in the mid-Eighties, enlighten us on the tendency to treat certain structural elements as *design* on the architectural scale. Not coincidentally, large multinational banking and industrial groups have always found the *high tech* language ideal for their own self-

representation. Designs for museums, like the aforementioned Sainsbury and Beaubourg, remain an exception. The numerous factories or office buildings are by far the predominant type: of the many, and in addition to those already mentioned, there are the Fleetguard plant (1981), the Inmos microprocessor factory (1982) and the building at 88 Wood Street (1999) by Rogers, the Bank of China Tower by I.M. Pei & Partners (1990), the Ladkarn laboratories (1985) by Nicholas Grimshaw, and the Renault factory (1983) by Norman Foster. It could then be said that all of the *high tech* suggestions have already been investigated over the twentieth century: the great lights of constructive nineteenth-century rationalism, from the Crystal Palace by Paxton to the Galerie des Machines by Dutert and Contamin; the technological expressionism of Russian constructivism, from the building for *Pravda* by Vesnin to the radical fantasies of Chernikov; the industrial detail typical of several experiments in dry mounting, from Jean Prouvé to Buckminster Fuller; finally, through the generalized use of the *curtain wall* in its various forms, the typically "modernist" paradigm of transparency, whose emblematic embodiment is the famous Maison de Verre by Pierre Chereau and Bernard Bijvoet. Aesthetic quotation allows us to define *high tech* as a fully postmodern phenomenon. It is often referred to as a distinctive feature of postmodernism, the recovery of languages derived from the past, combined casually and ironically. But it would be more correct to adopt the definition of Charles Jencks, who instead speaks of "radical eclecticism". In this sense *high tech* is just one of many possible variants of an architecture that has become a mere tool of communication. The cold smoothness of the covering and the bold structures spectacularize a technological image that has nothing of the unsettling materiality of the "brutalist" tradition. The homogeneity of the aluminium, the painted steels and reflective *curtain walls* radically contrasts the unsettling and desecrating pop polychrome by Archigram. *High tech* is in fact an aesthetic and reassuring response to the contemporary debate against technology as a form of architectural expression. Along with the dream of an unreal past celebrated by Strada Novissima at the Biennale of 1981, *high tech* offsets an equally ideological return to the future, in the illusion, cultivated perhaps for the last time in the 1980s, that technology could still be the common language of architecture on a global scale.

*Frei Paul Otto (1925), made famous by his tensile structure projects with metallic skeleton and synthetic materials, of which the German Pavilion in Montreal in 1967 should certainly be mentioned.

Bibliography
Banham R., *Megastructures: Urban Futurse of the Recent Past*, Thames and Hudson, London 1976.
"Being Norman Foster", in *Abitare*, n. 507, Novembre 2010.
Cohen J.-L., "The neo-Futurist optimism of high tech", in *The future of architecture. Since 1889*, Phaidon, London 2012, pp. 438-449.
"Engineering & Architecture", in *AD*, November-December 1987, vol. 57.
Jaeger F., *High Tech*, in Magnago Lampugnani V. (edited by), *Dizionario Skira dell'architettura del Novecento*, Skira, Milan 2000, pp.198-199.
Jencks C., *The Language of Postmodern Architecture*, Rizzoli, New York 1977.
Kron J., Slesin S., *High tech: The Industrial Style and Source Book for The Home*, Clarkson N. Potter, New York 1978.
Rice P., *An Engineer Imagines*, Artemis, London 1994.

Richard Rogers, Lloyds
of London, 1978-1986

Page 241
Renzo Piano, Richard
Rogers, Centre Georges
Pompidou, Paris, 1971-1977

Page 242
Norman Foster, Hong Kong
and Shanghai Bank,
Hong Kong, 1984-1985

Luca Molinari

La Tendenza

In 1973, the fifteenth edition of the Triennale in Milan opened with an event that was to have a significant impact on the Italian and western architecture of those years. The exhibition was directed by Aldo Rossi with Gianni Braghieri and Franco Raggi, and accompanied by the book *Architettura razionale* (*Rational Architecture*) by Ezio Bonfanti, Rosaldo Bonicalzi, Aldo Rossi, Massimo Scolari and Daniele Vitale. With the exhibition, the birth of the Tendenza movement was made official, in a turbulent historical and cultural period marked by a variety of fringe phenomena.

Behind this edition was the 1968 Triennale curated by Giancarlo De Carlo. It was dedicated to the "Grande Numero" (Great Number), which included some of the most interesting architects from Team 10 and the Radical period, but the exhibition was "born dead" because of the student occupation on the day of its inauguration.

The exhibition, curated by Rossi, immediately presented a change in cultural perspective with respect to the two editions of the 1960s. There was a strong return to architecture as an independent discipline and a turning away from reality and the undue pressure of phenomena considered to be outside its re-foundation.

Looking carefully at the list of architects invited, we can see that there were at least four cultural spirits that illustrated the complexity of the moment: the group recognized as the Tendenza experience with Gianugo Polesello, Bruno Reichlin, Fabio Reinhardt, Arduino Cantafora, Carlo Aymonino, Salvatore Bisogni, Giorgio Grassi, Antonio Monestiroli, Max Bosshard, Massimo Scolari, Rosaldo Bonicalzi, Daniele Vitale and Vittorio Savi. There were the New York Architects who in those same years Tafuri identified as the Group of Five with Peter Eisenman, Charles Gwathmey, Michael Graves, John Hejduk and Richard Meier. The group made up of European architects included Leon Krier, James Stirling, Leslie Martin, O.M. Ungers, Robert Krier, Colin Rowe, Ludwig Leo, Jurgen Sawade, Dolf Schnebli, J. Charters Monteiro, Ernst Gisel, Max Bill and the Halle Collective. And finally, there were two architects of the radical season, Adolfo Natalini from Superstudio and Franco Raggi.

The exhibition opened at the beginning of a very problematic moment in history, that of the great energy crisis, the end of the Vietnam War and the beginning of European terrorism. Illusions and hopes that had been stirred up by the student protests during the

Sixties were somewhat deflated. However, they had been a driving force in the reorganization of universities in Italy.

The reform of courses, teaching and lectures in many faculties of Italian architecture made it possible to experiment, carry out research and undertake graduate theses that were consistent with the construction of a new generation's approach toward architecture and urban design. It was particularly strong in Milan, with Aldo Rossi, Guido Canella and Giorgio Grassi, Pescara, where the campus was designed by a collective of many of these architects, and Naples, with Siola and Renna.

Therefore, it seems to be significant that the unprecedented section at the Milan exhibition, showing the work of the Faculty of Architecture of Pescara (Umberto Siola), Rome (with the thesis of Laura Thermes, Umberto Zagari), Naples (Filo Speziale, Umberto Siola and Agostino Renna), ETH Zurich (Aldo Rossi and Max Bosshard) and Milan (texts by Cristofellis, Braghieri, Bonicalzi, Vitale and Monestiroli) bore witness to the widespread political and cultural presence of the Tendenza group within some of the major universities.

But there are two other background elements that must not be forgotten in the reinterpretation of this period: the participation of the most senior members in the preparation and in the *Casabella-continuità* Center for Studies directed by Ernesto Nathan Rogers until 1964, and the common political community within the Italian Communist Youth.

The first element, in particular, is a fundamental cultural premise because *Casabella-continuità* at the beginning of the Sixties, and *Controspazio* a decade later, were the two basic conceptual and cultural workshops that allowed many of these architects to make contact, carry out the research, publish the first projects on an international scale and write some of the texts that later became seminal in the development of a possible theory of La Tendenza, as in the writings of Rossi on Lombard Neoclassicism, Ledoux and Adolf Loos.

The second half of the Sixties seemed to conceptually prepare the 1973 exhibition with the publication of *Il sistema teatrale a Milano (Milan's Theatres)* by Guido Canella (1965) *Architettura della città (City Architecture)* by Aldo Rossi (1966) and *La costruzione logica dell'architettura (The Logical Construction of Architecture)* by Giorgio Grassi (1967), which, together with the designs by Grassi for the reconstruction of the Castle of Abbiategrasso (1967), the residential housing project at District San Rocco in Monza by Grassi and Rossi (1966) and the Mount Amiata-Gallaratese project by Aymonino and Rossi (1967-1972), introduced a series of innovative visual and conceptual elements that recorded the emergence of a specific research group. As Massimo Scolari explains in his essay *Avanguardia e nuova architettura (Avant-garde and New Architecture)* within the volume for the Triennale of 1973, which actually saw the birth of La Tendenza, after analysing precedents in Italian post-war architecture, the core elements are represented by the "close relationship with history, the priority of urban studies and the relationship between building typology and urban morphology, monumental architecture, the importance of form."

There is a strong affirmation of the idea of an autonomy of architecture that reconsiders the disciplinary tools and concepts of the project and its renewed role in the project for the city at a moment when the very idea of architecture seemed to be deeply questioned by the international radical culture and the rapid growth of cities throughout the world.

247

The need to strongly affirm, visually and conceptually, the autonomy of architecture in this historical moment seems to be one of the last and conscious efforts of a generation of modern architects who were still considered to be a continuation of a militant avant-garde that had been called into question by the events and the emergence of a post-modern vision of reality.

In addition to these elements, there was a stylistic and representational method of architectural design that stands in total contrast to the pop and radical drift of the previous decade with "the indication of simplicity and formal rarefaction" that mark many of their designs due to the strong volumetric power and a use of shadows and highly expressive traits.

In this exhibition there were also indications of the precedents and noble fathers selected through a critical reinterpretation of the Modern Movement, considered to be the main reference for Tendenza. In the exhibition, this was represented by the work of Hannes Meyer, Max Bill and Karl Ehn, Tessenow, Loos, Beherens, Hilberseimer as well as Italian neoclassicism, Boullée and Antonelli, recalled in the great table of *Città analoga (Similar city)* composed by Arduino Cantafora, which became one of the most visionary and powerful visual manifestos of La Tendenza.

The presence of the works of the Five, a clear graphic and linguistic consonance in addition to the stated willingness to critically review the legacy of the Modern Movement, also opened up a series of exchanges and comparisons with New York. The nerve centre was to be found in the magazine *Oppositions* (1973 -1984) and the Centre for Urban Studies, directed by Peter Eisenman (1967-1984).

Oppositions at this stage became one of the most important cultural and experimental workshops for contemporary architecture,

and probably one of the arenas for Tendenza's most original research. Here, coherent and influential development could be found in an international context, sighting many of the reflections of these young architects to a form of postmodern criticism that was particularly influential in the following decade.

As Biraghi rightly said, Rossi's central presence in the definition of the 1973 exhibition was also the start of his shift away from the "dry" language in which many of the Tendenza architects would soon get stuck, and from the sense of a strong limit in the relationship between urban analysis and the form of the project.

With the experiences following the 1976 Venice Biennale directed by Gregotti and Raggi, and the exhibition of the 1978 "*Roma interrotta*" projects, the limits to a morphological approach to the architectural project became apparent. Together, the formal and linguistic elements that within a few years decreed the affirmation of postmodernism in the Strada Novissima of the 1980 Biennale became evident. In this same edition, Rossi designed one of his most visionary and problematic works, the Teatro del Mondo, in which the relationship among history, the idea of monument and the project of autonomy were poetically connected, allowing this unlikely contemporary *fabrica* to navigate the waters.

Bibliography
Biraghi M., *Storia dell'architettura contemporanea II*, Einaudi, Turin 2008.
Bonfanti E., Bonicalzi R., Rossi A., Scolari M., Vitali D., *Architettura razionale*, Franco Angeli, Milan 1973.
Hayes M. (edited by), *Opposition readers. Selected essays, 1973-1984*, MIT Press, Cambridge Mass 1989.
Megayrou F. (edited by), *La Tendenza. Architectures Italiennes, 1965-1985*, Centre Pompidou, Paris 2012.
Rossi A., *L'architettura della città*, Quodlibet, Milan 1966.
Savi V., *L'architettura di Aldo Rossi*, Franco Angeli, Milan 1975.

studio x il quartiere Gallaratese.

AR 1969

Aldo Rossi, Residential
building in Quartiere
Gallaratese, Milan,
1969-1970

Page 249
Aldo Rossi, San Cataldo
Cemetery, Modena,
1971-1978

Carlo Aymonino, Residential
building in Quartiere
Gallaratese, Milan,
1967-1972

Simona Galateo

Postmodernism

In the introduction of his book *Complexity and Contradiction in Architecture,* Robert Venturi somehow outlines the main features of postmodern architecture very accurately, and ahead of his time. Claiming to move against the precepts of the Modern Movement, whose exasperated functionalism and approval of the International Style he rejects, he promotes a more hybrid, inclusive, contradictory approach, the product of compromise and therefore more complex to manage. This is the moment in which the first architectural experiments break with what had hitherto been not just a stylistic reference but a veritable social and cultural program.

And it was with those changes in society, which in those early Sixties were growing more intense, that more open and dialectical attitudes were generated in the architectural debate. The world economy was growing, and for the first time in history reached planetary dimensions. Financial markets began to build international relations by changing the scale of their interests and the consequent political geographies. In addition, with the transition to the post-industrial age and the dissemination of information on computer networks, advertising messages, and the same information flow and television

were becoming more aggressive and invasive, with the consequent loss of the centralization of knowledge in favour of a pluralistic and complex vision.[1] In architecture, all of this was measured by the desire for a return to a more disenchanted history, as the reservoir from which to draw inspiration for a new architectural language, removed from any finalism. The writings of Robert Venturi, the aforementioned *Complexity and Contradiction, Learning from Las Vegas*, written by the same author with Denise Scott Brown and Steven Izenour, *The Language of Postmodern Architecture* by Charles Jencks, and his next volume *Postmodernism, the New Classicism in Art and Architecture*, are the main points of reference in an attempt to define the forms and language of postmodernism, a turning point with a more positive approach than the previous Modern Movement, which finds nothing so volatile, in any discipline, such as literature or philosophy[2] for example.

Postmodernism thus proposes a new interpretation in which architectural forms are conventional and symbolic, and must be defined in relation to history and context, and cannot therefore be either universal or abstract. The same Jencks uses the term

252

The Museum of Modern Art Papers on Architecture

1

Published by The Museum of Modern Art, New York in association with
The Graham Foundation for Advanced Studies in The Fine Arts, Chicago

Robert Venturi, *Complexity
and Contradiction
in Architecture*, New York
1966

Charles Moore, Piazza
d'Italia, New Orleans, 1978

Complexity and Contradiction in Architecture

Robert Venturi

postmodern for architecture that is ambiguous, metaphorical, layered and contradictory. In principle then, there is a return to a communicative expressive architecture that interacts with the historical archetypes. In fact, it does not always lead to concrete results in line with these assumptions, but leaves to freedom of expression, often ironic, the ability to draw on the styles of the past, thereby depriving progress of a linear and coherent history, to return to an eclectic form of decoration, to the superfluous and the recovery of local building traditions.

Initially, postmodernism developed in the United States before moving to Europe. Emblematic and significant, some of the most important examples of this period are: Anna Venturi House, by Robert Venturi, the first building-manifesto of postmodernism, a sort of mannerist evolution of classicism; the Piazza d'Italia by Charles Moore, which represents the kitsch deviation of the new language; the Sony Building by Philip Johnson, called by its author "the testimony to the changing times"; the Humana Building by Michael Graves, an architect who manifested a purely eclectic interpretation of traditional elements; the State Gallery by James Stirling and Michael Wildorf, an urban complex that seeks a dialogue between the contemporary and history.

In opposition to functionalism, postmodernism in Italy reconsidered architecture as an aesthetic process that was not exclusively utilitarian, with a return to ornamentation and widespread hedonism. It can be said that in our country, the start of postmodernism was marked by the exhibition "La presenza del passato" (The Presence of the Past) by Paolo Portoghesi, within the International Architecture Exhibition at the Venice Biennale in 1980, where the author was the director. At the Corderie dell'Arsenale, with staging by Constantino

Aldo Rossi, San Cataldo
Cemetery, Modena,
1971-1978

Opposite
Rem Koolhaas and Madelon
Vriesendorp, *The City of the
Captive Globe Project*, 1972

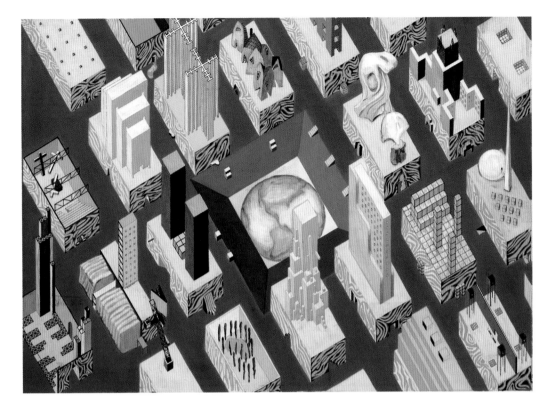

Dardi, the Strada Novissima was created, emphasizing the importance of the historical dimension of postmodern architecture, as a reservoir of images and ideas from which to freely retrieve forms, features and decorative elements, emphasizing the urban vocation. In Italy, some of the names that stood out were Aldo Rossi, whose Teatro del Mondo remains the emblem of the new architecture rich in historical references, Giorgio Grassi, Franco Purini, Paolo Portoghesi again, and Mario Botta. But in Italy the real postmodern exploits were found in the context of design, which chose not to make a wholesale reference to the classical, but to seek to recover the aesthetic value and quality of the surfaces and structures of the perceivable objects, working on colour and decoration,

freed from the modernist dictates. It was in those years, in fact, that the first experiments by Alchimia and Memphis in radical design took place, fundamentally important and recognized in the international arena.
In his text *The End of Prohibition*, Portoghesi asserts that the postmodern condition is a total cultural phenomenon, not reducible to stylistic-disciplinary formulas. And, in fact, it is precisely on this assumption that the debate focuses in defining its size and complexity: it is varied with a combination of different attitudes and trends. We cannot say that it is a real movement, and positions in this respect often oscillate between a pluralist and anti-ideological attitude (Venturi) and a stronger and more determined position, to be exacerbated into a sort of

anti-modern ideology (Jenks and Portoghesi).

Recently, in his book *The New Paradigm in Architecture*, Charles Jenks tried to understand how the lines of postmodernism came to define the current architectural trends. Designers, among others, such as Frank Gehry, Peter Eisenman, Daniel Libeskind, are mentioned for the use of technology and advanced construction techniques, which make it possible to bend forms to new geometries, and create varied fluid volumes. The goal is to create a sensual, engaging, communicative architecture, representing a new architectural paradigm, dedicated to pluralism and the heterogeneous nature of the modern urban reality and globalization, so that we can say that everything today is postmodern.

Notes

[1] It was Jean-François Lyotard who identified the post-industrial age with cultures of the postmodern age, in addition to providing a clear definition, towards the end of the Seventies, of the phenomenon of postmodernism still in place.
[2] "Let us disrupt then without bowing toward the desolation of modern architecture, and the destruction of our cities, like a kind of Martian tourist on Earth, visiting the archaeological sites with a superior indifference, absorbed in thought at the sad but instructive mistakes of a previous architectural civilization. After all, since it is completely dead, we could also dabble in examining the corpse." By C. Jencks, *The language…*

Bibliography

Jencks C., *The language of Post-Modern Architecture*, Academy, London 1977.
Jencks C., *The New Paradigm in Architecture*, Yale University Press, New York-London 2002.
Lyotard J.-F., *La condizione postmoderna. Rapporto sul sapere*, Feltrinelli, Milan 2014.
Portoghesi P., *The end of Prohibition*, in Portoghesi P., *Catalogue I of International Architecture Exhibition, Venice*, Venice Biennale, 1980.
Venturi R., *Complessità e contraddizioni nell'architettura*, Dedalo, Bari 1993.

Philip Johnson, Sony Building, New York, 1978

256

Arata Isozaki, Civic Center,
Tsukuba, 1978-1983

James Stirling, Staatsgallerie,
Stuttgard, 1977

259

Paolo Portoghesi, Mosqe
and Islamic Center, Rome,
1975-1985

Ludovica Vacirca

Critical Regionalism

Using the term introduced in the architectural debate by Lewis Mumford and used again by Alexander Tzonis and Liane Lefaivre in the 1981 essay, *The Grid and the Pathway. An Introduction to the Work of Dimitris and Suzana Antonakakis*, the architecture critic and historian Kenneth Frampton, in 1983, published *Towards a Critical Regionalism: Six Points for an Architecture of Resistance.* In this work he defined the "cultural strategy" of critical regionalism and outlined its main "attitudes." This approach seems to have united several generations of architects from Second World War onwards. First and foremost, it is an attempt to resist the homogenisation that was set into motion by the modernization process, recovering, in architectural practice, a project's specificity in relation to place. It was precisely this specificity that modern architecture had given up on, relying on abstractions and reductive general designs. However, while the postmodern position is based on the substantial rejection of the Modern Movement's legacy, taking refuge in a historicist attitude, critical regionalism, on the other hand, is based on the "unfinished project" – quoting the title of an article on modernity published in 1980 by the philosopher Jürgen Habermas – and it

conceives of contemporaneity in new and not idealized terms. The attention given to the context – whether physical, cultural or social – and to the tactile qualities of the space, as well as the interest in the structure of the materials and the local building traditions, become themes at the centre of a design trend that emerged with similar urgency in a number of countries, albeit in different ways.

Experiments in this direction by architects who in the Fifties were involved in renewing the paradigms of Modernity, posed some questions that were more closely examined by later generations at various points in time. Architecture as a tactile experience, whose substance lay in the quality of the material and that was the result of a solid knowledge of craftsmanship, was the objective behind the research of Carlo Scarpa (1906-1978). His work consisted mostly of small-scale projects, museums and exhibitions, the Fondazione Querini-Stampalia (1961-1965), the restoration of the Castelvecchio museum in Verona (1964), and the Brion chapel in Treviso (1970-1975).

The Danish architect Jørn Utzon (1918-2008), on the other hand, who worked for a time in the studio of Alvar Aalto, synthesized various references in his work, based on his studies of architecture for the masses in various countries. The shell-shaped roof of the Opera House in Sydney, for which he won the competition in 1957, probably draws on the oriental designs he became acquainted with during his many travels. This could also be true of the curved concrete surfaces inside the Bagsvaerd Church near Copenhagen (1976), which reinterpret the pagoda roof in Chinese architecture. His architecture thus became – according to Frampton – an emblem of the "capacity to generate vital forms of regional cultures, while absorbing external influences both in terms of culture and civilization." The Iberian Peninsula, culturally isolated until the mid-seventies during the authoritarian regimes of Franco in Spain (1939-1975) and Salazar in Portugal (1933-1974), is an interesting field of architectural experimentation where modern tradition contrasts with popular tradition in the constant quest for a regional identity. In Barcelona, the work of José

Antonio Coderch (1913-1984) synthesized a design approach where, all abstraction having been abandoned, the required forms were found through the functional demands of the project and the characteristics of the environment that provides their setting. One example is the Casa Ugalde in Caldetes (1952) and the residential building for the Instituto Social de la Marina (ISM) in Barceloneta (1951-1955). In fact, while the Casa Ugalde spaces are freely distributed in relation to the topography and landscape, in the eight floors of ISM building, he interrupts the orthogonal nature of the elements in the design to make the most of the available surface space. The shutters of full height that provide a rhythm in the ceramic-covered façades, reinterpret linguistic elements of Mediterranean architecture and are reminiscent of the solutions adopted by Ignazio Gardella in his building for Borsalino employees in Alessandria (1951-1953). In the complex reality of the Portugal that

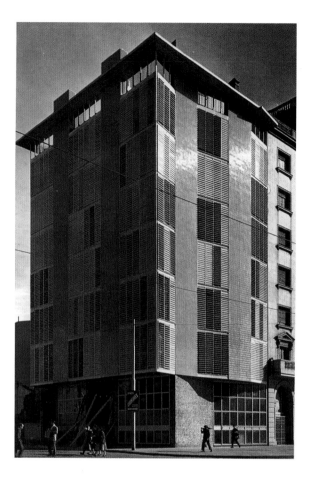

José Antonio Coderch,
Residential building ISM,
Barcelona, 1951-1954

Opposite
José Antonio Coderch,
Residential building ISM,
plans

Page 263
Atelier 66, Residential
building, Distomon, 1969

was still under the dictatorship, a fruitful research project developed around the figure of Fernando Távora (1923-2005) and his student Alvaro Siza Vieira (1933), in which the study of folk architecture and its principles, closely related to the real characteristics of the site, becomes part of a formal system that is rooted in the experience of the Modern Movement. Siza's work, which reached beyond national borders thanks to a 1972 essay by Vittorio Gregotti on *Controspazio*, is the result of a "tactile and tectonic" approach – according to the coordinates identified by Frampton to define critical regionalism – and reflects a profound relationship with place. In the Barrio of Malagueira in Évora (1977-1997), a public housing project built immediately after the Carnation Revolution, the theme of place was expressed on the urban scale as well. Here, the settlement of high-density, one or two-storey residential units is organized along an overhead conduit infrastructure that makes the site particularly characteristic, evoking the aqueduct of the ancient walled city, and interacting with the historical remains in the area.

The Swiss canton of Ticino, in its difficult quest for a unique identity, within the architectural landscape of the Second World War, is an interesting experimentation ground where different influences from the outside converge, connected as much to its French side as the German and Italian sides. There is a reference to Italian Rationalism, which returned as a reference point in Ticino's architecture of the seventies, and whose most active proponents were Luigi Snozzi, Livio Vacchini, Aurelio Galfetti, Ivano Gianola and Mario Botta. The architecture of Mario Botta (1943) – in particular the residential projects such as the house in Riva San Vitale (1972-1973), and Casa Medici in Stabio (1980-1982) – appear as pure, solid, sculptural volumes. The attention

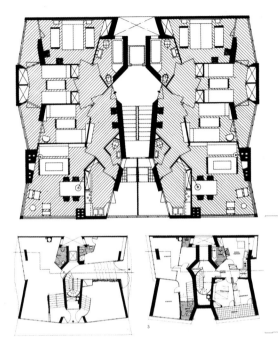

developed an approach that began with the topographic and climatic characteristics of the project site and went on to rediscover vernacular architecture, while maintaining a strong bond with the Modern Movement. Some examples are projects by Dimitris and Suzana Antonakakis, such as the holiday home in Oxylithos in Euboea (1973-1974), the residential building on the Benaki road in Athens (1975) and the Lyttos Hotel (1974-1976). Of the many projects outside of Europe where an approach of critical regionalism can be found, those by Australian architect Glenn Murcutt (1936) are worth mentioning. The houses he designed, built with poor materials and drawing on the Aboriginal tradition, are the result of his constant attention to environmental issues related to place and construction aspects that Murcutt always resolved with simple systems and standardized elements.

Bibliography
Cohen J.L., *The Future of Architecture Since 1889*, Phaidon, London-New York 2012.
Dal Co F., *Mario Botta (1960-1985)*, Mondadori Electa, Milan 1989.
Frampton K., *Storia dell'architettura moderna*, Zanichelli, Bologna 1993.
Frampton K., *Studies in Tectonic Culture: the Poetics of Construction in Nineteenth and Twentieth Century Architecture*, The MIT Press, Cambridge Mass 2001.
Jenks C., Kropf K. (edited by), *Theories and Manifestoes of Contemporary Architecture*, Academy Press, 2006.
Lefaivre L., Tzonis A., *Critical Regionalism. Architecture and Identity in a Globalized World*, Prestel, Munich 2003.

to the inherent qualities of the materials, to the detail and to the local building traditions, draw directly from the teachings of Carlo Scarpa. This essential architecture, by carving and cutting into the surfaces, selects the landscape and becomes an instrument capable of "creating the place." Moving away from the context of Ticino, the concept of a form of architecture as a "tectonic fact", developed by Frampton in one of his six points, finds its concrete expression in the work of the Swiss architect Peter Zumthor (1943) whose most significant example is the Therme Vals (1991-1996): a monolithic-looking building, its expressive power relies on the material quality of the local stone used to cover the surfaces and the effects of light on surfaces.
In Greece too, since the early seventies, when the quest for a national stylistic identity had been abandoned, there

Peter Zumthor, Spa, Vals, 1991-1996

Mario Botta, Round House, Stabio, 1980-1982

Opposite
Jorn Utzon, Bagsvaerd Church, Copenhagen, 1973-1976

Antonello Marotta

Deconstructivism

In 1988, the exhibition "Deconstructivist Architecture" at the MoMA in New York, curated by Philip Johnson and Mark Wigley, triggered new dynamics in composition in a moment in history when the housing market crisis led intellectuals, promoters and artists to question the meaning of the architectural project. No longer was it the image of the historic city to dictate the rules. New places, interstitial spaces, the philosophy of *between*, and the crossing now prevailed. The protagonists in this period were Eisenman, Gehry, Hadid, the firm Coop Himmelb(l)au, Koolhaas, Tschumi and Libeskind. The exhibition changed the guidelines: no longer was it history as a completed self-referential document that established the boundaries of composition, nor was it a consequential and hierarchical idea tied to structure, both in lexical and urban terms. The city was dissected, memory was sundered, unhinged. In the Eighties, memory was, in a battle of ideas of the Modern Movement, brought back to the ordered spaces of classicism, while deconstructivism was re-examining the most powerful figures of the early twentieth century: Boccioni, Balla, Duchamp, Melnikov, Tatlin, El Lissitzky, Terragni, Le Corbusier, Mies van der Rohe. Returning to the identity of this season was the explosive force of the futurist, constructivist and supremacist Russian periods, in which re-emerged spirals, dynamic structures, jutting and suspended, loaded with a utopian quality that for years had remained unexpressed.

The deconstructivist movement saw a central hub in the Jewish culture and certainly Derrida in philosophy, and Gehry, Libeskind and Eisenman in architecture were able to nourish this idea, echoed in the thinking of Franz Kafka and James Joyce. Those authors spoke of a human being who had lost his sense of being in the world, his balance, his identity. In parallel, philosophers like Foucault and Deleuze traced out an analytical method in philosophy that directed the interpretation of history onto thresholds, temporal fractures, onto the trace or mark as an interpretative value, and finally onto human beings as being de-territorialized, undermined by a system in which the categorical certainties of the past had vanished. Space was no longer understood as an *a priori* conception, as an absolute and objective value, on the contrary, it spoke of an overlap of information, of a layering that expressed the complexity of the present. In the Seventies in the United States, the development of a new trend had shifted the axis of interpretation in terms of history.

Postmodernism had focused its attention on classicism, excluding modern research. With the advent of the deconstructivism of the late Eighties, it took central place in the iconographic, spatial and cultural unconscious of modernity, but in a new spirit. While postmodernism had overtaken modernism, proposing a return to classicism, deconstructivism focused its attention on the heroes of modernism, such as the above-mentioned Melnikov, Terragni, Le Corbusier, and Mies van der Rohe. The tools employed by the new current were aimed at design projects that split, accumulated, built interstitial spaces. Modernism was in fact divided, crushed, broken and rebuilt according to new figures. Postmodernism had worked to build a list of citationist possibilities, an archive of memory from which one could recover, with freedom of movement, the words of the past, which were transformed into columns, pediments, pilasters, arches, Renaissance windows, reassembled in a new compositional construct. But the return to the original myth necessarily went through a period of irony and paradox, inasmuch as the time that had passed could not be brought back to life as an archaeological dig, but rather as an eclectic text whose function was to recall and produce a state of serenity in the observer, a world that was once again welcoming. By contrast, deconstructivism operates through phrases, contained space recovered by modern architectures, dismantled and rebuilt according to new compositional processes.

The process of deconstruction in fact implied actions of disassembly and reassembly and opened the way to new spatial figures, in which the space became deformed, full of sharp edges. It triggered surprise, and definitely denied the classical balance of proportions.

Certainly Frank O. Gehry had the historical weight of anticipating deconstructive research with the design for his home in Santa Monica, in 1978, ten years before the MoMA exhibition. The American architect worked on a traditional house and built a metal casing around it. It is a huge sheet of metal that reshapes the previous volume and creates spaces full of light, like the kitchen, where a luminous prism lets the light penetrate. Everything speaks of poor materials, in relation to the duration and position of a new spatial energy. The space lives in the continuity and the crossing. Memory is deformed and split like a metal mesh, invoking the world of the informal and non-finished in art. Imperfection and the ephemeral have replaced modernism's ideal of perfection.

Now we shall look into the interpretations of some historical works of the deconstructionist current, in order to understand the complexity and richness of the movement.

With the Parc de La Villette in Paris (1982-1998) Bernard Tschumi created one of the works that provides us with a new way to understand urban space, together with the compositional processes. The dissociation and decomposition go beyond the idea of a synthesis, of a two-way relationship between form and function. The competition required that the design be for a "twentieth century urban park", located in the north-eastern suburbs of Paris and located between the metro stations Porte de Pantin and Porte de La Villette. Tschumi interprets the park as a text, on the basis of the experiments conducted in 1976-1977 on the literature of Joyce at the Architectural Association in London. Joyce's gardens were built from a grid on which students had to create a park inspired by the novel *Finnegan's Wake* by James Joyce, conceived as a stream of consciousness. The architect for Parc de La Villette created three structures called *points*,

269

lines, and *surfaces*. The idea is that the park no longer represents the romantic image of the nineteenth-century city, but is a potential place for social and urban connections. The three structures are autonomous and interconnected. The *points*, created on a grid, resulting in red metallic structures (10 x 10 x 10 meters) denominated the *folies*. These are temporary machines waiting to assume a certain function. The *lines* are the result of the intersection of two main elements, with a 5 meter covered path, which allows access to the various *folies*. Finally the *surfaces* create entertainment spaces for festivals and markets. Tschumi proposed an open organization where there was the cardo, the main street, and the decumanus, whose functions were to connect the park to the city. The deep structure of the *points,* when they meet the *lines,* creates connections for theme gardens that were to be created by other designers. It is no coincidence that *Point, line, surface* is one of the most important texts by Vassily Kandinsky, the Russian artist who worked in Walter Gropius' Bauhaus and who inspired an idea of the park as something with overlapping layers and interconnected functions.

Deconstruction as a movement became formalized, as mentioned in the MoMA exhibition, but certainly the Austrian couple Coop Himmelb(l)au anticipated a certain iconography. The Rooftop Remodeling Falkestrasse in Vienna (1983-1989) appears as a parasite that dominates the historical building on which it is installed. The penthouse, a law office, becomes a machine that simultaneously evokes a certain science fiction cinematography. The meeting space becomes the terminal part of the design, like an alien being that in its organic and crystalline form, declares independence from the body with which it cohabits.

Peter Eisenman with the Wexner Center for the Visual Arts in Columbus (1983-1989) brought to the fore the urban theme of the towers that recall the history of the place, while in parallel, in the three-dimensional structure of the frame, which is grafted between the existing buildings, he broke the symmetrical and self-referential mould of the nostalgic postmodern languages and opened the way to the idea of deconstructivism.

In 1993, Zaha Hadid completed the Fire Station in Weil am Rhein in Germany, where Frank Gehry had built the Vitra Design Museum in 1989. The design is a thunderbolt in the landscape, with oblique slabs of concrete, and a slender projecting roof that seems to pierce the massive body. The thin pilotis hold up the projecting roof and recall modernism, but in an architectural construct that disregards function. It is a building-sculpture that translates itself into landscape. Deconstruction, interlocking lines: the shape is reminiscent of a collision and recalls, in its nakedness, the lesson of the Russian Constructivists, so dear to the architect of Iraqi origin. The fragmented taut image is reminiscent of designs by Tatlin, or Rodčenko, in the season of the Russian avant-garde that challenged previous historical models. But here the construct, in the liberation of the fragments and the elements, is reassembled to create an unstable and dramatic image.

Certainly the Villa Dall'Ava in Paris by Rem Koolhaas, completed in 1991, fully illustrates the deconstructivist season. The house consists of three connected bodies. The two external volumes are suspended from the ground and supported by slender pilotis, while the central connecting body resolves the issue of the leap in height on this sloping site. Koolhaas reinterprets modernity, merging Le Corbusier's Villa Savoye and the Farnswort house by Mies van der Rohe into a single system and changing the direction. The deconstruction is done on earlier texts, where the reference to the works of modern

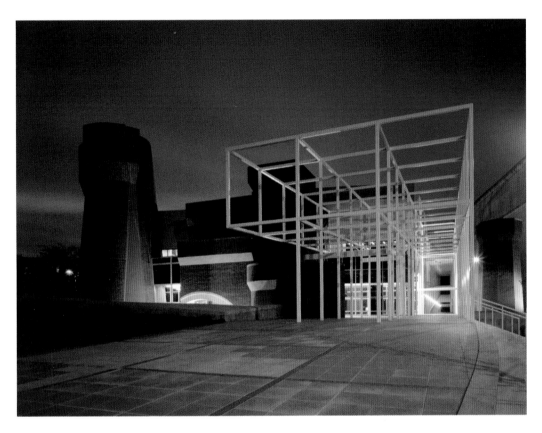

masters is no longer a quote so much as a fracturing of the spatial principles, reassembled in a new building. The pilotis become a forest of slender supports, while the front is reminiscent of that of Le Corbusier's Villa Savoye. Finally, the central body, designed on the one hand as a Miesian glass surface, contains a ramp, which serves the function of connecting the parts. In the main building are the kitchen and the dining area. The house communicates an ambiguity in the use of metal plates. On the roof, a swimming pool completes the design. Here, deconstruction is not aimed at processes to deform the shape, so much as an intellectual and cultured revision of modernism.
With the Guggenheim Museum in Bilbao,

Peter Eisenman, Wexner Center for the Arts, Columbus, 1989

Gehry (1991-1997) expressed himself spectacularly. As a futurist work, the museum follows the lines of the city's throughways, resulting in an urban sculpture, an icon-landscape in the public space. In a disused industrial zone, the American architect created a complex interplay of conflicting masses, creating dynamic spaces like the great fifty meter-high atrium, where installations come to life. The museum itself is transformed into a work of art. Completely covered in titanium, it has the plastic look of a sculpture on the outside, while dynamism prevails on the interior. Gehry's Guggenheim becomes quickly recognizable as an icon of deconstructivism.

Certainly, we are obliged to Daniel Libeskind and his Jewish Museum in Berlin (1989-1998) for giving us one of the highest points in late twentieth-century architecture. Libeskind had to take on a still-painful history and in 1998 in Berlin, contrary to everyone's wishes, he created a new organism which goes against the rules and transforms the urban plan of the city into a map made up of lines, lines that connect the places in which Jewish intellectuals, poets, and artists had lived. He then connected these lines in a casual design that transforms the place into a scheme of universal memory. The result is a compressed zigzagging lightning bolt that in its movement discharges its energy. The museum, in the void that runs through it, recalls the wound of the names cancelled out, and emanates the silence of the painful text. The American architect put all his compositional research into this work, from the Micromegas designs, 1978 onwards, to the Typewriter designs for Palmanova at the Venice Biennale of 1985, curated by Aldo Rossi. The designs provided him with the archaeological scheme to generate the plan, while the typewriter, consisting of 49 mechanisms of memory, is transformed into the garden of exile, consisting of exactly 49 inclined columns in reinforced concrete, and an olive tree planted there as a symbol of life. Libeskind, the son of Jewish survivors, deconstructs his life and, in parallel, the Soviet literature of Melnikov and his manifesto: the Soviet Pavilion at the USSR Exhibition of Decorative Arts in Paris in 1925. He breaks down the text of the Russian architect and disassembles the parts that take on life in the museum. We think of the great staircase on which the beams are stuck like knives, and the column of the pavilion, which is transformed into the Holocaust Tower, where light penetrates from a slender cut positioned on the top. From an interpretation of the works and the deep underlying reasons, it follows that deconstruction has worked on several fronts, recovering the sources not only of the architecture of the past, but also philosophy, literature and cinema. In some cases it has worked to deform and sunder form, in other cases it recounts the breakdown and reassembly of spatial fabrics, assembled to generate a confrontational, critical and often dramatic composition.

Bibliography
Culler J., *Sulla decostruzione*, Bompiani, Milan 1988.
Derrida J., *Della grammatologia*, Jaca Book, Milan 1969.
Ferraris M., *Introduzione a Derrida*, Laterza, Rome-Bari 2003.
Johnson P., Wigley M. (edited by), *Deconstructivist Architecture*, The Museum of Modern Art, New York 1988.
Marotta A., *Daniel Libeskind*, Edilstampa, Rome 2007.
Wigley M., *The Architecture of Deconstruction. Derrida's Haunt*, Mit Press, Cambridge Mass 1993.

Bernard Tschumi,
Parc de La Villette, Paris,
1982-1988

Zaha Hadid, Vitra Fire Station,
Weil am Rhein, 1991-1993

Frank Gehry, Guggenheim
Museum, Bilbao, 1997

Rem Koolhaas, Dall'Ava House,
Paris, 1991

274

Luca Molinari

Digital Architecture

In the spring of 2013, the CCA (Canadian Centre for Architecture) launched the first of a series of three major exhibitions entitled "Archaeology of the Digital", curated by the American architect Greg Lynn, the recognized mind behind "Blob architecture" and one of the most provocative and brilliant theorists of this specific period of contemporary architecture.
The exhibitions were produced with the declared intention of launching the digital architectural archive for this important institution and, at the same time, of beginning to historicize and critically interpret one of the more complex and turbulent phases in the architectural culture of today.
The first exhibition, which opened on May 2013, featured the work of four architects who looked to the computer and the first design applications, not only as a means to quickly develop their own professional work, but above all as an opportunity to experimentally explore the relationship between the emerging digital culture and the architectural design project.
The works of Frank Gehry for the Lewis Residence (1985-1994), Peter Eisenman for the Biozentrum (1987), Chuck Hoberman for Expanding Sphere (1992) and Shoei Yoh for a building in Odanara (1991) and for the

Galaxy Toyama Gymnasium (1992) are recounted by Lynn as the beginnings of a problematic mental and creative attitude that began to look at the architectural work not as a static object, but rather as a dynamic phenomenon, solicited by reality and the flow of information and emotions that the world produces and emits into the atmosphere.
We must not forget that in 1989 the exhibition on Deconstruction at the MoMA in New York was inaugurated. The first two architects took part in this. The dematerialization of bodies and the deconstruction of their forms was already taking place, both from the point of view of formal and conceptual research, and also thanks to the introduction of digital technology in the creative process.
Historically, it was the beginning of a period of an international economic boom and there was a gradual shift from an economic idea based on "heavy" modern production to intangible assets like information and data regulated by a digital and global finance that was becoming firmly consolidated. During the 1990s, this "New Economy" reached a peak, mainly due to the rapid growth of the digital industry, and sales of its securities that led the Nasdaq to a record high of 5132 points in March 2000, crowning the final

confirmation of a productive and social phenomenon that started in the late Seventies and eventually affected every part of our existence.

In 1979, Sony launched the Walkman that allowed for private individual music listening without being connected to fixed domestic appliances; MTV was born in 1981, the first channel capable of imposing a different and generational way to look at, think about and make music integrated with video and moving images.

In the second half of the Seventies, Apple was founded, followed by the presentation of Windows 1 in 1985. These two electronic language systems were to have a decisive role in simplifying and bringing into the home technology that once seemed totally limited to a small community, starting a true global revolution that was to have decisive consequences in architecture.

In 1987, came the presentation of ArchiCAD 3.0, a programme for designing virtual buildings. In the early nineties, the CAD system and the CATIA program came into use, making designing and creating forms easier, forms that were impossible to check in the past, due to costs and times that were unsustainable for the majority of the professional studios.

In 1985, the American architect and computer scientist Nicholas Negroponte founded the Media-Lab at MIT in Boston, the first research facility that investigated the relationship between new media, digital culture and the different areas of our lives. In 1993, *Wired* was founded in San Francisco by Louis Rossetto, Jane Metcalfe and Negroponte. It was the first magazine capable of looking at the digital world as an unprecedented cultural, economic and social dimension, which was capable of bringing, almost in real-time, the research and innovations from nearby Silicon Valley.

In the early Eighties, efforts were made to begin expanding the Internet with the creation of the first stations and communities that connected computers to each other. Towards the end of the decade nearly 100,000 stations were already connected, and in 1991, CERN announced the birth of the World Wide Web; Mosaic, the first browser for the network was presented in 1994, and from this phase came a frantic rush that actually saw 5 billion people online worldwide.

This powerful and exciting historical period had a very important effect on part of the new international architecture and university teaching because it gave a new generation of architects the possibility of experimenting, processing and exchanging information with a rapidity inconceivable only a few years before, raising the issue of a radical rethinking of the formal and linguistic system of architecture.

Those that Italian critic Luigi Prestinenza Puglisi called the "silent avant-garde" had actually carried out a noisy transformation and questioning of traditional tectonic certainties of modern architecture, looking at digital technology as a tool for the radical transformation of the world in perfect harmony with the revolution that seemed to be happening on a global scale in the societies of the great metropolises.

In 1996, when Greg Lynn wrote the text *Blob, or why Tectonics is Square and Topology is Groovy* for *ANY*, it opened up what had been called for several years "Blob architecture", giving a theoretical form to a process in place all over the western world that was seeking an experimental relationship between the digital culture and architectural design.

Lynn was part of a group of innovative professors who were called to Columbia University by Bernard Tschumi, director of the GSAPP between 1988 and 2003, and that saw some of the greatest talents in the new North American architecture give shape to one of the most advanced research nuclei in the U.S. along with the Sci Arc in California. The group included the likes of Hani Rashid, founder of Asymptote together with Lise Anne Couture, Jesse Reiser, with Mark Wigley and Stan Allen for theoretical research. In the late Nineties and the turn of the new century, some of these architects experimented with the relationship between CAD and design and their potentials, how the algorithms and new forms of calculation could implement new architectural forms, exploring the relationship between biomorphism and built space, questioning the emerging catastrophe theory as a track for producing potential linguistic materials for the foreseeable future. They delved into the relationship between the programming of new software and innovative construction. In 1997, the Dutch studio NoX designed the H20 Expo and two years later Greg Lynn built the Presbyterian Church in Queens, New York with Douglas Garofalo and Michael McInturf. These first two built works immediately illustrated the contrast between the visual smoothness of the digital architectural representations and the possibility of actually building them. But above all, it was the Dutch pavilion that highlighted the potential of a space where the visitor's experience, the controlled irregularity of the dynamic forms, new construction techniques and the integration of different media could give shape to a different space.

Even more extreme was the pure research of architects such as Karl Chu, Bernard Cache, dECOi, ONL, Marcos Novak and Neil Spiller, who worked obsessively and with very different results from each other on the complex relationship between machine language, uncontrolled production of forms, fluidity of materials and new mathematics in relation to architecture.

Probably one of the clearest visual and formal representations of this phase is the design for the New York Stock Exchange Virtual Trading Floor and Operation Centre designed by Asymptote between 1995 and 1997. It is a virtual augmented reality project conceived to give visual form to the flow of information and data processed continuously by the New York Stock Exchange and in which the ambiguous threshold between the real and the virtual is taken to the necessary extremes, establishing an interesting relationship between experience, immersive emotion, variable geometry and the use of colours. The same research was developed by the duo in New York for a new virtual Guggenheim in which to host a section devoted directly to digital artists, but the effort was not followed up. From this stage, the digital wave experienced a major critical and academic success that crossed all continents. From the London studio of architect Zaha Hadid for Future System, to Ben van Berkel & Bos with the project for the Moebius House and the first urban research of MVRDV, to Toyo Ito, with writings on Blurring Architecture and its first built projects, the French François Roche (DVS & Sie) and Didier Fiuza Faustino, the Austrians Coop Himmelb(l)au who walked the line between digital and deconstructionism to a monumental scale that was not always controlled, and the Americans Hariri & Hariri, Neil M. Denari, Diller & Scofidio and Morphosis, who had an important influence on the university works and teaching. The theoretical writings of Derrick de Kerckhove, William Mitchell, Lynn, Eisenman, Tschumi and Ito, on the other hand, tried to give conceptual and critical form to the research that was taking shape in real time.

The Venice Biennale in 2000, directed by Italian architect Massimiliano Fuksas, became perhaps one of the most interesting moments in which digital culture, a glimpse

of the new urban landscapes, and architecture all came together, establishing a public consecration of this phenomenon, and posing a serious question about the relationship between these cultures and the possible formal implications.

In Italy too, in those years, the advent of the digital culture was welcomed, especially by the new generation of students and designers, as an opportunity for a linguistic and conceptual updating far from the traditional academy. In March of 1995, Marco Brizzi founded *Arch'it*, the first fully digital magazine of Italian architecture, which opened up to new authors and to the international debate. At the same time, the exhibition "Radicals" of 1996 short-circuited the digital language and the political rediscovery of radical experiences creating a national phenomenon in which the original definition of new language tools, various

Asymptote, New York Stock Exchange Virtual Trading Floor and Operation Centre, New York, 1995-1997

Page 281
Massimiliano Fuksas, New Convention Center, Rome, 2008

forms of communication and exchange, and a notion of direct participation in the urban phenomena blended together with great vitality, shaping the work and experiences of designers and theorists such as Stalker, Cliostraat, Ventre, Brizzi, Gomorrah, Multiplicity, Luigi Prestinenza Puglisi, Antonino Saggio, Massimo Ilardi, A12, Luigi Centola, MaO, Ian+, HOV, Gianluca Milesi, 2 A + P, Metrogramma and Marialuisa Palumbo.

"I said (to Jim Glymph): 'I want to deal with more complex forms.' He replied: 'No problem, we'll use the computer'."

Frank Gehry

In recent years there has been a relativization of the digital phenomenon that has unfortunately led to a limitation of the forms of research and experiments as well, or that has transformed the insights of electronic design into *market-oriented* tools as in the case of Gehry Technologies, founded in 2002 after the construction of the Guggenheim in Bilbao. Within some English and North American universities the experimentation on parametric forms continues, but with the feeling that by now it is a formalism often difficult to understand except in an exaggerated form of technical and linguistic virtuosity. One of the most important consequences of this phase is certainly due to the explosive growth of the web, that has led to the emergence of communication tools, exchange and criticism that are more transparent, horizontal and democratic, tools that have permanently changed the way we think about communication and the culture for architecture. The digital season in all its extreme and free forms has ferried us to a different world which has formalized the economic, social and symbolic revolution that is the twenty-first-century experience.

Bibliography
2 A + P, Brizzi M., Prestinenza Puglisi L., *GR la generazione della rete. Sperimentazioni nell'architettura italiana*, Cooper & Castelvecchi, Verona 2003.
Lynn G., *Folds, Bodies & Blobs: Collected Essays*, La Lettre Volée, Brussels 1998.
Mitchell W.J., *E-topia*, The MIT Press, Cambridge Mass 1999.
Prestinenza Puglisi L., *Silenziose avanguardie*, Testo & Immagine, Turin 2001.
Riley T. (edited by), *The Un-private House*, The Museum of Modern Art, New York 1999.
Sacchi L., Unali M. (edited by), *Architettura e cultura digitale*, Skira, Milan 2003.
Toyo Ito, *Blurring architecture*, Charta, Turin 1999.
Tschumi B., *Architecture and Disjunction*, MIT Press, Cambridge Mass 1994.
http://www.cca.qc.ca/en/exhibitions/1964-archaeology-of-the-digital

Neil M. Denari, "Interrupted
Projections", exhibition at
Toto Gallery MA, Tokyo,
1996

Opposite
UNStudio, Mobius House,
Netherlands, 1993-1998

282

Antonello Marotta

Minimalism

Minimalism is an art movement that in the United States during the Sixties was opposed to the subjective nature of informal art and abstract expressionism, and communicated an objective, impersonal and absolute vision. The exhibition "Primary Structures", held in 1966 at the Jewish Museum in New York, showed that artists had reached a new understanding of the artistic process, based on elementary forms and industrial materials. Minimal Art, in the works of Donald Judd, Robert Morris, Carl Andre, Sol LeWitt and Dan Flavin, provided an understanding of the importance of sculpture objects, the environmental context in which the installation was positioned and the weight attributed to the material, amplifying the perceptual and sensory aspects. In architecture, minimalism has been developing from the Eighties until now as a reaction to postmodernism and deconstructivism.

The battle of the minimalists was directed at breaking down the use of the architectural quote and the decorative excesses of postmodernism. At the same time, it also denied the role of the architect as an artist, according to the deconstructivist vision. The idea of form as a happening, as a futurist expression, was also rejected. In minimalist architecture, the composition is oriented toward reducing the internal complexities and details in favour of a clear design. The revolution brought about in the early part of the twentieth century, that of Kazimir Malevich's concrete art and Mies van der Rohe's poetics of reduction, generated deep echoes in this vision, to the point that ornament and its memory were eliminated. In 1986, when Mies van der Rohe's Barcelona Pavilion was rebuilt by Ignasi de Solà-Morales, Cristian Cirici and Fernando Ramos, all the power of thought given to necessary space, space that was at the same time fluid, resurfaced on Iberian soil. It was not so much a case of rebuilding Barcelona's modern architecture as it was of more intensely rewriting Spanish history after decades of Franco's dictatorship. In fact, with this manifesto, there was a revived and profound focus on the quest for the essential at the end of the Eighties, and this was to produce a new season in minimalism.

It follows that minimalism's great expression was through corporeal massiveness and transparency, which found its life's blood in modernism. Working with the essential means interpreting the project as an act of subtraction, a reduction in complexity that maintains a few winning features, in a place

David Chipperfield, Am
Kupfergraben 10, Berlin,
2007

that welcomes the new. The plans are often enclosures, magical spaces, without any intention of making an architectural quote. Subtracting, removing material: the enclosure is still an archetypal, mystical, and ritualistic place. These designs call for silence in terms of drama. The surface often becomes a diaphanous field, a distorting lens in which things appear veiled.

It was Rafael Moneo who recognized a first great achievement in the work of Herzog & de Meuron, when in the Eighties they focused on materials and formal simplicity. Between 1986 and 1987, the architects, who trained at the Zurich Polytechnic with Aldo Rossi, their tutor, proposed a radical design with the Ricola warehouse in Laufen in Switzerland, a design which sweeps away postmodern formalism and deconstructivist excess. The construction returns to speak of artisan features in the system of expanding wooden strips that culminate in a crowning feature. The building is primitive and abstract, defining an elemental environment and creating an interesting space in relationship to its rocky wall. With the Goetz art gallery in Munich (1989-1992), Jacques Herzog and Pierre de Meuron have achieved a minimal, abstract design with calibrated proportions. The materials (concrete panels and glass plates) communicate their nature without any falsification. Yet nothing in their work conveys the obvious and usual. The gallery is an abstract body set in a birch grove, and declares its independence from its environment. The building seems to float in the air, held up by a band of transparent glass. Effectively, a basement floor contains the exhibition galleries, and the light penetrates through the sections of the windows anchored to the ground. What comes through so strongly is all of Mies van der Rohe's modern utopia of transparency, but risemanticized and cleared of all illusion, particularly the logical basement-siding-roofing sequence. The concrete outer sections are contrasted by the use of wood panelling on the interior, which gives the gallery a private atmosphere. As noted by Moneo, there is a return to the themes regarding materials developed by Louis Kahn.

Tadao Ando was certainly the architect who in the Eighties and Nineties designed necessary essential spaces, spaces in which the light becomes the true narrative material. There is a profound relationship between the Eastern tradition and minimalism.

It was the great poets, intellectuals and architects, such as Wright and Taut, and before them Baudelaire and the Impressionist artists, who recovered the ancient principles of modern thought from the east. It was a two-way reciprocal exchange of information and culture. From 1933, Bruno Taut, as Manfred Speidel reminds us, stayed in Japan for several years, reinterpreting in the Katsura Palace in Kyoto (XVII century), the highest aspiration of the modern ideals, where the living space and the natural space blend into a relational system, losing their respective differences. The oriental garden for Taut was the perfect synthesis between the indoors and the outdoors, between the abstraction of thought and the beauty of nature. Following this came the travels of Gropius in 1954 and Le Corbusier in 1955 to the same place. Gropius, after visiting the Katsura Imperial Villa and the garden of Ryoan-ji, wrote to his friend: "Dear Corbu, everything we have fought for has its parallel in the ancient Japanese culture. This thirteenth-century rock garden of the Zen monks – raked white pebbles and stones – could have been designed by Arp or Brancusi – an intoxicating haven of peace. You would be as enthusiastic as me about these 2000 year-old remains of cultured wisdom! The Japanese house is the best and most

modern house I know and it is genuinely prefabricated" (Katsura 2004, p. 388). The West was looking to the East for principles of simplicity and nature, such as the use of structures separated from the ground for good ventilation and the flexible and measured use of the living space, while the Oriental architects were looking to European masters to recover the principles of modernity, in an intertwining journey. Some contemporary oriental masters whose research merits mentioning are Tadao Ando and Kazuyo Sejima. The work of Tadao Ando, between the Seventies and the Nineties, is strongly connected to minimalism in art. We only have to think of the experiments with the grid and cube that were applied in different works: Matsumoto House (1976-1977), the Multipurpose complex and art gallery in Tokyo (1977), up to the Rokko Residential Complex I (1978-1981). Ando wrote in the text *On the architectural project*: "A homogeneous space created by a uniform structural grid is the first principle of modern architecture" (*Domus*, no. 783, 1992, p. 20).

Some years before Arata Isozaki designed the Museum of Modern Art in Gumma (1970-1974). References to Isozaki and Ando can be found in the work of minimalist artist Sol LeWitt who had made a series of works based on the subdivision of the grid, such as: *Cube without a cube* (1968) and *Structure* (1973-1983). The artist and the architects are interested in the objective rule of the cube and the grid that allow for infinite variations: we think of the complexity of the typology and system of the Rokko I housing complex, with nine different living units in it. In an issue of *Quaderni di Casabella* dedicated to the housing complex, Vittorio Gregotti wrote that Ando's references could be found in the minimalist work of Carl Andre and Richard Serra and the complex material of Louis Kahn. To be precise, Kahn

Sanaa, Century Museum
of Contemporary Art,
Kanazawa, 2004

Page 288
Gigon Guyer Architekten,
Kirchner Museum, Davos,
1992

287

is Ando's secret poetic reference in the research on the wall and light: a mysterious luminousness, as can be seen in the house designs such as the Koshino House (1979-1980) and the Lee House (1991-1992). The Japanese architect wants to communicate the essential nature of the material in the slabs of concrete, thanks to the geometrical rigour and the knowledgeable control of the light. Again one finds the same material and the same research on light that Louis Kahn transposed to the Salk Institute for Biological Studies in La Jolla, California (1959-1965), where the designs, as noted by his collaborator Thomas Vreeland, recall the Piranesi plan for the Campus Martius in the Ancient Rome of 1762. Kahn had designed a system of great

purity, in the square crossed by a stream of water and in the laboratories where the rotated windows sensitized by the use of wood offered a softer material, which contrasted with the absolute and metaphysical spatiality of the great courtyard. In 2002, Tadao Ando, with the creation of the Modern Art Museum, had the opportunity to take on Kahn's manifesto: the Kimbell Art Museum. It is a museum conceived as an oasis to create an intense relationship between the exterior and the interior. A dual line of thinking informs the project: the theme of simplicity and transparency and the relationship between construction and landscape. From the main atrium it is possible to understand the new institution, the idea of resting the pavilions on a film of water and making the exhibition halls an aesthetic reflective experience, which is then combined with the interpretation of the works of art. It is a space that is all about suspension. What is more, the pavilions have the characteristic of being glass boxes with the distinctive sharply projecting roof that is supported by Y-shaped structure. The enclosure and transparency are born from the idea of creating a meditation place for art. Again, there is a re-emergence of the research on the repetition of pure geometric units.

The theme of essentiality or simplicity, the reduction of the sign, and evanescence, was investigated by the Sanaa studio, formed by Kazuyo Sejima and Ryue Nishizawa. In the New Museum of Contemporary Art in New York (2007), the process generates the form. Starting from a small urban lot, the choice was made to use the space in a dynamic and complex way. The museum design entailed the superimposition of seven boxes of different heights and sizes, which slide onto the vertical axis, creating a neutral exterior, covered with a mesh made of anodized aluminium. Through slits made in the volume, light penetrates in a diffused way, while the walls are opaque and can contain the works to be exhibited.

In 2004, in Kanazawa, Japan, Sanaa designed and built the Century Museum of Contemporary Art. The L-shaped building contains annular internal enclosures, cases of memory. The geometry is made of simple essential bodies which allow for a free movement between the art installations. The curved glass, positioned on the edge, generates a warped perspective of the exterior and makes the interior immersive and soothing. Built in the centre of Kanazawa, it contains a library, a conference room, places for workshops and exhibition rooms. The glassed-in courtyards create a strong relationship with light, while the galleries, which are of various sizes, offer a dynamic and highly flexible environment. The ancient geometry is reborn in this design that combines abstraction with the metaphysical space.

Minimalism has found fertile ground in England: think of the works by David Chipperfield, John Pawson and Tony Fretton. John Pawson created the Palmgren House (2006-2013) in Drevviken, in Sweden, where the extent of the reduction is carried to an extreme in the white volumes that from the exterior penetrate the interior of the house. In 2009, Tony Fretton completed the British Embassy in Warsaw, Poland. Here the passion for the American designs of Mies van der Rohe re-emerges. The building declares its urban weight, its structural simplicity, the clarity of its plan.

David Chipperfield reveals his passion for Eastern culture, which has nourished his architecture from the time of his earliest works, reflecting an interest for research into simplicity and minimalism. The works for Japan such as the Toyota Auto Kyoto (1989-1990) and the Matsumoto Corporation Headquarters (1990-1992) perfectly describe his international leanings, shaped by Japanese culture. With the project for the Neues Museum (1997-2009) in Berlin, the English architect takes a real leap in scale, taking on Museum Island with the work of Friedrich August Stüler, built between 1842 and 1855. In a state of ruin, following the Second World War bombings, the Neues Museum was completed and rebuilt. Chipperfield took two main directions: reconstruction of missing parts, re-using Brandenburg bricks, and restoration and reinterpretation of the interior. The staircase becomes one of the cores of the design. Its grandeur is revived through an essential body, which excludes any decoration, and restores the original values. The two courtyards, Egyptian and Greek, become special places for the staging and recovery of material memory. In the Egyptian courtyard, the architect has made some very interesting integrations: a minimal frame of slender pillars capable of creating new spaces and providing new functions. The project, through the linguistics of subtraction, enhances the complexity of the neoclassical monument. Chipperfield shows that the minimal project finds its highest aspiration when it has a historical comparison. In Berlin, in front of the Museum Island, the Gallery Building "Am Kupfergraben 10" was completed in 2007. The proposed solution is a grafting of the historic buildings in a void caused by the bombings of World War II. The new gallery stands next to the historical monuments and restores the relationship between mass, height and urban limits. The architect has created a clear and dynamic plan, characterized by the presence of a large exhibition room for the works of art. The space is continuous and open, with a minimal choice of environments and materials used, making the light the real protagonist. The 5.5-meter high exhibition rooms create sites suitable for perceiving contemporary art. The full-height windows frame the urban space, and are fitted with panels in order to be able to direct the light. In Swiss culture, some significant contributions to minimalism have been made by the architects Diener & Diener, Gigon Guyer and Peter Zumthor. The studio founded by Marcus Diener and his son Roger in 1980 offered a concrete response to the minimalist trend through essential works where the relationship with the environment has been resolved with balance. The Galerie Gmurzynska (1990) in Cologne remains a manifesto for having reworked the Bauhaus research by Johannes Itten. The famous lithograph by Itten, *Haus des Weissen Mannes* (1920) is analysed and re-proposed for the gallery: a red rectangle, divided into basic volumes, in which the light penetrates through narrow slits, while the interior space opens onto itself, like an inner action. In Davos, Switzerland, in 1992, Gigon Guyer Architekten designed and built the Kirchner Museum Davos: it is an essential space, dictated by enclosures made of reinforced concrete panels, illuminated by a system of overhead lights. The building is sharply detached from the valley behind it and recalls, in elementary geometry, the abstract season of the historical twentieth-century avant-garde protagonists, who worked with similar formal and figural principles.

There is certainly more complexity in the work of Peter Zumthor, where the essential is always combined with sensory experiences. In 1997, the architect designed the Kunsthaus in Bregenz, consisting entirely of cubes made with frosted glass panels, making it an impalpable and diaphanous volume in the city. Behind a smaller body, perpendicular to the museum, are the offices and the library, in addition to the ground-floor bookshop and café. The vitreous body is a container that preserves the interior. In the veiled transparency, one can make out the load-bearing structure of reinforced concrete. A double casing lets the air circulate in the cavity for a perfect climate control. The plan provides an exemplary resolution for the requirements of the exhibition spaces, which are placed on the three higher levels. On the ground floor is the entrance, and on the first underground level are the conference hall, workshops and offices. With this work, Zumthor shows that research into the essential is not a starting point, but a point of arrival. The interior denies the relationship with the outside world and everything becomes intimate. The ceilings are in glass plate and the walls are in visible concrete. The space becomes absolute, in a battle to find essentiality, simplicity.

Mansilla + Tunon, Museo
de las Colecciones Reales,
Madrid, 2006

291

In Spain, finally, we find poetics that are strongly inspired by the essential in the interpretations of Alberto Campo Baeza and Mansilla + Tuñón. Campo Baeza identifies the theme of light and the gravity of the project materials. The references range from Mies's Farnsworth to Le Corbusier's Villa Savoye, in that the architecture is white and absolute. This is how he describes his idea of architecture: "A naked, intelligent, simple beauty, capable of capturing our minds" (Campo Baeza 12, p. 40). In 1992 in Zahora, at Cadiz, he completed the Casa Gaspar, which was soon to become an icon of research into the essential. It is a *hortus conclusus*, bounded by four 3.5 meter-high walls. The volume is divided into three parts; the central one is covered and 4.5 meters high, enhancing the core of the house. The living space inhabits the interior in the two courtyards, in this white and absolute cloister. In the work of Mansilla + Tuñón the relationship with minimalism is very intense. An exhibition of sculptures by Donald Judd, held in Madrid in 1989, attracted their attention. Through the pursuit of minimalism in art, they were investigating themes that relate the architecture to its context, by analysing the mediation space. The Museum of the royal collections in Madrid, nearing completion, is an extension of the base of the Royal Palace. The architects are working with respect to the open space of the Plaza de la Almudena. The construction is almost invisible from the Plaza, while the historical wall is being carved into sections for three exhibition levels. The building extends outward to the gardens of the Campo del Moro. The exhibition halls have a regular shape, 20 x 150 meters. The museum will therefore become part of the historical image of the city. Special attention has been given to the façade, with a double frame of pillars. These, together with the beams connecting them, create a strong and rhythmic internal structure that recalls the sequence of Philip Glass's music, repetitive and different, doubled and staggered in its levels. The design reveals the character of the place, creating a relationship with the city and the historic gardens behind it.

A wealth of the different souls of minimalism is uncovered, with an awareness of the increasingly active role that the research into the essential, into simplicity, will play in the years to come.

Bibliography
Campo Baeza A., *L'idea costruita*, Lettera Ventidue, Siracusa 2012.
Didi-Huberman G., *Il gioco delle evidenze. La dialettica dello sguardo nell'arte contemporanea*, Fazi, Rome 2008.
Kipnis J., *A Conversation With Jacques Herzog*, in "Herzog & de Meuron 1993-1997", *El Croquis*, n. 84, 1997/II, pp. 6-21.
Pawson J., *Minimum*, Phaidon Press, London 1996.
Poli F., *Minimalismo, arte povera, arte concettuale*, Laterza, Rome-Bari 1995.
Ponciroli V. (edited by), *Katsura. La villa imperiale*, Electa, Milan 2004.
Zabalbeascoa A., Rodriguez Marcos J., *Minimalismos*, Gili, Barcelona 2000.

Aires Mateus, Residential detached house, Leira, 2008-2010

Chiara Ingrosso

New Urbanism

At the end of the Eighties, a group of American architects and urban planners set themselves the objective of remedying the rampant suburbanization of their territories, and generally attempted to move beyond the *urban sprawl* model that was so widespread after the Second World War. The intensive inner city settlements had turned out to be harbingers of pollution, soil consumption, and social decline, and they were unsafe. The solution was found in a new balance between nature and urbanism in the city, based on public transport, with the aim of ensuring a good quality of life for its inhabitants.

In 1993 in Alexandria (Virginia), at the Congress for the New Urbanism (CNU) there was a meeting of some of the architects who shared these ideas and some who had already experimented with alternative urban models at the "villettopoli": these were Peter Calthorpe, Andrés Duany, Elizabeth Moule, Elizabeth Plater-Zyberk, Stefanos Polyzoides, Dan Solomon and Peter Katz.

Since the early Nineties, the CNU has been meeting periodically to discuss in working groups made up of architects, but also *developers*, economists, academics or simply citizens, specific issues that are based on the principles of the *Charter of the New Urbanism,* the movement's manifesto drafted in 1996, which lays down its cornerstones. For the New Urbanism movement, the metropolitan region is a reservoir of great environmental but also economic importance, whose life is closely connected to the metropolis and vice versa. What follows is the interconnection of the various levels of design, from regional planning to the design of the block. The neighbourhood or district is the privileged human habitat, central to the community and social integration, meriting the greatest care in the design of the balance and location of the functions, in any case mixed, and in the design of the public spaces. Transport planning is a central theme on all scales, particularly with regard to public transport at the expense of the car. In terms of architecture and landscape, the priority is a design approach that takes due account of the climate, topography, history and local construction practices.

For its innovative research aimed at seeking alternative social forms, the New Urbanism is considered by John A. Dutton to be not an antithesis but a continuation of the modern theories on City planning, so that the CNU could be said to share many similarities with the CIAM. Nevertheless, the architectural response of New Urbanism to urban *sprawl* is influenced by the theories of the anti-modern and neo-traditionalist architect Leon Krier and inspired by the study of cities and pre-modern buildings. According to Jill Grant, New Urbanism is one of the American movements (not only) based on *community design*, namely on *mixed uses*, on the study of neighbourhood units and public and pedestrian spaces, the liveability, quality of *design*, social equity but also amenities.

Overall, New Urbanism fully subscribes to the American cultural and technological tradition and, in general, the Anglo-Saxon one, from Olmsted, Howard and Unwin to Geddes and Mumford. A reference text on the theories of New Urbanism is *Death and Life of Great American Cities* by Jane Jacobs (1961), for the value that it gives to the urban variety and attention to people and everyday life, but other references may be found in the work of Christopher Alexander and Kevin Lynch.

On the technological side, there is *Traditional Neighbourhood Development* (TND) by Andrés Duany and Elizabeth

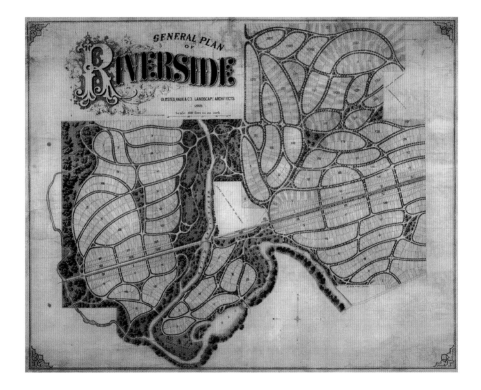

Master plan, Riverside, 1889

Page 297
Urban Sprawl in America

Plater-Zyberk, which begins with the historical model of the *neighbourhood unit* formulated from the Twenties by Clarence Perry (1923) and applied to the Regional Plan of New York (1929). The *neighbourhood unit* is calculated based on the maximum distances travelled on foot between the civic centres, and therefore services, and residences. The fundamental principle of *walkability* that emerges is a real unit of measurement of the plans by the Duany Plater-Zyberk & Company (DPZ) studio. The limited use of the car combined with "compactness" understood as the density of the urban centres and the introduction of traditional and recognizable public spaces characterizes numerous settlements designed by American architects who founded the CNU.

As for regional planning, the Transit Oriented District model (TOD) by Peter Calthorpe, applied in the study Region 2040 for Metro Portland in Oregon, summarizes some of the founding principles of the movement. Overall, TOD is an integrated (social, economic, ecological) and sustainable polycentric model, since it proposes a large investment in public transport, at both regional and district levels, and is based on containing land consumption by applying Urban Growth Boundaries (UGB). Limiting the *sprawl* with UGBs helps to ensure the necessary quota of natural areas and aims at a balanced growth of built-up areas at the regional level. A case of *urban infill,* namely suburban completion in this case, is Orenco, designed as a regionally integrated Transit Oriented District. Other notable projects for completing urban or suburban neighbourhoods have been designed by Dover &Kohl at 'On (South Carolina), Winter Park Mall (Florida) and Winter Spring Town Centre (Florida).

The Duany Plater-Zyberk & Company studio,

with the assistance of Leon Krier, designed the project for Seaside (1985), the Florida town founded by Robert Davis on land owned by him. It became the symbol of the New Urbanism movement. The urban plan, configured according to the *Traditional Neighbourhood Development* model, is compact and deliberately reminiscent of a traditional town, with a clearly defined system and hierarchy of streets, parks and blocks and a central plaza open to the sea, where the principal axes converge. Architectural regulations were made for the town, providing quantitative guidelines for the project but also the typological features of the architecture. The *Seaside urban code* was designed as a reference framework that would allow different designers to interpret style and form in different ways, to guarantee the diversity of individual buildings without affecting the overall coherence of the system, as well as ensuring a balanced relationship between the public and private spaces. Most of architecture (including some villas designed by renowned architects, including Aldo Rossi, Leon Krier, and Steven Holl) explicitly incorporates the traditional and vernacular styles, such as "Charleston", "Victorian", "Antebellum" or other revivals.

The criticism that is often levelled at New Urbanism is that of having a nostalgic and populist approach that would place the movement within the broad category of postmodern historicism. The most postmodern of the New Urbanism settlements is definitely Celebration, the town built by the Disney Corporation and designed in 1994 by Cooper, Robertson and Robert A.M. Stern near Orlando, Florida and next to the famous amusement park. Although it could be ascribed to the movement for a number of features, including the "compact" design of the system, with well-designed public spaces

and parks, community buildings that are accessible on foot, and the use of electric cars, as well as its "Twenties style" architecture, on the whole, Celebration is a city for the *upper classes*. Therefore, unlike what is proposed by New Urbanism, Celebration lacks social integration that on the other hand would be in contrast with the speculative *mission* of the Disney Corporation that has strategically diversified into real estate. The maximum number of inhabitants, the strict rules that prescribe the aesthetics and maintenance of the buildings' exterior spaces (façades and gardens) and common areas, as well as the capillary

security system, makes the town one of the most successful *gated communities* in America. In this case, the city contains a number of designs by renowned international architects, such as the post office by Michael Graves, the offices by Aldo Rossi, the City Hall by Philip Johnson, and the cinemas by Cesar Pelli.

Bibliography
Duany Plater-Zyberk & Company, *Lexicon of the New Urbanism*, 2003 (www.dpz.com/uploads/Books/Lexicon-2014.pdf).
Dutton J.A., *New American Urbanism*, Milan 2000.
Grant J., *Planning the Good Community: New Urbanism in Theory and Practice*, London 2006.

Disney Development
Company, Celebration, 1996

Disney Development
Company, Celebration, 1996

299

Maria Vittoria Capitanucci

Landscape Architecture

The meaning of landscape architecture is extremely broad. It connects different fields and disciplines with specific features that range from the design of the public, private or interstitial space to infrastructure systems and actual masterplans. This discipline's strong sociological connotation has meant that the term "landscape architecture" is no longer synonymous with landscaping or the art of creating gardens, but with a multidisciplinary field that involves and integrates areas such as botany, horticulture, fine arts, architecture, industrial design, geology and other scientific disciplines, as well as environmental psychology, geography and ecology. This subject area, depending on the scale of intervention or its complexity within predefined urban and territorial dynamics and flows, multiplies and fragments into a series of new or traditional specificities. These range from urban agriculture to edgelands design (border territories or city limits), to gardening – in its most multifaceted variations including that of "guerrilla gardening" – to the more general urban design and landscaping. The latter in its "classic" or "more contemporary" version is aimed at managing large wilderness areas or recovering degraded landscapes, from mines to landfills. Moreover, the presentation page of the Department of landscape architecture at the Harvard Graduate School of Design (one of the oldest dedicated to the discipline, dating back to 1900) reads as follows: "Its mission is to advance research and innovative design practices in the natural and built environments, as they intersect with processes of urbanization". This meaning goes far beyond its original roots, somewhat elitist, aristocratic, and bound to tradition, and the passion for botany and gardening.

Or it is that broader meaning, identified with the term "landscaping", interpreted, according to the times and the preferences, as British, French or Italian. A practice and a "science", it began in the Renaissance when the great masters of design expressed their visions with unsurpassed heights (Francesco di Giorgio Martini in Serlio, Filarete, Leonardo, Raphael, Bramante and Palladio) with those "ephemera" related to ceremonies and celebrations or "monumental" and "picturesque" works (caves, fountains, pavilions, but also lakes and canals).

In the centuries that followed, one "style" or "manner" prevailed over another when it came to designing the greenery, in the style

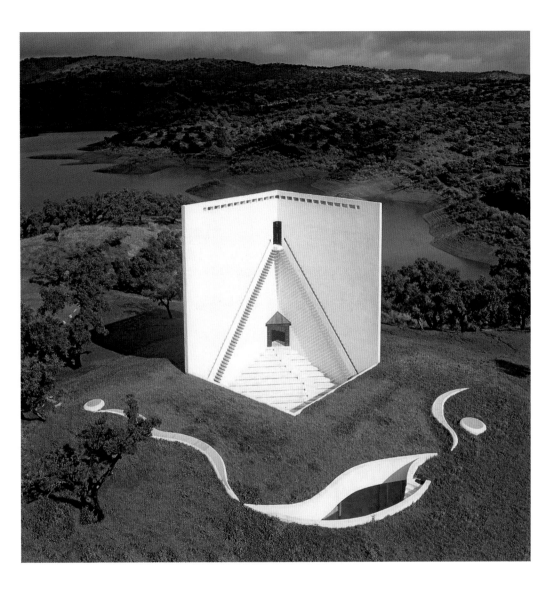

Emilio Ambasz, Casa de
Retiro Espiritual, Seville,
1975-1978

Page 302
Emilio Ambasz, Master plan
for Seville Exposition, 1992

Page 303
Emilio Ambasz, Fukuoka
Prefectural International
Hall, 1990

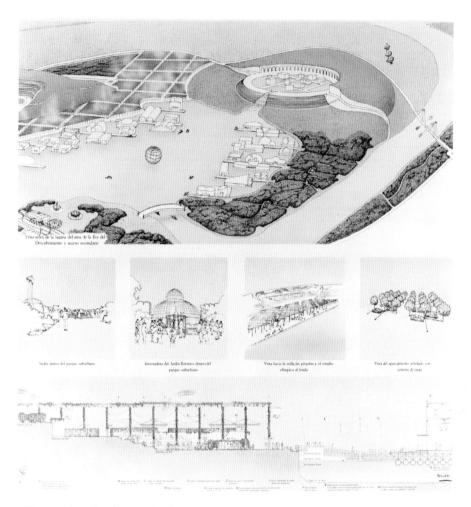

Vista aérea de la laguna del área de la Era del Descubrimiento y acceso secundario

Jardín dentro del parque suburbano

Invernadero del Jardín Botánico dentro del parque suburbano

Vista hacia la orilla, las pérgolas y el estadio olímpico al fondo

Vista del aparcamiento arbolado con sistema de riego

of the woods and spaces in absolute harmony with the architectural trends of the different eras. The architectural incursion of those charming eighteenth-century "follies" became emblematic in the balance between romance and neo-classicism, dotting wonderful private parks and later, public parks in Europe. Eventually these were followed by the 'modern' greenhouses, structural and linguistic fields of experimentation for cultivated types like William Chambers (the Palm House and the Pagoda at Kew Gardens in London) or ingenious builders like Joseph Paxton and what was to be the Crystal Palace in Hyde Park. And then there was the Guell Park by Antoni Gaudí, a visionary and epic fantasy interpretation of an Art Nouveau language, Catalan modernism and medieval tradition that opens up to the twentieth century. The Modern Movement, however, represents the true watershed between two great epic moments in the conception of landscape architecture starting with the first projects by

Bruno Taut and Walter Gropius in the Germany in the Thirties and from there onwards. Certainly we cannot overlook the intrinsic relationship, generating space, views and architecture, between the interior and exterior in the works of Frank Lloyd Wright (particularly in the period of the Prairie Houses and then the Usonian period), where the green areas and landscape are always meticulously conceived and designed.

The interest in the complexity of urban design, public space, the management of full and empty areas in the landscape beyond the city limits, and sometimes even in the heart of historic centres, starting in the Thirties and Forties, represented a new challenge for a series of designers who were ready to share the dictates of the new architectural language. Some of these, more than others, were capable and interested in combining their own botanical and scenic sensibility with the essential nature of geometric modernism. Some names that stand out are Roberto Burle Marx (São Paulo, 1909 - Rio de Janeiro, 1994), a German-Brazilian master who, in his work – Ibirapuera Park, in São Paulo, 1954, the monumental Axis of Brasilia in 1961, the Aterro do Flamengo area in Rio de Janeiro in 1962, and the recent KLCC Park in Kuala Lumpur – showed a scientific interest in the landscape and a relationship with the environment, combining the International Style with the nature and cultural traditions of Brazil.

Burle Marx, indicating a new aesthetics for landscape architecture, opened up an entirely contemporary approach for large scale projects as well. In these projects, he also worked with designers like Oscar Niemeyer, Lucio Costa, Hélio Uchôa or Milton Roberto. But this discipline drew in many other designers from different backgrounds and with varying sensibilities,

perhaps more notably dedicated to the architectural project *tout court* as in the case of Luis Barragán. The Mexican maestro oversaw the Jardines del Pedregal project in the Thirties, and in the Fifties, oversaw the restoration of the cloisters of the Convento de las Capuchinas Sacramentarias in Tlalpan, the plan of the Jardines del Bosque in Guadalajara and the Torres de Satélite (in collaboration with the sculptor Mathias Goeritz, 1957). With this mark on the territory, shortly after he advanced a theme that was dear to the universe of land art, with works by Richard Long, Christo, and Robert Morris. This inheritance was also transposed into architecture in the Seventies by *Radical Architecture* and *Metabolist* movements in a large-scale territorial vision, like the project for the Bay of Tokyo by Kenzo Tange or in the many mega-structural works, of which the plans for Algiers and Rio de Janeiro by Le Corbusier were the forerunners.

In Italy, a leader in this disciplinary renewal and approach was certainly Pietro Porcinai, born in 1910. After early experience in Gio Ponti's *Domus*, he chose the international route and in 1948, founded, at Jesus College, Cambridge, the IFLA (International Federation of Landscape Architecture) in order to raise awareness of architectural culture and more. Capable of making great changes in scale and unexpected leaps, the Florentine designer took on wonderful private gardens as well as the landscape plan for the Brenner highway pass between the Fifties and Sixties. He designed the landscapes of the Olivetti headquarters, the Ina-Olivetti neighbourhood in Pozzuoli and the park in Berlin's Hansaviertel between buildings by Alvar Aalto, Walter Gropius, Le Corbusier, Luciano Baldessarri, and Oscar Niemeyer. Niemeyer was also the author of the Mondadori headquarters in Segrate where Porcinai oversaw work on the park.

This great teacher was responsible for bringing to Italy the methods, techniques and formal solutions of the most important European garden architects (Fritz Enchke, Karl Foerster, Gustav Lüttge, Russell Page, Geoffrey Jellicoe, René Pechère, and Gerda Gollwitzer). Of course, it is possible to trace an attention to the redefinition of the landscape (even in the absence of greenery) in many contemporary works. In this sense, some exemplary work would be that of Peter Eisenman for the City of Galiega Culture in Santiago de Compostela (1999) as well as the Memorial to the Murdered Jews of Europe in Berlin (2005). The work of Tadao Ando as a whole and in particular, some of his museum structures like the Japanese world in general, is traditionally sensitive to the relationship between interior and exterior, nature and artifice. Also interesting is the position taken by Kazuyo Sejima at the XIII Biennale of Architecture in Venice, curated by her in 2012. Even the postmodern theorist par excellence, Charles Jencks, in his second life, entirely "Scottish", became an effective landscape architect and recently, in Milan, was responsible for designing the green area of the former Alfa Romeo industrial area in Portello, assisted by the Land Study, in its turn engaged in planning the landscaping for one of the major areas for transformation, Porta Nuova Varesine, based on the masterplan by Cesar Pelli.

In this multi-faceted discipline, the socio-economic connotations move in parallel along compositional, scientific, eco-sustainable and urban lines in a broad sense. This is demonstrated by numerous and frequent contemporary interventions that integrate these aspects into a unique and complex programme. One of the flagships, but certainly not the only one, is the Dutch West 8 Urban Design & Landscape Architecture studio, founded in 1987 by Adriaan Geuze as a laboratory for landscape architects and urban planners. The studio has worked on some major projects including the masterplan for the Borneo-Sporenburg area in Amsterdam, the Jubilee Gardens and Chiswick Park in London in the late Nineties. More recently, it has worked on projects for the waterfront of Toronto and the development plan for Governor's Island, off New York.

With a different language and training but an approach that ranges through related disciplines, Kathryn Gustafson works along the same lines, engaged, in recent years, in the Park of City Life in Milan's former Fairground. This American landscape architect has formed the Ecole Nationale Supérieure de Paysage de Versailles – a leading school for training contemporary landscape architects. She is also the architect behind the recent Les Jardins de l'Imaginaire in Terrasson, the Square of Evry in France, the memorial to Princess Diana in Hyde Park (London), the Lurie Garden in Chicago and landscape plans for the headquarters of Shell Petroleum (1992) and Esso. It is clear that today more than ever, the boundary between architectural design and landscape architecture is very slender, perhaps even non-existent. Signs on the territory that can be read according to different layers or levels, where an integrated design is used to change the complexity of the landscape, are points of departure and arrival for advanced design visions that involve many disciplines. This is the case, for example, in the design by Norman Foster for Masdar City, the first Zero Impact city, in the desert, 20 km from Dubai.

Bibliography
Cavalcanti L., El-Dahdah F., Rambert F. (edited by),
Roberto Burle Marx. The Modernity of Landscape,
Actar 2011.
Kassler E.B., *Modern Gardens and the Landscape*,
Museum of Modern Art, New York 1964.
Matteini M., *Pietro Porcinai architetto del giardino e
del paesaggio*, Electa, Milan 1991.
Simonds J.O., Starke B., *Landscape Architecture: a
Manual of Environmental Planning and Design*, Mc-
Graw Hill 2006.
Walker P., Simo M., *Invisible Gardens, The Search for
Modernism in the American Landscape*, MIT Press,
Cambridge Mass 1994.

West 8, Jubilee Gardens,
London, 2005

Page 304
Roberto Burle Marx,
Garden of Edmundo
Cavanelas House, Pedro
do Rio, 1954

Norman Foster, Masdar
City, Abu Dhabi, 2007

Diller Scofidio + Renfro,
in collaboration with James
Field Corner Operations
and Piet Oudolf, High Line,
New York, 2004-2009

Index

311

313